D1575349

My Father's Name

My Father's Name

A Black Virginia Family after the Civil War

LAWRENCE P. JACKSON

The University of Chicago Press *Chicago and London*

LAWRENCE P. JACKSON is professor of English and African
American studies at Emory University. He is the author of *The
Indignant Generation: A Narrative History of African American
Writers and Critics, 1934–1960* and *Ralph Ellison: Emergence of
Genius.*

The University of Chicago Press, Chicago 60637
The University of Chicago Press, Ltd., London
© 2012 by Lawrence P. Jackson
All rights reserved. Published 2012.
Printed in the United States of America

Portions of chapter 1 appeared in an earlier version as "To
Danville," *New England Quarterly* (Winter 2007): 150–67.
Portions of chapter 8 appeared in an earlier version as "The Will,"
Southern Quarterly (Summer 2009): 57–87.

21 20 19 18 17 16 15 14 13 12   1 2 3 4 5

ISBN-13: 978-0-226-38949-3 (cloth)
ISBN-10: 0-226-38949-9 (cloth)

Library of Congress Cataloging-in-Publication Data

Jackson, Lawrence Patrick.
   My father's name : a black Virginia family after the Civil War /
Lawrence P. Jackson.
      p.   cm.
   Includes bibliographical references and index.
   ISBN-13: 978-0-226-38949-3 (hardcover : alkaline paper)
   ISBN-10: 0-226-38949-9 (hardcover : alkaline paper)
   1. Jackson, Lawrence Patrick—Family.   2. African
Americans—Virginia—Biography.   3. Slaves—Virginia—
Pittsylvania County—Biography.   4. Freedmen—Virginia—
Pittsylvania County—Biography.   5. Pittsylvania County
(Va.)—Biography.   6. Reconstruction—Virginia—
Pittsylvania County.   7. United States—Social conditions—
1865–1918.   I. Title.
   F235.N4J33 2012
   975.5′041092—dc23
   [B]   2011034713

⊗ This paper meets the requirements of ANSI/NISO Z39.48-1992
(Permanence of Paper).

This book is dedicated to my parents,
Verna & Nathaniel Jackson Jr.;
my brother, Greg Carr;
my sons, Nathaniel & Mitchell;
my grandparents, Christine & Vernon Mitchell
& Virginia & Nathaniel Jackson

CONTENTS

ACKNOWLEDGMENTS

This project arose from my relationship with my father and my sons, and I am thankful to my ancestors for their immaculate guidance. Greg Carr gave me the spirited words "I knew my father," and the work of David Bradley helped me to grasp the necessity of visiting children whose parents had been enslaved.

I am indebted to everyone who helped me to collect the research and who shared their time. Chanel Craft and Rev. Dan Ricketts provided valuable assistance to me in Pittsylvania. Lisa A. Lindsay generously gave me a place to stay in Chapel Hill.

In the fall of 2010, I benefited from the enthusiasm and candor of members of Freshman Seminar 190, "Autobiography African American Style." In the spring of 2011, graduate students Anthony Cook, Yoshi Furuiki, George Gordon-Smith, and Diana Louis from the seminar "Rewriting Agency in Slavery and Reconstruction in Southside Virginia" read primary source documents, especially the US census, with deep insight. I would like to thank Emory librarian Erica Bruchko, who always enthusiastically answered questions and helped to find sources; Randall Burkett and the librarians at the Manuscript, Archives and Research Library at Emory University; Michael Page, the Emory GIS librarian who created the Pittsylvania County maps; Marie Hansen of Emory's interlibrary loan system; Kyle Fenton of Digital Curation; and Richard Luce, Vice Provost and Director of Libraries at Emory University.

Library professionals and scholars outside Atlanta were most considerate and include Naomi Nelson, Director of the Duke University Rare Books, Manuscripts and Special Collections Library, and her staff; the National Humanities Center, Research Triangle Park, North Carolina, where the project was conceived (special thanks to Israel Gershoni, Jeff Kerr-Ritchie, and Tim Tyson); the Albert and Shirley Small Special Collections Library at the University of Virginia; the Library of Virginia, Richmond; the Pittsylvania Historical Society, Chatham; the Virginia

Historical Society, Richmond; historians Drew Swanson and Martha Katz-Hyman; and Pittsylvania County Clerk H. F. Haymore.

I thank Stephen Donadio and Douglass Chambers for publishing versions of this early work. Robert Devens of the University of Chicago Press, the press's anonymous readers, Robert Steptoe, Michael Elliott, Nathan McCall, and Delores Dwyer have all helped to make this a better book. I also thank Horace Porter, Arnold Rampersad, Houston Baker, James West, Keith Gilyard, Mark Anthony Neal, Al Yasha Williams, and my sister, Col. Lynn Jackson-Dorman of the US Army, for believing that this journey was important.

This book about the Old South was written in Richmond, Virginia; Durham, North Carolina; and Atlanta, Georgia.

1 · To Danville

When my wife and I learned that we were going to have a baby in the summer of 2004, we thought it would be fitting, if we had a boy, to name the child Nathaniel for my father and grandfather, and in honor of American patriot Nat Turner. Six weeks before the baby was due, I drove up to Danville, Virginia, in Pittsylvania County, the rural point of origin for the Nathaniels of my own family saga. More accurately, I drove just north of Danville to the outlying town of Blairs. I thought that walking the terrain of my forebears would put me in a paternal frame of mind and that, with luck, I might unearth my grandfather's old house by the railroad tracks. Now that I was on the verge of contributing to another generation that would carry that puzzlingly common surname for American blacks—Jackson—I was curious about how my father's people saw the world. In the back of my mind, I wanted to better understand my father, such a formidable presence in my own memory.

My father, as an old Virginia saying goes, "went back to Guinea" in 1990, the year I finished college. Ours was a relationship filled with the anguished complexity of fathers and sons. I wanted to be like him, but never felt I could achieve his magnificent serenity. On the other hand, he desperately wanted me to build the emotional strength to be myself. By the end of his earthly life, my father and I had overcome the sore feelings and failed moments: I know that he loved me, and my love for him grows every day.

After he had gone, I tried different things to enhance my memories of him. On his birthday in 2001, I drove from Richmond, where I then lived, down Route 360 to Danville. I wanted to see the place where my grandfather had lived, which I hadn't been to since the last time my father had taken us there when I was seven years old. During that visit I had gone to the Danville tourist bureau and looked at telephone books from the 1960s and 1970s to see if I could find my grandfather's address. But I had forgotten a crucial fact: Grandpa Jackson had lived in Blairs, not nearby Danville, the comparatively robust city of fifty thousand on the Dan River. So I spent an hour in Danville's colored cemetery, vainly looking for the headstone. I remember the trip mainly on account of pictures. Every ten miles or so on the route to and from Richmond, I stopped to shoot rolls of film, taking color photographs of every tin-roof barn and chinked wooden cabin that looked as if it, like my grandfather, had had its beginnings in the nineteenth century.

My father was not particularly close to his paternal family, so after my grandfather died in 1975 we visited Blairs only one more time, the next year. My final and most complete memory of the place is from that summer trip. Most of my time was spent sitting on my great-aunt Sally's front porch while the adults talked. My sister, who was eleven that summer, had been able to stay with a classmate in Baltimore, leaving me by myself. In the sweltering August heat I spent an hour alone on the porch and swatted about seventeen flies. I was just getting coordinated enough to swat a healthy fly, and the insects seemed to me the most no-account form of animal life I had encountered: uglier than ants, vicious and stubborn. Sometimes, while I was waiting for the adults and wishing for other kids, I would jog up and down the road outside the simple white clapboard house. In the living room, Aunt Sally had only hard candy in a bowl, and I remember moaning and pleading for a Popsicle.

Our trips to Danville in the early 1970s were unremarkable—always. At 11 a.m. we would leave our home in Baltimore, outfitted to survive in case the Volkswagen broke down and we wound up stranded outside Fredericksburg, Virginia, as regularly happened. Well beyond the point of miserliness, my father resisted eating at roadside restaurants, whether Howard Johnson or Tastee Freez. In an insulated sack, my mother would pack fried chicken legs, ham sandwiches, and frozen sodas on the verge of exploding. Danville was about four hundred miles from Baltimore, and if we got what was, for the four of us, an early start at eleven in the morning, we'd arrive there about a quarter to nine, which in summer was just before dark. My father kept the speedometer needle of the Volkswagen at fifty-five, which was probably the best way to coax the old fastback down the road without repairs. My grandfather had wanted my father to buy a top-of-the-line automobile, to let everyone know that his son had prospered in the city. My father, though, was content to wear English caps, penny loafers, and khaki trousers, to marry a black Episcopalian, and to have preschool children who could read and swim.

Grandpa Jackson lived simply, sharing a two-room bungalow owned by his sister, Mary, and her husband, John Kesee. The house sat only about a hundred paces from the railroad tracks of the old Southern line, and inside there was a coldwater tap. The toilet was outside.

I spent those visits listening attentively for the carrying whistle and chugging wheels of the locomotives, anxiously looking down the tracks at the overpass for Route 29, and collecting the spikes that railroad men drove into the crossties to hold the iron rails in place. After painting them gold, I used to give the spikes to my godfathers and male relatives as holiday gifts. Grandpa had been a railroad man, though I can only remember him as a large-bellied, tobacco-brown man, smiling and joking, flashing a gold tooth on the side of his mouth, and wearing a stocking cap and an apron, with his belt buckle on the side of his pants instead of over the zipper. Whenever we came into the house he would be performing some caregiver's duty for his brother-in-law, who was ill. A comfortable and easy man, my grandfather called me dutifully on birthdays and holidays from a telephone in his house, I always assumed, speaking a staccato but cheerful version of black Virginia speech. He always sent me a card with at least five dollars, an extravagance to me. My memory tells me that Grandpa Jackson had signed his name—though not with the flair and precision of my own father, whose signature remains an architectural mystery to me.

The most joyful part of the Danville trip for my sister and me was our stay at the newly built Holiday Inn, with its buckets of ice and soda machines overflowing with Dr Pepper and Royal Crown Cola. The hotel's swimming pool had a slide, and my sister and I would play briefly at dusk when our visit to our ancient relatives had ended, or we would brave a dip in the morning, when the water was still chilly. I don't know how long the hotels had been integrated; interracial marriage had gained legal sanction in that part of the world only the year before I was born, and in 1968 small-town Danville had had the distinction of hosting one of the largest race riots that had ever taken place in North America. As a child of five or six, I didn't think much about how the waitress acted when we entered the restaurant or about the clerk's attitude when we checked out of our rooms, or why we stayed mainly at large national franchises instead of the smaller privately owned places. I do remember, though, that my father always had us wait in the car when he went in alone to the hotel registration desk, and sometimes I'd get a bit fidgety, waiting for him to return. My strongest memory of public dining experiences with my father in the 1970s and '80s centers on one recurring episode: my father's forcefully objecting to being seated by the kitchen door. But I can still recall the ritual dinner of chicken fingers that we always had at Long John Silver's, a "treat," because it was white meat without any bone.

◆　◆　◆

In the fall of 2004, I was working on a book at the National Humanities Center and living in Durham, North Carolina. At the tail end of the sabbatical and as the season began to change, I looked at a map and noticed that Danville was perhaps no more than fifty miles away. Almost on impulse, I decided to steal a visit. A short drive through the countryside would be a small price to pay, to gain a surer sense of the earth and the trees, the sky and the birds; an act to renew my family memory. With any luck, I would tread the old ground of my father's fathers. Sunday was the day of ritual, and I was called.

For my country visit, I started off the day at Biscuitville with a cheese-and-scrambled-egg biscuit, driving past Durham's prized eateries, Foster's and Guglhupf. Everybody at the drive-thru was pleasant, and I got directions to the interstate. After only four miles on Interstate 40, I picked up Route 86. My watch told me that it was about 11:30, the right time for a Jackson ride to Danville. Driving through forests and alongside farms, I observed the early winter dress of the passing trees: oak, maple, poplar, and pine.

Going through the town of Hillsborough, I scanned the colonial-era historical markers and saw that George Washington once billeted there, and that Tories and patriots alike had swung by their necks. The somber past reminded me of a man I had been reading about named Odell Waller, who had shared a last name with my grandmother's mother, and who had been electrocuted in Richmond in 1941 for shooting a white Pittsylvania County farmer. Odell Waller had claimed he wasn't a violent man, but was defending himself from a white landowner who had stolen seventy-two bushels of his wheat. The incorporated city of Danville is, by tradition at least, in Pittsylvania County, and I wondered if this man had been kin to me. I also wondered, as my thoughts drifted into abstraction, if anyone related to me had been around to see George Washington. How could I determine that?

I drove past the Hillsborough Historical Society and Welcome Center, a delightful stone building dating back to the colonial era, and it occurred to me that the stones it was made of don't come from a quarry. I had known houses exactly like this in two places in Maryland: at the junction of Falls and Old Court Road, and in Ellicott City, the hometown of the mathematician Benjamin Banneker. They were the types of stones you would find if you had tilled several hundred acres of ground and had upturned and collected, one by one, every troublesome rock that had stood in the path of your plow or hoe or shovel.

Yanceyville, some twenty miles further on, was smaller than Hillsborough—not much more than a water tower, a cattle farm, and a filling station combined with a general store. I could remember how much fun it was as a child to go through a well-stocked old store, with grooves on its wooden floor like lane markings telling you where you could run and how fast you could go. My grandfather, who had a reputation as a ladies' man, probably made more than one little trip to Yanceyville, after Danville and Blairs had unfolded all their delights to him. He must have made the journey on foot, I thought, as I drove along holding the speedometer at fifty-five while drivers behind me, even the big rigs, signaled and swerved into the oncoming traffic to get around. As a teenager driving with my father, I would become desperate for him to propel the car down the highway so as to keep up with the pace of traffic, and once I asked him, in my typical beleaguered way, "Why do you go slower than fifty-five?"

This time he answered me. "I like to look at the trees."

The roads must have been alive at night in the 1910s, when my grandfather would have been at his most obstreperous, and when the night air would have been filled with the sound of the owls and waddling low-slung beasts moving through the dense brush. I looked over the hills of the countryside passing by, and picked out the curious geometries of the frame houses, and the materials used to build their roofs.

The first time I checked my watch, I saw that it was getting past 12:30. I opened up the atlas on the seat next to me a couple of times and eyeballed the Virginia map again. Danville edged the North Carolina border, obliging me to flip back and forth between the N map and the V map to get a clear fix on it, which I felt a bit unsafe doing while at the wheel of the car. Besides, where the little dot should be designating the location of the town of Blairs, the map in the atlas has a rectangle labeled *See inset*—a map within a map showing the city of Danville proper. The "See inset" rectangle obscured Blairs. I flipped the map closed and kept driving. Something in my blood resisted stopping the car until I'd achieved my destination.

In the nineteenth century, Danville had been a highly profitable tobacco crossroads, the center of two states' worth of tobacco farmers' Bright Leaf special. The key to the town's early success was its strategic location on the Dan River, named in 1728 by the eminent Virginian William Byrd, who once had punished his slave butler by forcing him to drink a pint of urine. The river runs from Pittsylvania County through Halifax to Mecklenburg, all on the edge of the state border, and now, courtesy of the US Army Corps of Engineers, it empties into the huge reservoir at Lake Gaston.

On a lark, I decided to avoid Danville proper altogether and to take my chances searching for Blairs. After about four miles, I recognized that I was lost, and my errand itself began to seem ill-considered. Not a soul knew I was on the road, and I wouldn't even know anyone here to tell that I'd arrived in their neighborhood. My mother had lost track of our Danville relatives years ago, even the ones that had moved to Washington, DC. Besides, in the early 1960s, my grandmother's father, Arthur Joyce, had pressured her to move a heavy crock when she was pregnant with my sister, and she still carries the image of him and the whole Piedmont clan as a group of mean boors. Since the old man lived in the city of Roanoke, my mother suspected that the country folk were even cruder.

Disoriented somewhere between Danville and Keeling, I saw that it was a little after one o'clock; there wasn't a cloud in the sky, and I figured I could burn a little daylight. Then I asked myself: What am I really looking for? A house? A man? A family? A memory?

I couldn't answer right away. My quest had at least a minor source in purposeful envy. The day before, after a brief conversation with two white colleagues who were African American history professors—a Brit and a North Carolinian whose next-door neighbors once had lynched a black man—I realized that I couldn't afford to miss my own family's history when it was this close at hand. It seemed to me a kind of betrayal to conduct conversations with grown-up white men who had traveled the world and written books about the subtle interiors of the lives of black people in Virginia and North Carolina and be black myself, with only the vaguest awareness about specific ancestors in those same places, really only one generation removed. I exited the highway and resolved that I would find, at least, the old house where Grandpa Jackson used to live with his sister and brother-in-law. Finding that place would make the day a success.

Driving southeast on 726 in the direction of Ringgold, I passed rows of mobile homes, their front lawns already gaudy with plastic Christmas decorations, their rear yards loaded with small sheds and barns. The new dwellings reminded me of the old house. I felt positive at that moment that Grandpa, Aunt Mary, and Uncle John lived in a mobile home resting on a cinderblock foundation. The only thing disturbing my fantasy was the missing railroad tracks. Every one I saw looked familiar.

I spied several young men in overlarge sweatshirts lolling in the front yard of a house; they looked up at me with mild interest as I drove by. Next door a man toiled over the hood of a Lincoln, applying soapy water. He too looked up, curious about the stranger with Georgia license plates. On the other side of the road I noticed a man in a sharp brown jacket walking the yard of the Christ's Deliverance Baptist Church. After another mile, I made an about-face and decided I would ask the Baptist for some directions. Pulling the car slowly into the church's gravel driveway, I saw a house in the rear with a hulking, shimmering maroon Humvee parked on the grass, among half-a-dozen other rusted-out cars from various epochs. A sure sign that they were "country," I thought to myself, while I measured the glamour amid ruin. I walked over to the man, who at first seemed to have the stature of a man in his early forties; but as I got closer I saw the worn face of a person twenty years older. Making a small wave, I kept my hand in close to my body, as if I were covering him with a pistol.

"Hello, my friend," I said with professional cheerfulness. "Can you tell me where the train tracks are around here?" From the time I was a very small boy, constantly and to my annoyance, my mother has instructed me to be polite to strangers. At times like this I recognize I am embarrassed to hear my own voice.

The man smiled. He was about my size but looked as if he had recently been shrunk. Heavy folds of skin hung around his eyes, but otherwise he looked healthy. Until he opened his mouth.

After I looked critically at his teeth, I altered my syntax and asked for more precise information. "Haven't been back here in thirty years. Sort of hoping to find my people; you don't know any Jacksons, do you?" Toward the end of my question, I ran my words together a bit, and as I reached the end of the sentence my voice rose an octave.

He looked at me pleasantly. "Go back down this here, I fuhget name, cross Twenty-nine, take a right. Railroad there. But I ain't been here long myself; don't know many people."

I thanked him profusely and repeated his directions as I understood them. I had missed a couple of his words, but I thought I had the gist of what he had said. I walked back across the front of the church toward the car; he followed about ten yards behind me, smiling, and this attachment made me more uncomfortable. I waved him off twice and would have preferred that he not return the wave before I pulled out in the direction in which he had pointed me. I was not sure that I trusted his directions, and I was not sure if that was because my teeth, which my dentist told me are on the verge of gum disease, were nonetheless all in my mouth, or if it was because he told me he was new to the neighborhood.

Back on 726, I noticed that the local name for that road is Malmaison. This made me wonder if the "bad house" was a brothel or a tavern set off the road somewhere. Maybe it had been a place that catered to the antebellum fancy trade? Not imaginative enough to consider an adolescent female relative coerced into the life of the whore, my prurient curiosity about the eighteenth and nineteenth centuries was unleashed. Reaching the intersection with the business district of Route 29, I was still at a loss to identify the railroad. So I headed away from the city, hoping that the road would angle toward a train track, but after a mile I appeared to be leaving Blairs way behind, so I came about again, thinking that perhaps I should get to a gas station and ask for some help. I thought that I really didn't have any more time to waste; I was almost forty years old, and it didn't make sense for me to stay lost for this long.

The Race Track gas station was hosting many black folks, which eased my mind. I hadn't gone too far, nor had I wandered into a Ku Klux Klan nightmare—black urban Americans' rationale for why their relatives left the rural South. "Folk," as they would say in Georgia, were coming home from church, and there was also a retinue of black men and shiny cars from the local auto-body shop. The brothers had at their disposal a gray Mercedes sedan, another lustrously detailed Humvee, and two 1957 Chevrolets, refinished and with delicious two-tone paint jobs. Inside the store there was a long line, in which I noticed a woman wearing a fur coat like the one my mother's aunt from South Hill, Virginia, had stored in our basement. Behind her stood a man I took to be in his middle fifties; he was dressed like a sport, including brand-new construction boots, baggy jeans, and a heavy gold-link chain. Dressed in my idea of country walking attire—khakis, forest-green barn jacket, hiking boots, and wool fedora—I achingly comprehended that I was likely to look pretty stodgy to people with a demandingly contemporary sense of style. On this trip I thought it would be important for me to show my age, but when I saw those groups of fifty- and sixty-year-old black men dressed up like sports, I lost my sense of what was appropriate and decided it might be best to ask the white counter clerk for help.

"Pardon me," I said when it was my turn at the counter, loud enough to be heard but no louder. "Pardon me, but can you tell me where the railroad tracks are?" A thin, dried-up-looking white woman stood behind me. I had the sense that she was fiftyish but began to wonder if all my age guesses were overestimates by a decade. She was impatient, I was sure of that. The clerk looked up and said, in a clear and not especially Southern accent, the kind I had been conditioned to think of as intelligent, "If you take Twenty-Nine to Danville, after about a mile you'll see a large Baptist church on your right. Then you're at a bridge, and the railroad runs right there."

The woman behind me put down her chips and sodas and pushed them along the counter, doing her best to end my conversation. I was about to ask the clerk for more explanation but thought better of it and walked out. Outside I tipped my hat to two older black women in a car. What the hell, I shrugged, and decided to ask the old boys nearby for an opinion.

There's a scene like this in Toni Morrison's novel *Song of Solomon*. The lead character, Milkman Dead, arrives back in Shalimar, the town of his long-lost grandfather Solomon, who is the key to Milkman's ancestral past and the originator of the family myth of slaves flying back to Africa. Milkman's personality and his life's work are caught up in the myth, and he is preoccupied by his kinfolk. But when he returns to rural Virginia, initially he has a painful encounter—a violent confrontation, in fact. Disrespectful, crude, and selfish, he seems to be a big-city guy ridiculing small-town ways and people, insulting them and putting them down without being aware of it.

When I approached the sports outside, who were all facing the highway, I had Milkman in mind. I walked behind the group and prepared to make an admiring remark about their car. Looking over the men, I tried to determine which of them was most likely to give me the directions I needed. "Sure have them looking good," I offer, in a voice that strikes me as much too loud. Milkman or not, all black Americans I have known appreciate stentorian clarity, but my ordinary speaking voice is mild like a librarian's. The end man of the group heard me but turned around the wrong way, looking down for me, and this drew the attention of Gold Link, who was talking into a cell phone. Gold Link ignored me, but in turning caught the attention of the tallest and leanest man—about fifty-two, I thought, with freshly trimmed salt-and-pepper hair and a fluffy mustache. The man looked in my direction and opened his mouth for a second, exposing full rows of gleaming white teeth.

I understood that my moment onstage had arrived. All my life I had admired and felt it necessary to indulge men exactly like this one; only their sporting women have claimed a fuller devotion from me.

"Tell the truth, I have another question. Can one of you tell me where the train tracks are? Put it to you like this. If you lived in Blairs and your house was by the train tracks, where would you have to live? I haven't been here in thirty years and I'm trying to find Granddaddy's old house." I spoke to strangers in a most deliciously familiar and unpretentious way, which itself was a minor performance of dishonesty. I pushed the words together and closed off the endings like I had been drinking. Without any prompting, I would have started to add little aphorisms and bits of color, and it wouldn't have been long before I started to make cozy assumptions and to offer opinions on things that were really none of my business.

The tall man looked at me and the other man gave him some room. Gold Link remained completely absorbed in his cell phone conversation. "Sure. It must be 719. You just go down road Twenty-Nine back to Danville and make a left at 719. You can't miss the railroad." He was pleasant and assured and I picked up his aura of confidence. By then I was wishing I had on a new pair of expensive sneakers, baggy jeans, an ample-sized collegiate jersey, and a sweatband. Everyone was quite friendly, and who wanted to let them down? As I climbed into the car, I smiled to myself and wondered if this was what Toni Morrison had had in mind.

Not far beyond the gas station, I hit a new portion of the road. I saw 726 and wondered if this was it, and then thought he might have said 729. The next light was 719, and I figured that was close so I would give it a shot. A sign on the right side of the road said SOUTH SIDE ELEMENTARY, so I took the left, back across the expressway and toward the town of Ringgold. After two blocks I was seeing fields of tall grass and mobile homes on cinderblocks; this might be what I was looking for. I made right turns into the small streets, and found it promising when I stumbled upon a run of mobile homes that seemed to dead-end at a railroad. In thirty years they might have added other trailers, I would guess. There were signs that said Only Residents and Their guests Permitted, which, in the African American sectors of the United States, means that people sell or take their narcotics outdoors. Driving over the speed bumps, I reached a cul-de-sac but failed to see any train tracks. As I was coming back up the hill, a young girl went into one of the barracks, and then a man in a white knit hat trotted outside and stared at my car.

Back I went to 719. Although a couple of the streets looked promising, except for the one with the bounding black Rottweilers, it was clear that I was getting nowhere. After a couple of miles, I came up to a T intersection; a car was bearing down behind me, so I pulled off into the gravel lot of what appeared to be a nameless convenience store. I got out of the car and locked the door. As I approached a cinder-block building, a Chihuahua stood sentinel and barked loudly while retreating. The store was open, and a screen door kept out the bugs. Since two young whites had been driving the car behind me, I began to wonder if I had crossed into a different neighborhood; but inside the blockhouse, two youngish African American men stood beside a pool table. There was a bar in the far depths of the store, and a television secured by a chain to the ceiling blared out the latest teen video. One of the men was meriny colored like Malcolm X, and short and stocky; the other stood about medium height and was slim, with ancient scars around his eye sockets, and he had what people searching for runaway slaves used to call a "scanty beard." I asked the fellas where to find the railroad tracks.

The stocky guy must have been around my age, but he wasn't showing any gray in his goatee. He had the high-pitched voice that I associate with contented black Southern men. "I only moved here last month. If my brother was around he could tell you. Poochie here, he's from around here, he might know." He pointed to the nicknamed man, who backed up to the edge of one of the pool tables. His mouth was slack, and I saw the canyon descending from his gums. "I ain't been up here but six months, come down from Lynchburg." I jawed back and forth a bit, telling them what I was looking for. They were helpful, polite, and earnest, but they didn't know anything about the local history or geography. "Maybe try Malmaison road. Might be out there." I pointed my finger outside the door, assuming that Malmaison was parallel to 719, the road I had just been on. "I never tried to get there that way," the thickset man said.

Starting out again, I picked up my cell phone and dialed my mother's number. I felt like this was cheating a bit, but it was now almost two o'clock in the afternoon. After several rings she answered the phone, and I told her where I was, after telling her about the baby shower that my colleagues had held for me the previous night. She was in a good mood and talkative, and — this surprised me — she was pleased that I had come to Blairs. At the end of the day, my mother believes that you can never do enough for family. She told me that my father's Aunt Sally lived in a white clapboard house across the street from an elementary school; I immediately remembered passing South Side Elementary earlier, so I turned the car in the other direction, away from Keeling, and headed back the way I had come. When I reached the Blairs end of the Malmaison road, the day turned in another direction.

As I covered the same ground I had traveled an hour earlier, back to the business road heading into Danville, my mother provided me with a crucial piece of information: my grandfather didn't live on a regular blacktop road. It was possible, I knew, that the road he lived on might have been paved sometime in the past thirty years, but when I drove down Blair Street and saw the train tracks I was inspired. I was close now, close to that symbol of social mobility and locomotion, the way in and out. If someone were writing about my own early life in Northwest Baltimore, it would be impossible to ignore the significance of the B&O line and the elevated subway train a few blocks away, though the subway appeared only around the time I entered high school. Would an outside observer understand the closeness of the rail lines to my parents' house, a good furlong, to be a measure of my family's nearness to poverty or despair? In all my childhood in Baltimore, I have no memory of the train.

But the road I was on did not lead to houses by the tracks; instead, it merely took me through an underpass that allowed only one car to pass at a time. I turned around and tried another street, Depot Road. This time I saw white families, and the houses were separated by only about twenty-five feet. I remembered that Grandpa Jackson had few neighbors. His outhouse was shaded by trees and visited by crawling things, so he must have lived near a forest. This couldn't be right. When I reached the crest of the hill, there were huge piles of crossties and automobile-sized mounds of gravel: the railroad tracks were in plain sight now. A dirt road led off in one direction toward what looked like a commune, a circular cluster of houses on a hill with what appeared to be a junkman's inventory littered throughout the yards. The clutter and the neighborhood violated the essence of my memory, and so I went on. I rejected Learner Lane because it was paved and seemed too small. Besides, a black couple had made eye contact with me, and I didn't want to appear so witless as to have driven down a dead-end street and to have to turn around in someone's driveway. Certainly they would say, "You're not from around here. Lost?" I worried that I would fail in life because I dwelled on what other people thought. Soon I would have to go to the bathroom.

I spotted another choice, the Mountain View Road, which became the Warehouse Road. I saw two young, bosomy black women walking lethargically, but I didn't ask them any questions. I doubted my ability to reach beyond their defensive armor, and I doubted their ability to contribute to the story I was trying to piece together, since they appeared to be only in their twenties. Far along the Mountain Road, much farther than the house could be, I saw a marvelous wooden bridge across a small creek, then a small two-story white house with round dormer windows on a small rise just before the forest grew dense.

I imagined my grandfather on a starry evening, walking with my grandmother Virginia Joyce in the cool woods—no, that would have been when he was already my age. So I imagined him further back, when he would have been a teenager, strutting with some coltish young woman. I considered the sublime beauty in those nights. Reversing my course once again, I let a car pass and returned to Route 29, headed toward Danville. It was getting on toward three in the afternoon now, and when darkness came down I knew that people around here would be more suspicious of strangers, and that it would be impossible for me to square my old memories with the actual layout of the neighborhood.

Without cause, I turned in at the Dallas Car Wash, a line of do-it-yourself cinder-block bays resting on the same lot with Bryans Brothers and Johnson, an old grocery store. The store was on Landrum Road, and behind it was a gravel path. I followed the macadam past two houses occupied by whites, and then, in front of a not-indecent log cabin house, the gravel path broke off into a rutted mud lane. But I would be damned if the log cabin didn't directly overlook the railroad tracks. It seemed impossible to me that I had forgotten so significant a detail as that my grandfather had lived in a log cabin. I tried to adjust my memory, and a vivid recollection emerged. In 1992 my Cincinnati cousin Elizabeth had shared with me a photograph of her mother, my great-aunt Sally, standing in front of a timber-and-chink frame cabin. She had used that picture to tell the story of how far we had come as a family.

Since it was getting late and I had had such rotten luck getting even this far and finding the railroad, now that I was here I decided to walk the train track and see what was what. I parked the car behind a building near the car wash so as not to attract attention, and as I made my way past the first two houses and up to the log cabin, a white man in a blue mechanic's jumper and a billed cap walked out the cabin door and scampered around back. He didn't acknowledge me. Seconds later, when I reached the front of the cabin, another man strolled outside, quart in hand, wearing an acid-wash denim jacket. He had a long beard, like those worn by farmers in the 1860s. I waved to him, and he came over. "Hello, there," I said. "I was looking for the house my grandfather lived in. I haven't been here in thirty years." The man looked at the ground and not at me, so it took me a minute to realize he had heard me. "What's his name?" he asked.

I told him I was looking for the Jacksons, which is really like saying nothing sometimes, because the name is so common. The bearded man called to the mechanic, who arrived with alarming speed. I figured I could handle two drunks, if it came to that, but I remained very wary, wondering if they were armed, remembering that worse than the pain that's inflicted during a brawl is the lingering sense that you have been inappropriately touched, handled, had your privacy violated. I would not like to have these two men eternally lodged in my memory that way.

"He says he looking for his folks." The bearded man spoke in a friendly tone, articulating his words in a way that evokes the Southern elite, though his diction was casual. I imagined that Custer defeated his ancestors in March of 1865 at Waynesboro, one of the only battles I was aware of taking place so far west in Virginia. The other man, whose teeth had dwindled to a handful, spoke more plainly. I tried to describe to them what little I remembered of my childhood visits to this place, recognizing that I didn't know any of the last names of my relatives, and that I could barely recall their first names. So far as I knew, all my folks had been dead for at least twenty years, and these white men seemed to have been drinking so much they would barely be able to recall anything that happened last week. It seemed futile to talk seriously to them, and to require that they talk seriously to me—as if I were in the Senegalese city of Dakar asking the baggage clerk to look at me and tell me where my ancestors were from.

In spite of my reluctance, the story intrigued the man, who pulled on his quart bottle; he held up his end of the conversation. "Cody, he might know, and Charlie up there remembers all kinds of folks."

We were walking downhill now on something like a muddy cattle path. My guide pointed to a house immediately after his, painted yellow, with a porch and a second story and a tin roof, an elaborate home compared to the others, even though it looked as if it had been abandoned.

"They was white," he informed me, offhandedly and randomly. Unsure of a safe route through the minefield, I had not mentioned race at all.

"But black people did live around here?" I continued, uncertain of the exact protocols of this place and time and wondering if I've crossed a line. In the end, I decided I was obliged to rely on the sense of kinship and honesty that the inebriated and the manual laborer are known for.

Using the bottle as a microphone and holding his cigarette in the other hand, the bearded man replied, "Oh yeah, used to live all up on that hill." Then he pointed to a large man on a porch. "See that man up there, he might be able to tell you, or the other fella."

Up on the hill sat a tiny house that the circular dirt road linked to the others situated in the grove. On the face of this clock, the car wash was at midnight and the train tracks were at six; the house, which looked to have been one or two bedrooms, was at about nine. I have arrived back at the domestic junkyard I encountered earlier. The yard was teeming with every conceivable cast-off item of the imagination, all laid out as if corresponding to the intricate, abstract design of a Roman phalanx or an elaborate Asian garden. The booty was immense, and it included a basketball backboard, goal and post, highway signs, construction barriers, old tires, three rusted iron wood-burning stoves, a table filled with athletic trophies, a sewing machine, and a plastic barrel jammed full of empty liquor quarts. Sitting on the slab porch with what looked like a guitar was a bear of a brown man with red-streaked skin.

At the foot of the concrete stairs, I could see that he was dressed like a hunter: orange cap, fatigue shirt, black vest, khaki trousers coming apart at the crotch, muddy boots. In his fist was a wine bottle with a metallic screw top. He opened his mouth and I saw, for the fourth time that day, only canines and molars; but he was young and ample enough that no appreciable slackness was yet manifest in his full mouth.

Without offering any greeting, the two white men began to relate the general elements of my story, but I decided, with a burst of courage, that I should tell it myself. I cut off the drinking man before he got very far. I guess I did it because these two seemed to me just lowdown drunks and, well, white Virginians whose ancestors fought for the Confederacy. Then I wondered about that move: was my sense of basic human feeling giving way to the calculations of status that have become increasingly important to me since I began my career, got married, became a stepparent, and purchased a home? Was this worth any soul-searching at all? Weren't the men only toothless drunks, barely keeping a roof over their heads, and living out in the country to boot? Their grove of dwellings on this messy road by the CSX railroad tracks called to mind a hobo camp. What I had seen before that compared to it were the giant squatter camps of the townships of Guguletu, in Cape Town, South Africa.

I got down to business, explaining what I wanted but not paying enough attention to get Bear's name correctly, which I knew was rude and sadiddy. "I think my grandfather used to live around here. You ever hear of Nathaniel Jackson?"

"No. Can't say as I do. When was he here?" He took a pull from the jug.

"He lived in a little house with my aunt Mary and my uncle John. Must have been 1973, '74. I haven't been here in thirty years. All I remember was we could walk up and down the train tracks."

After I had gotten out these words and the atmosphere eased, the bearded man ambled diffidently up the path with his quart of beer, dragging on his cigarette. He was the one who had suggested I talk to the man at the top of the hill. His cabin-mate in the blue mechanic's smock asked for a taste from Bear.

"Let me have—let me have a sip of that wine." Bear ignored him.

"He lived right chere, he did! Mary and John Gizee was living on here quite a time, and then Carnel come but she was Stevens by then and CD and Clyde, they Mays, she the oldest..." He rambled elliptically from name to name, and I was unable to follow the rapid connections. After a while, he found a familiar vein and went off into a deep account of his epic life and my family that I struggled to follow. I had always prided myself on my ability to speak Southern vernacular, or at least to understand it, but now I was listening to what might as well have been Haitian Kreyol. Overall, though, it was good to see this man beaming and excited and telling his story. He was certain that this was my grandfather's house.

Just to be sure, I tried to press for more information, and again the mechanic insisted, "C'mon man, gimme a drink."

"You better get you a cup of water," drawled the large man, eyes still on me as I explained the story I'd heard. Suddenly, Bear rushed inside and returned with a packet of wadded paper. He'd been unable to recall the spelling of the surname of Aunt Mary and Uncle John, and I had had no idea what it might have been and offered a bad imitation of what he had said. He showed me a year's worth of electric bills, still in the envelopes, bound by a rubber band. This is the practice that I've invariably known at home, where the billing address is always left in the name of a person who might have been twenty years gone. On the bills that Bear showed me, the last name is spelled "Kesee."

John Kesee, husband of Mary. Well, I've documented proof that I finally found it. My memory, capable of having my grandfather living in a mobile home one moment, or a log cabin in the next, was obviously an instrument operating on principles that I had not quite mastered.

Bear seemed happy for the conversation, and he shifted our talk into a new groove. "Yeah, I do what I can here, not too much. Roof leaks and I tried to patch, water still comes through."

I knew how to respond; after all, I was from Baltimore. "Hat's off to you. What can you do? You're only one man."

He rattled off the phone number of the woman he was renting the house from, and I took some notes with a pencil on a yellow Post-it. Bear was from Alabama and Florida, he said, but was trying Danville for a while.

"Hey, if there's somewhere else to go, I'll go! Nothing holding me here! I don't need much and I could live anywhere. I mean, I'm from Tampa

Nathaniel Jackson's house, Blairs, Virginia, 2003. Photograph: Lawrence Jackson.

where it's not country, you know, people might say, 'How he done it,' but up here it is kind of country, you know, 'How he done did hit,' people talk country like that." He effortlessly read my mind and was, in his own way, keeping up with the Joneses.

The mechanic heartily agreed with Bear's comparative analysis of the local idiom and kept his eyes fixed on the wine jug snug in the brown paper bag. I told the men I would return with a camera and that I would try to find them a taste. Cutting across about thirty square yards of freshly plowed ground, I edged away from three barking dogs on chain leashes and got back in my car. Back on Route 29, I thought I understood my father a whole lot better. At the convenience store a black patron told me I couldn't get beer on Sunday. So instead I purchased Funyuns and a Seagram's ginger ale for myself, and I planned to make a cash gift to the storyteller later in the day.

From the convenience store I drove north, back to E. Witt Road and South Side Elementary, where I hoped to locate Aunt Sally's house. There were four houses across from the school. One of them had a roof and porch, and even though the strongest memory that I had was of killing flies in the hot sun, I chose the house with a screened-in porch and a Volvo in the driveway. I rapped against the doorframe. A man emerged from the doorway, almost exactly my age, I thought, and dressed in a white shirt and creased black pants. He had his head turned in the direction of a woman he was talking to who remained sheltered behind the door. I explained to him quickly that I wanted to know if this was my great-aunt Sally's house, though I did not know her married name. Without opening the screen door, he bid the woman come to the doorway. Whereas the man was tall and inclining toward portly, his apparent spouse was petite. Both of them had the complexion of a Hershey bar and looked exactly like movie extras for a family reunion film. They resembled well-fed, shy members of the church choir, the people who we would claim universally as kinfolks without any reservation. I wondered how they took me, talking proper and with a wool felt hat like men wore sixty years ago.

"Oh, you must mean Miss Sally Younger. All them Younger peoples lives right next door, on the other side of the yellow house," the petite woman said, and she gestured to the four houses on her left. I asked her to repeat herself, unable for some reason to make out what she said without watching her lips move.

Next door was a weather-beaten yellow bungalow, with a roof about ready to collapse. Beside it was a house in slightly better shape, although I couldn't be sure that people lived there. Further down the road, the small dwelling directly across from the elementary school had a sign over its front door that appeared to read Keep Out. The cinderblock foundation for the porch remained, but there was no longer a concrete slab covering the blocks. Instead, the space had the look of an open grave waiting to be filled in. Still, this was the place to which I had been directed, and I walked up the gravel driveway to the door. Everyone used the back door to get in, I was sure, but I did not want to lose my status as a kind of guest, a pilgrim maybe, anticipating what I hoped would be a polite, if restrained, welcome. The flat rocks making the path through the lawn were painted white, I noticed, as were the first three feet of the two trees in the middle of the yard.

I knocked on the door, fairly confident, perhaps, because I had by then introduced my story to a dozen people. After a moment or two, I heard stirring inside, and then the door opened to reveal an older woman with a broad nose and ginger-colored skin. It was hard to place her age, but she had an efficient quickness and energy about her.

"Hello?" she asked querulously.

I was formal and a little bit apologetic. "Good afternoon. I'm sorry to bother you. I was wondering if my aunt Sally used to live here."

And then, finally, as if I had been seeking these words for a long time but had been unable to utter them until now, I said, "I am Nathaniel Jackson's grandson."

"Who's that you say?"

"My grandfather was Nathaniel Jackson and my father was Nathaniel Jackson, but everybody called him Junior." Across the chasms of my memory, I could hear my grandfather's sister, Aunt Mary, saying "Junior," which she pronounced "june year" and in one syllable.

Slowly, the woman opened the door and allowed me into the front room. It had been a mild day, about fifty-nine degrees; and when I walked into the house, smelling the cabbage and beans and salted pork, the overpowering steam heat fogged my glasses. I didn't see the man seated in front of me, immobile and with his mouth open, until I wiped off my glasses.

"You don't know who be at your door nowadays; people act so crazy," the woman apologized to me, and then marched speedily into the kitchen. Just as quickly, she returned.

"I had to get something on the stove. So you say your last name was Jackson and you was looking for Sally?" She beamed at me. "That's her son right there. William Younger. And I'm Lillian."

I didn't catch on immediately, but I don't have any doubt that these people knew Aunt Sally well. I remembered my great-aunt as having a complexion lighter than my grandfather's and my twin great-aunts, Mary and Martha. From my mother's description I can remember mainly Sally Younger's gregariousness and ample bosom. Smiling at the woman who invited me to sit down, I took off my hat but left on my coat.

"I haven't been here in thirty years, but my mother told me that there was a school across the street, and I remember playing out in front of my aunt Sally's yard, across the street from the school. Somebody I am related to used to work at the school."

"That was me!" Lillian Younger responded. Her youthfulness intensified as she warmed to the conversation and as I became less of a stranger. She was thin and bristling with energy, wearing slippers and a Mother Hubbard, and her hair was already set for Monday's business. William still hadn't said much; he appeared immense, seated in a recliner, gripping the chair's remote control and fixing his eyes on me purposefully.

"He's eighty-four and I'm eighty-one," Lillian went on, joyful now, flashing her teeth. She had a golden incisor tooth, next to the canine, the golden adoration I admire most because the flash is subtle. My father had a front tooth chip in gold, but it fell out in the middle 1970s, and he had it

replaced with porcelain. Over the years my sister has reminded me that
Grandpa Jackson was fond of gold work in his own teeth.

I told Lillian the reason I had come and she drank the story in, responding with animated facial expressions, gestures, and steady eye contact to let me know she was really interested in knowing about me and
not at all put off by the gulf in our ages, though she and William were
about ten or twelve years older than my own father would have been,
had he lived.

My cousin Lillian reeled off the names of my great-aunts and uncles—
Willie, Ed, Johnny, Burt, Hugh, Sally, Mary, Martha, and Lil—with a
nod or a word or two from William in confirmation. I never really had
considered my grandfather's brothers and sisters beyond the ones I had
met personally; despite the fact that I had known all of my maternal
grandmother's living siblings, my paternal extended family had been abstract. Of course, then I fully understood my relation to William seated
before me—he was my father's first cousin, the son of Sally—and I was
a bit stunned to have bungled onto my second cousins this way, after so
many years in absence, to have connected directly with my own bloodline. I pressed Lillian to tell me anything she could concerning my great-grandparents, their land and the work they did, and where it was that
they came from originally. "We used to know more," she said, bashfully,
"but we've forgot so much."

I asked if I could take their picture, and I prepared a single-use camera
I had bought for this purpose at the local store. Cousin William was immediately game, but Lillian was a bit reluctant; and when she finally consented to have her image captured, she wheeled around the corner into
the other room to take the curlers out of her hair. I can't quite get into
words what I wanted to say to her. "Don't go to any fuss for me," I stammered, not wanting her to put herself out for an unannounced stranger.
Yet I admired her wish to perform the ritual act of making up, because
neither one of us knows where the picture will wind up someday. What
if this image turns out to be the only connection my grandchildren have
to this place? Lillian wanted to be proud of the image she left to posterity, and I very much wanted her to take pride in the idea of her own
memory.

After I had spent some time attempting to make small talk with William, she returned. She had quite a lot of black in her hair, which haloed
her face and made it seem like the center of a delicate mushroom. I
snapped the picture and prepared to leave. Before I could, she telephoned her niece Carnel, but got the answering machine on the first

ring. My aunt Sally, she told me, used to live right next door, where Lillian's son, Sally's grandchild, now lives. Lillian had imagined he would have repaired the house before Christmas.

"It takes every penny and always something to fix. You can't do much on social security," she said. I nodded my head in agreement, thinking of my own mother who retired that year, and whose house was certain to require some looking after. "I spend every free minute I have and every penny on the house," she went on. I was sympathetic, knowing how much of my take-home salary had gone into my own house, after the twin mortgage payments and utility bills.

As I made for the door to go in search of Carnel's house, Lillian's son, William Jr., was coming in. He was an extraordinarily distinguished-looking man, almost a twin of former Maryland congressman and NAACP executive Kweisi Mfume, but taller. He greeted me warmly and, apparently the kind of person never at a loss with strangers, said he remembered me as a child.

"I tore down the porch of Aunt Sally's house and I'm fixing the place up," he continued, conveying the message that he was a man who got things done.

"I've got a daughter just turned thirty-two," he told me. This news seemed unbelievable, because William Jr. gave the impression of being in his midforties, maybe. He was wearing a starched denim shirt and denim pants, new Timberland hiking boots, and a wool-billed cap. He had a thick mustache, exactly like the one I remember my father having when he was in his middle forties, and like his mother and father, he was the color of rich almond and ginger, the same color as Anwar Sadat, as if his complexion emerged at the exact geographic center of Africa and Europe. Repeatedly insisting that he'll be sure to stay in touch with me, he walked me over to his cousin Carnel's house, next door to his.

"Carnel!" He rapped on the locked screen. The door was unlatched, and a retreating figure moved away from the general arc of the front door. "Oh hey, Clyde," William Jr. said, shouldering past a man into the house. "Carnel, look who I found." A middle-aged woman appeared, medium size and a bit stooped. She had on a Caribbean carnival T-shirt, and since she stood next to a colorfully lit Christmas tree that dominated the living room, I had a hard time making her out. As soon as he announced my visit, William Jr. turned and left the house.

"I just drove up from Durham today, but I live in Atlanta," I explained to Cousin Carnel. "We're having a baby, and if it's a boy I'm going to name him for your cousin Nat, and I wanted to come up and see the old house, where Grandpa Jackson used to live." I was not sure what part of what I said registered with value to Carnel.

She was Aunt Martha's daughter, and I met Aunt Martha maybe twice. But I saw her twin sister, Aunt Mary, more than anybody who came out of the union of my great-grandparents. The memory of the two sisters has stayed in my mind for many years. In fact, I once told my wife that she reminded me a little of Aunt Mary, though I doubted there could be any connection between what my wife looked like on the day we got married and my memory of a woman who was in her seventies when I first met her. I thought of this when I asked, "Excuse me, Cousin Carnel, but do you have any pictures of Aunt Martha?" She directed me to the television set that doubled as a bureau top and handed me a framed color picture of a high school graduate, which held another small black-and-white snapshot tucked into the upper corner. The picture showed a gleaming dark-brown-skinned couple, and especially because of the young man's tie, the photograph looked like it dated from the 1940s. But the face of the woman staring out of the picture was so young that it could only be from the 1920s. I suspected that for Carnel both the '20s and the '40s were before her time and thus, for all it matters, the same time, so I didn't ask her to date the picture. Besides, I got the sense that she might not have gotten along very well with presumptuous William Jr., and that as a consequence of his taking the liberty to show me in I might be only slightly welcome in the house. As I looked at Aunt Martha's photograph, what struck me about her youthful face was the way her upper lip dimpled in the center, making her seem simultaneously shy and sensual.

Carnel and I talked a bit; she told me that at the beginning of the year both of her sons were stationed in Iraq. Then something else occurred to her. "Oh, wait a minute," she said. "Come here. I've got another picture in here." She walked toward the back bedroom of the two-bedroom house. Carnel's brother Clyde was sitting against the room's light-blue wall, watching a basketball game on a floor-model television. I didn't even have time to utter a greeting before an old picture dominating the bedroom overwhelmed me. It was my grandfather and his brother, in their very early twenties.

I had no memory of ever having seen a picture of my grandfather as a young man. As an older man he had become portly and gray, and it wasn't possible for me to imagine him in his prime. But if I had ever seen it anywhere, I would have fixated on the picture hanging over Clyde's bed. The family resemblance was so definite and strong that seeing that face was very much like seeing a ghost. I was astonished by the way my

Nathaniel Jackson Sr., ca. 1918.

grandfather's expression favored someone in particular—my own sister. Over Thanksgiving I had found myself staring at her, trying to figure out the murky origins of her looks and wondering whose appearance the baby would reflect.

The picture was remarkable for another reason. The two young men were both wearing their hair shaved along the sides, furry on top, and sloping into a peak at the right. I too had worn my hair like that, in high school and in college, seventy years after these two men. *Avum aethiopem regeneravit.* My grandfather was clean shaven and handsome, and his eyes sparkled with purposefulness. It was a marvelous picture, and I had not wanted to have something so badly in a very long time. The double portrait was sepia tinted, larger than an eight-by-ten, and housed in an oval wooden frame that reminded me of the winged clocks popular during the eighteenth century. The glass of the frame was concave, so I needed to stand almost on top of Clyde's bed to see the image properly, which I knew was the crown of rudeness in a day of putting myself and my story first. Obviously, the picture occupied a deliberate place of prominence in the home. The portrait of the two Jackson brothers made the house familiar and reminded Carnel and Clyde of their ancestry and gave meaning to their existence. The picture was a sanctuary and a relief from the insistent flatness and plainness of day-to-day life, and I don't doubt that the clear-eyed purposefulness of the two dandy young men offers an inspiration to their descendants. Still, my excitement could barely be contained; this was so much more than I had hoped to encounter—the house, my own kin, and now the very man at the center of this history.

I asked permission to take a picture of the picture on Clyde's wall. Then I turned back to my cousin. "Well, what do you think, Carnel, do I favor him?" I showed my own profile, obscuring the television screen, and she could only answer yes. As we made our way out of the room, having left the taciturn Clyde in peace, I found myself to have grown drunk on pompousness by nightfall. I demanded assurance from my cousin: "You have to promise me that you'll keep that picture in the family." That picture turned out to be a window that let the air of the past rush in.

2 · "I Knew My Father"

I can't remember exactly why I had wanted to see my father's birth certificate around the time I published my first book. I had written a biography of the writer Ralph Ellison, and it was a demanding struggle to obtain the man's public records. But with my own father's records, I presumed I would have unfettered access as next of kin. Thinking it would be a simple matter, I went to the Virginia bureau of vital records, which was in Richmond, just down the street from where I then lived.

The occasion turned into a miniature odyssey filled with surprises. Because of the commonness of the surname Jackson, the clerk asked me to look at the original record to help the computer distinguish my father from one or two other men. The tattered index card that the clerk eventually produced gave my father's birth year as 1932. As long as I had known my father, I thought he was born in 1933: that date was on his passport, social security card, driver's license, and gravestone.

The torn old record contained a trove of additional personal information, including the street in Danville, Virginia, where my father had been born. I had never known that before. I later found a writer's description of that area as consisting of the "tumbled-down Negro shacks of Jackson's Branch" and the "poor little Providence Hospital for Colored." In the hard times of the Depression, women from Poor House Hill close by were thought to eat dirt.[1] But most revelatory on the unusual card was my grandfather's inclusion of the names of his parents, Ned Jackson and Less Hundley Jackson, both of them aged but still living in 1932. When I indicated that this was the correct Nathaniel Jackson record, the clerk asked me to return the card, and a minute or so later gave me an official birth certificate bearing the state seal. But none of the precious information about my father and his grandparents was included on the computerized form. I asked to see the original record again, but he refused to show it to me a second time.

I had to insist on a meeting with an assistant to the registrar, and then had to entreat this woman for another chance: that I was actually a credentialed research professional in addition to being my father's next of kin, and that I had a right to at least take notes from this pertinent family information. Her first response was to refuse to admit that I had seen an original form. Then she denied any qualitative difference between the computer-generated certificate and the original index card from 1932. The scene struck me as odd, my having to importune and supplicate in a cloying kind of way so that I could see a dynamic living record scribed by a human being. That the clerk and the assistant registrar, and indeed the registrar, were white, and that the bureau sits on Monument Avenue in Richmond, with its legendary marble statues of Confederate generals Lee, Stuart, and Jackson, and that I am black did not register in my mind on that day.

Like the great majority of Americans, like the Richmond assistant registrar I guess, I grew up in a world that still needed to believe the quaint, comforting Thomas Nelson Page image of slavery. Page, the best-known postbellum broadcaster of literature nostalgic for the plantation era, described the period of black servitude in Virginia as a time when "the heart was light and the toil not too heavy."[2] Page's romantic view of slavery became a cornerstone of what might stand as the American national religion when Margaret Mitchell's book *Gone with the Wind* became a successful film in 1939. During my childhood, my family regularly watched the annually televised film *Gone with the Wind* with the same ritual devotion that we gave to the Easter pageant film *The Ten Commandments*. (By contrast, the television series *Roots* came on one time.) *Gone with the Wind* opens with images of black plow hands jostling with one another in the bright sun for the privilege of announcing, "It's quitting time!" The strong undercurrent of the film is that slavery was a job, like any other, and devoted hard work produces success. It is not difficult to see why the movie would be popular not just with whites but with blacks too.

My grandmothers were both living in 1977 when *Roots* was broadcast. I don't know if they saw the program, but even if they did I am fairly certain that all my grandparents had a more intimate relation with the film *Gone with the Wind*. All of them, born in the rural South, at one time or another, for some of or all their working lives, served in parlors and kitchens and sickrooms and in front of furnaces. The film's key black characters, Mammy, Prissy, Pork, and Big Sam, must have presented as interesting a challenge to them and their memories of their grandparents as it did to my own conception of what slavery would have been like. The film embodies three powerful concepts about enslavement: black people were childlike (Pork and Prissy), they were faithful (Mammy and Big Sam), and mixed-race people did not exist. In other words, if you have lived several hundred years in a country known all over the world for the ethnic range of its population and the possibility of accumulating fantastic wealth, what being a member of a powerless but highly visible minority group descended from ex-chattels means is to look at yourself, your past, through the myths, the joys, the guilt, and the fear of someone else. It is possible to identify with that person and his or her point of view, but whether or not it is your own, or is one that the people who have created you would recognize or acknowledge, that is something else. Under such circumstances, looking for yourself might not be impossible, but it is a task with stalwart and jagged obstacles.

It can take a while to achieve your own vision. At my Catholic high school on the same day that Martin Luther King's birthday became a federal holiday, the Irish-American class president stopped me in the hallway and said that he and some of the athletes thought that Booker T. Washington should have received the recognition instead of Martin Luther King Jr. My scholarship to the school notwithstanding, my classmate told me that Washington, not King, "really did something for black people." I had been to the US Capitol with my dad, my sister, Stevie Wonder, and others to gather for a day in King's name. But as the seventeen-year-old president of my high school Black Student's Union, I didn't really know enough history to counter my schoolmate's unflattering point. I simply dismissed his remark, because I knew that what he meant was that he opposed the national holiday.

And honestly, when I was in high school during the early Reagan years, I accepted King's struggle and work as largely complete. The success of the civil rights movement, as I understood it then, was that my racial background would not hinder me if I lived an immaculate, cautious life. The hallway conversation took place immediately prior to some quite ordinary events that I had been sheltered from that would pierce the myth that slavery was like a job, and that being black in America amounted to the same kind of difference as being of Mexican, Irish, or Jewish descent: a white American called me "nigger" to my face; a white American in a position of power told me my background was inadequate to be admitted to a school; and white (at first) American police began to demonstrate precisely how cheap to them my life really was.

In college, when I learned that American slavery was a genocide involving tens of millions of people, I became prouder of my heritage, because I understood more about what my ancestors had survived. I doubted if I could have survived it myself. I was also confused, because it had never been a topic of much conversation among the black people I had then known. In spite of the magnitude of American slavery, since it was more than a century in the past, I was forced to conclude that my slave-born ancestors would ever remain a complete mystery to me.

An ordinary black American had three chances to learn about the past, I thought. You could have ancestors who had been vicious desperadoes tried before the bar of justice and had their deeds transcribed in a court and exposed by the press, generating a paper record for posterity. Or, wealthy planters who left extensive farm books, correspondence, or diaries might have owned your family. An ancestor might have been jotted down by name in a record when he or she received a peck of cornmeal, a blanket, a visit from a doctor, or thirty-nine lashes. Finally, and least probably, a black family might have stewarded a phenomenal African legend of some kind that had been passed down orally. But since most blacks merely tried to survive slavery, and served out that sentence with something like twenty-three fellow captives on a small farm and many of the group were children, and since so many black Americans are as uneasy toward Africa as are American whites, the chances for uncovering enslaved forbears seemed slight.

But really the profound difficulty to the entire prospect of finding my ancestors was in my surname, one of the terribly common ones among African Americans. In 2000, the US census reported something like 353,046 black Americans sharing the surname Jackson, almost one in every hundred. Black people made up 53 percent of all Americans named Jackson: only Washington and Jefferson had higher percentages among black Americans, though there are more black Jacksons than all the Washingtons and Jeffersons, black or white, combined.[3] In the roughly century and a half since slavery, these common names, evidence of "unrecognized and unrecognizable loves," have become tribal.[4] Even when they are ordinary, we make something of them and the story that they tell, because human beings are past-making machines.

In the eighth grade, a friend had impressed me with his own sense of past-making when he presented his Scottish forefathers' coat of arms to our class. I had not considered something like that, a remote but heralded lineage for my own English surname. I had grown to adulthood on a city block where black Americans with English surnames surrounded me, and having one seemed only a matter of course. My neighbors carried names like Carrington, Blow, Watkins, Travis, Parrot, Rawlings, Barber, Miller, Anderson, Smith, Jones, Holeman, Tubman, Grant, Speers,

Shelton, Sampson, Thompson, Hopkins, Washington, Dallas, Brown, English, Taylor, White, and Clayborne.

Of course, when you think about the whole of human history, surnames themselves are fairly new. In the English-speaking world, the common surnames came into fashion as people escaped from (or were pushed out of) the lands they had worked under feudal lords. This process confused genealogies and took the common man away from the landowners' church to a town or parish church that had to record men, their marriages, and their issue on rolls and keep them distinct, one from the other.

The most regular surnames evolved from the custom of being known as the son of a certain person. The custom gained in importance as people had something they wanted to make sure went from one generation to the next during the nasty, brutish, and short phase of English history. So the son of John, the most popular first name in England, took off and never looked back. John in fact was so popular a first name that it drew a derivative, Jack, and the sons of that family too clapped a mighty sound. The relation must mean something, because I once received a speeding ticket from a completely sober Baltimore police officer who wrote my name as "Lawrence Johnson." It's hard to even call it an error.

More typically, and arguably with more certainty, since the axiom "mama's baby, papa's maybe" cuts across race and time, English common folk took last names based on what they could be absolutely certain of: what they did for a living. The "smythe" of the early modern world was a "can-do" operator. Village life and early industry gave rise to all kinds of construction and merchant engineers and, consequently, surnames: archers, sawyers, coopers, carvers, carters, turners, joiners, tinkers, rogers, fullers, tuckers, and so on. Some people left the places they were born and called themselves after the region, the town, or my favorite, the general landscape of the places they'd left: hill, brown, green, blue, river, ford, brook, forest, and field.

Jack in English can of course be either verb or noun, a tool, money, or a lever to help lift something, or it can be the lifting itself. In the eighteenth century when the trade in men and women between Africa and the Virginia colony was regular, it was not unknown for the English masters to practice rough transliterations in naming their slaves. *Jack* also seems to have been an Anglicized version of *Quacko*, or the Akan name Kweku, for a boy born on a Wednesday. I was born on a Wednesday.[5]

African Americans were overwhelmingly owned by English descendants in North America by the nineteenth century. Several surnames register significant percentages from among a population that had no legal right to any for the greater part of the nineteenth century. They are Smith, Johnson, Williams, Jones, Brown, and Jackson.

Perhaps the simplest hypothesis is the best. At the conclusion of the Civil War and the reality of the general emancipation, let's just say by 1866, newly freed people would very naturally choose a surname like Freeman or Washington or Jefferson or especially Lincoln. Excluding Freeman, these names recalled revered national figures who seemed to embody the ideals of democracy and the franchise. Democrat Andrew Johnson was president of the United States when the emancipation became irrevocable and widespread. Johnson believed in a country and government for white men, but picking Johnson as one's surname must have been classy. The choice said, "Hey, look at me! Last week I was on the auction block with a mule, and this week I have the same name as the man who runs the White House!"

That is precisely the kind of noisy exuberance and merriment black Americans have been known for. Booker T. Washington was born in Franklin County, Virginia, in the later 1850s, and he claimed to have invented his own last name in a moment of classroom anxiety and inspiration. After hearing other children proudly recite two or three names, young Booker decided to join himself to the founding father of the United States. This was a boy with grey eyes and kinky red hair, who had worn mainly a rough flax shirt, gone barefoot all his life, and been known to the world heretofore as merely Booker. And of course, since black Americans continued to live in the South, Jefferson, Johnson, Washington, and Jackson were more strategically savvy choices than Freeman or Lincoln.

Thinking of himself and others he knew, Ralph Ellison once praised the complex adaptation that African Americans had made after slavery, naming themselves, like the educator Booker T. Washington, for presidents and the like.

> Perhaps, taken in the aggregate, these European names which (sometimes with irony, sometimes with pride, but always with personal investment) represent a certain triumph of the spirit, speaking to us of those who rallied, reassembled and transformed themselves and who under dismembering pressures refused to die.[6]

White masters in the eighteenth century had mocked the enslaved by giving them the names of Roman senators and consuls, but in the nineteenth century, with the pedestrian regularity of enslavement, blacks increasingly had exactly the same given names as whites. When the century changed and a generation of blacks came to lose the ties they had had with Southern whites, some of these whites being masters who had undoubtedly sustained particular African Americans during slavery, a pretentious ambition crept in that countered the miserable social reality, the era that the historian Rayford Logan called "The Nadir" in race relations. Thus, Ida and Lewis Ellison named their son Ralph *Waldo* Ellison. Added to this, eastern and southern European immigrants coming to America in large numbers assisted in a remarkable shift in ethnicity among white Americans. Consequently, given the opportunity to choose, black Americans took the most widely recognized English surnames, and in the process the holders of the names Jones, Johnson, Jackson, Jefferson, Washington, Brown, and Williams became remarkably dark in hue.

There were blacks in Pittsylvania County named for the president of the Confederacy, Jefferson Davis—that was irony—but even Ellison had difficulty revealing all the outlandish practices connected to black naming. When giving names to their children, African American farmhands and cooks, wet nurses and woodcutters resorted to a conspicuously divergent symbolic terrain that appeared to be casual and extemporaneous, but which was deeply defiant. So they named themselves Sukey and Doctor, Febby and Boocey and Morning. A tradition determined to resist white norms and arguably the legacy of bondage at the hands of English people themselves persists in such modern-day names as Lakeisha and LeBron.

Another moment of nominal differences between black and white occurred at the first full census in 1870. The white officials in the rural places where Negroes had served out their enslavement began to record surnames and given names as they seemed to be pronounced, spelling in official documents the English words spoken by black Americans the way that they sounded, and often enough using minstrel shows and print culture doggerel as their phonetic guides. Lighthearted perhaps, the practice complicated tracing the old lineages, the blood relations and the nominal evidence of the people and place where bondage had occurred.

Ex-bondman Martin Jackson described his own unique passageway to the common surname. He decided to name himself Jackson because his father had carried a tradition that the family stemmed from an African forebear who had been named Jeaceo; at the general emancipation, young Martin picked Jackson for himself.[7] There was also Andrew Jackson, popular president from the 1830s, frontiersman, and slave owner, who was rumored to have had some African and Indian blood. He appeared on the Confederate one thousand dollar bill. Moreover, he had addressed black troops and breastworks contractors at New Orleans in 1815, a deed that might have gotten around. Jackson embodied the ideal of the vigorous common man unequaled in the presidency to this day. To top it off, his wife, Rachel Donelson, was born in Pittsylvania County. I don't like to think of black people actually naming themselves for Confederate general Thomas "Stonewall" Jackson, but I am sure that some did. I suspect, however, that most newly freed people took the name of either their former owner or a nearby person, white or black, who commanded personal respect. I doubt if, with the exception of the name of the proudest of them all—Freeman—they wanted to be genuinely unusual in the new practice. I would be surprised if a goodly number of people didn't keep the names of their former owners, which had, for good or ill, become their identity by the general emancipation.

As I pondered the idea of finding my ancestors, the details I had secured from my dad's original birth record were, in fact, a bit deflating. If I was going to take advantage of Virginia archives and Pittsylvania County records to find my enslaved relatives, I needed more than the damningly popular Jackson surname and given names like Ned and Less. I knew the latter to be foreshortened proper names, but of what full versions, I could not imagine.

And yet, my grandfather's cryptic message—his own parents' names on my father's birth certificate—had stirred in me a delicate seed of curiosity. In the subsequent years, I would grow determinedly ambitious. I started to believe that I might uncover a figurative meeting place or switching station from the past where a very definite number of actors and episodes would collide. I couldn't stop myself from imagining about my ancestors, about what they must have done and known to survive, and the human beings who crowded their world and profoundly shaped the possibilities of their lives. I thought that with some sweat and some luck, I might even reach my family's last generation in slavery.

◆　◆　◆

My ancestors turned out to be waiting for me in a place a lot closer than I could have dreamed. In 2006, five years after learning the names of my great-grandparents, I prepared a family tree for my year-old son, Nathaniel. Since his own grandfather had passed away, I wanted him to have a good account of his Southside Virginia history and the origin of his own name. I couldn't travel very far into the past on my dad's side of the tree, and the empty spaces on the chart frustrated me.

Those feelings were also being rubbed raw during an early morning undergraduate class I was teaching on the slave narrative. My students—black and white—seemed complacently sluggish. They were disengaged from any problem of slavery, although they were sitting in a classroom in Georgia, on a campus named for the Methodist bishop who had created the "Southern" solution to the conflict between slavery and salvation. They were slouched at their desks only a few blocks from a street officially called Butlers Lane, where lived black servants and also slaves who had worked the land for two centuries. As a descendant of slaves, I was as disappointed by the black students having no discernible curiosity about their own near past as I was by the white students' refusal to understand how their extraordinary prosperity was owed to the nation's unhappy engraftment with servitude, to paraphrase Booker T. Washington, who was probably paraphrasing Thomas Jefferson.

I thought that I might make a presentation to the students on my own family's American past, or even on the difficulty of getting to that past, so they could see a firsthand connection to enslavement. The timing of the course coincided with the university library's subscription to an Internet database of federal census records that seemed as if it would be helpful. Thus, I began another kind of journey into the past, one shaped not so much by memories of my father and grandfather as by the occasional public records documenting their lives. On the afternoon I retrieved my grandfather Nathaniel Jackson from the census of 1900, I found my great-grandparents' official names and their ages, and another world of possibility opened up.

I had grown into adulthood knowing the names and lives of only the family members with whom I actually had relationships, who called on my birthday or played with me when I visited. But in one afternoon using the database Ancestry.com, I doubled the names of my known, direct-line ancestors. Then, after two days of a more thorough combing of the census records between 1900 and 1860, not only had I rescued my grandfather's parents and grandparents, but I had located a fair number of landholding farmers whom my ancestors had known rather well.

It turned out that both my grandfather's parents, Edward "Ned" Jackson and Celestia "Less" Hundley Jackson, had been born during slavery.

◆ ◆ ◆

I found my great-grandfather Edward Jackson in the US census of 1870 living in the southern portion of Pittsylvania County, Virginia. The census takers split the big county in two, and the dividing line was just south of the town of Competition, the county seat. In 1870 there were about one hundred and ten people named Jackson who lived either in the southern part of the county near the tobacco factory center of Danville, or in the subdivision north of the town, known as Competition between 1807 and 1874 and later renamed Chatham, for British prime minister William Pitt, first Earl of Chatham.

On the census form, I found out that my great-grandfather thought he had been born around 1855; he told the census taker he was fifteen. Over the years and in many official documents, he changed that date of birth, a fact he could never be certain of. But no other family member named Jackson was listed at the same address or even in the vicinity with Edward. He seems to have been quite alone, and he gave his occupation as "domestic servant."

My great-grandfather Edward Jackson was living with a black couple in their twenties named Isaac and Bettie Ferguson. I call the people "black," because that is how they were enumerated in the census. The other possible choices were "white" and "mulatto." The government was quite concerned about an accurate, scientific count of the "mulattoes."

Mulatto is the Spanish word for "mule," and as such it was a heartless metaphor for mixed-race Americans, because it equated human beings with creatures resulting from breeding horses with donkeys, animals from different species, whose issue was infertile. "Be particularly careful in reporting the class *Mulatto*," the 1870 census enumerators were advised by their commissioners. "The word is here generic, and includes quadroons, octoroons, and all persons having any perceptible trace of African blood."[8] An 1870 census taker undoubtedly would enumerate me as mulatto: skin color somehow not quite white but not really brown either is another kind of brand from the days of slavery.

I expect that my great-grandfather was born in a one-room "Negro house," a building of logs raised one wall at a time by hands during a pause in the work, a house which had a mud chimney. The mud chimneys were daubed with sticks, and they sometime caught fire. The celebrated hidey-holes in the cabin were the loft, which would have been warm and dry, and the root cellar, the earthen pit that housed food and

SCHEDULE 1.—Inhabitants in *Subdivision north of Dan River*, in the County of *Pittsylvania*, State of *Virginia*, enumerated by me on the 23d day of *June*, 1870. **83**

Post Office: *Ringgold & Laurel Grove*. *J. W. Cole*, Ass't Marshal.

		The name of every person whose place of abode on the first day of June, 1870, was in this family.	Age at last birthday	Sex	Color	Profession, Occupation, or Trade of each person, male or female.	Value of Real Estate	Value of Personal Estate	Place of Birth, naming State or Territory of U. S.; or the Country, if of foreign birth.	Father of foreign birth	Mother of foreign birth	If born within the year, state month	If married within the year, state month	Attended school within the year	Cannot read	Cannot write	Whether deaf and dumb, blind, insane, or idiotic	Male citizens of U.S. of 21 years and upwards	Male citizens of U.S. of 21 years and upwards, whose right to vote is denied or abridged	
1	2	3	4	5	6	7	8	9	10	11	12	13	14	15	16	17	18	19	20	
1	326 326	Bryant William W	46	m	w	Farmer	350	150	Virginia									✓		1
2		— Christina	42	F	w	Keeping house			"						✓	✓				2
3		— James	22	m	w	Farm Laborer			"						✓	✓		✓		3
4		— William W	18	m	w	at home			"						✓	✓				4
5		— Kate E	12	F	w	" "			"						✓	✓				5
6		— Sarah A	11	F	w	"			"						✓	✓				6
7		Gusley John W	32	F	w	without occup!			"						✓	✓				7
8		— Rebecca A	19	F	w	at home			"						✓	✓				8
9		— James	9	m	w				"											9
10	327 327	Daughtry John W	53	m	w	Physician		200	"											10
11		— Bettie W	44	F	w	Keeping house			"											11
12		— Charles E	9	m	w				"											12
13		— Sarah A	8	F	w				"											13
14		— Laura W	6	F	w				"											14
15		— John R A	2	m	w				"											15
16		Rice Laura W	21	F	w	without occupation			"											16
17	328 328	Jennings William H	26	m	w	Farmer	200	250	"										1	17
18		— Murla A	22	F	w	Keeping house			"											18
19		— Leora	4	F	w				"											19
20		— Robert A	3	m	w				"											20
21		— James W	1	m	w				"											21
22		White Lizzie	35	F	w	without occupation			"											22
23	329 329	Bullington James T	25	m	w	Farm Laborer		100	"										1	23
24		— Christina P	22	F	w	Keeping house			"											24
25		— Mary A	3	F	w				"											25
26		— Murla P	1	F	w				"											26
27		— Ann	60	F	w	without occupation			"						✓	✓				27
28	330 330	Hill Levi	41	m	w	Farmer	3000	3000	"										1	28
29		— William H	21	m	w	Farm Laborer			"										1	29
30		— Elizabeth A	20	F	w	House Keeper			"											30
31		Calvin James	2	m	w				"											31
32	331 331	Ferguson Isaac	24	m	B	Farm Laborer			"						✓	✓				32
33		— Bettie	22	F	B	Keeping house			"						✓	✓				33
34		Jackson Edward	18	m	B	Domestic servant			"						✓	✓				34
35	332 332	Powell Abram	29	m	B	Farm Laborer			"						✓	✓				35
36		— Delpha	25	F	B	Keeping house			"						✓	✓				36
37		— Charlotte	12	F	m	at home			"						✓	✓				37
38	333 333	Cole Leonard F	47	m	w	Farmer			"										1	38
39		— Jim F	31	F	w	Keeping house			"											39
40		— Elizabeth	4	F	w				"											40

No. of dwellings, 8 " " families, 8 " " white males, 30 No. of white females, 31 " " colored males, 3 " " females, 4 No. of males, foreign born, " " females, " " " blind,

No. of insane, —

14 14 10

6

Freedman's cabin. Note the stick-and-mud chimney. From *Southern Workman*.
Photograph courtesy New York Public Library.

North Carolina freedman's cabin. Photograph: Library of Congress.

contraband. The earth-dug hidey-holes were a gift carried over from Africa by the Igbo.[9] The house had probably been occupied by families before Edward's.

The teenaged Ned Jackson would have learned how the other half lived if he had worked in a weatherboard house made of split planks called "pales" and set on a fieldstone foundation. Since hand-hewn log dwellings with *V*-notched corners, chinked at the seams with some sort of mud mortar, were typical dwellings for rural whites in Pittsylvania, I assume he grew up in some lesser variation of that. Martin Delany, the black doctor, journalist, explorer, and Union officer, used the word *hut* to describe the dwellings of black Americans. Of course, the fact of four walls and a roof was not to be gainsaid: some black Virginians lived in wooden lean-tos.

My great-grandfather and the Ferguson couple were enumerated immediately after a fairly well-to-do white man named Levi Hall, whose land was worth $3000. They all lived in a post office designation called Ringgold and Laurel Grove, which I initially figured must be somewhere near the two nineteenth-century neighborhoods of the same names. Ringgold was northeast of Danville, on the north side of the Dan River and east of the White Oak Mountain, and it had a railroad depot. Laurel Grove was at best a crossroad off Birch Creek and nestled closer to the border with Halifax, the older Virginia county to the east. Perhaps Laurel Grove had a general store and a tavern, and one of the area's ubiquitous gristmills.

When Edward Jackson worked as a "domestic servant," his housemate Isaac Ferguson and yard mate Abram Boswell, black men in their twenties, were "farm laborers." All things considered, I expect that all these black males worked for the vigorous farmer Levi Hall, whose land and personal property combined were worth $6,000, and on whose land they seem to have lived. Hall, aged fifty-one, was also a "Male Citizen of the U.S. 21 years of age and upwards," whose right to vote had not been "abridged on other grounds than rebellion or other crime." He had probably been successfully paroled or taken an oath in favor of the federal government. Whether they took some sort of oath or not, none of the black males could read or write.

The black labor on Hall's moderate-sized farm brought in the tobacco crop, under some arrangement between ex-slaves and former slaveholders. In 1876, when he filed his homestead exemption, Hall claimed ownership of four thousand pounds of tobacco.[10] On the farm he kept a horse and buggy, eighteen hogs, four head of cattle, forty barrels of corn,

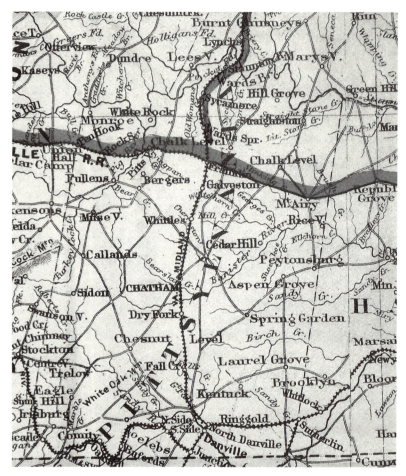

Colton's Map of Virginia, 1882; Pittsylvania County, detail. Photograph: Mahone Papers, Rare Books, Manuscripts and Special Collections Library, Duke University.

and plenty of oats and fodder. He also owned a clock and a gun. The relationship between workers like Ferguson, Boswell, and Jackson and landowner Levi Hall explains their sequential enumeration on the census. People who lived together were clumped on the census, and laborers tended to live quite close to where they worked in the days when the ownership of a riding horse was a prime luxury. In an era when crops, cash and staple, were cultivated by hand, the farmhands lived in cabins not far from the fields they tended, and virtually no freedmen owned any land. If Ned Jackson had worked in domestic service for Levi Hall during slavery, I would imagine he must have lived with his employer. But perhaps after slavery it had become unseemly to have an adolescent black male in a white person's home; perhaps, given the choice, Ned himself preferred some distance from his employers.

Property owners like Hall had been in the community a long time. In 1842 he married Mary Shelton (who owned eight slaves herself, two of them working age). The couple had lost an infant child named Daniel in 1857 and three years later buried twenty-three-year-old Henry, who may have been Hall's brother. Hall seems to have been well respected in the area. He had a taste for some things of the good life, such as coffee and refined white sugar, which he regularly purchased in 1855 and 1856 from the downtown Danville merchants Claiborne and Jeter.[11] In 1860, Levi Hall owned nine slaves, three of them "full" hands. Ten years later, after the debacle of war and defeat, he yet owned 458 acres in the area between Sandy Creek and the Birch Creek, near Old Richmond Road.[12]

For the census of 1860 for Pittsylvania County, however, Edward Jackson did not appear by name. The disappearance of his name from the census is tantamount to proving that he spent the years between 1855 and 1865 in bondage. That census, which included all free people by name and exact age, was a work of art in itself. It was also a marvel of racial compromise and accommodation to the South. The bottom of the first schedule handily summarized the nature of the United States at the time: total numbers of white males, white females, "colored males," "colored females," "foreign-born," "deaf and dumb," "blind," "insane," "idiotic," "paupers," and "convicts." If my great-grandfather lived in Pittsylvania in 1860, he was undoubtedly included in the record on Schedule 2 as one of 208 enslaved five-year-old black males, the tally of slave inhabitants being necessary for Virginia's congressional representation. On Schedule 2, under the name of each individual slave owner, the census bureau deputies logged the age, sex, and color of enslaved Africans and their descendants; but they never recorded the name of any individual enslaved person. Without the lines dividing the Schedule 2 columns, the notation marks for an enslaved five-year-old black male looked like *5. // B* .

But I had to pause before I could firmly place my great-grandfather in those ranks. I couldn't be all that sure he was in Pittsylvania County at the time. No slave-holding Jacksons in Pittsylvania in 1860 owned young boys. Additionally, the majority of the eighty-seven Jackson-named people lived on the Chatham side of the county, in the "Subdivision North of the Dan River." For my entire childhood, we went "to Danville" to visit Grandpa Jackson, one of humanity's more sedentary people, so I resisted searching the area twenty miles north of town for his forebears.

This line of questioning forces me to consider that in my examination of the 1870 records for young Edward's parents I might even be roaming through the wrong county. There were several families named Jackson in adjacent Halifax County. Raphael, Martha, and Charles Jackson all were in their forties or fifties and heads of household, with children and working-age teenagers living with them. Logically, they could all have had a parental relation to Edward. They lived about fifteen miles away, near enough to Halifax Court House to be enumerated with its inhabitants.

Two other possibilities in Halifax County would have been only about an hour's walk from the broad neighborhood where Edward was living, that is, if a straight road or unobstructed path were available. Thirty-year-old Andrew Jackson and his twenty-two-year-old wife, Millie, lived in Mt. Carmel with two very young children. Perhaps Edward was somehow connected to them? In Birch Creek lived George Jackson, born in 1815, his wife, Frankie (a favorite Tidewater name for black women[13]), their sons, Madison and George, and their daughter, Polly. Birch Creek was just barely over the Halifax line, a couple of miles from Laurel Grove. Pondering whether or not Edward Jackson had moved for some obscure reason from Halifax to Pittsylvania was a problem of curious probabilities.

But something about the Halifax connection didn't jibe with what I had learned about my great-grandfather. Certainly the numerous small families of Jackson freedpeople on the western side of Halifax suggested that he could have come from Halifax, but why, if his origins were there, did he never return?

My ancestor Edward Jackson proved to be a man of regular, dutiful habit. He spent at least sixty years of his life in one section of the county, south of Chatham and north of Danville, east of the White Oak Mountain. Once there, he apparently never moved very far from surroundings that had claimed him at least since 1870. This man, who never owned any property or never had more than five dollars' value to his personal estate, was in virtually the same place during every decennial census.

So if as a lad of ten or eleven Ned Jackson for some reason left home after emancipation, why did he never lodge an elder relative at a later date? As long as he was enumerated in the census, Edward was always the oldest Jackson in his house. Or perhaps he did house an older relative, and that person did not live to see the next census? Following another lead, closest to where Edward Jackson wound up in 1870, somewhere, I think, along the modern-day Ringgold Church Road, I found a twenty-eight-year-old white woman named Elizabeth Jackson. She lived with two children in the household of a man named Thomas Hancker, but it

Runaway.

RANAWAY from the subscriber about the 5th of June, a mulatto boy named JIM WIER, thirteen years old. Said boy was bound to me by the Freedmen's Bureau, and a reward of one cent will be paid for his apprehension and return to me. All persons are forewarned against employing or harboring him.

jul8 2t   BEVERLY LINDSEY.

Runaway indentured servant advertisement, *Danville (VA) Register*, June 1865.

appears that she did not own people in 1860. Maybe there was some connection? There is just no way of knowing.

I presume that my great-grandfather's life after emancipation lacked two elements: comfort and intellectual refinement. If young Edward had gotten to freedom without any immediate kin, as his living situation indicates, the Freedmen's Bureau may well have contracted him to apprentice with a local farmer. Things were so bad in Pittsylvania, where "a large number of freed children are bound or apprenticed to their former owner without the consent of the children's parents," wrote a Freedmen's Bureau lieutenant to his commander, that by February 1867 one hundred black parents applied to the bureau for help in regaining their children.[14] Edward may have been indentured to someone in the neighborhood—perhaps even to landowner Levi Hall, whom I had found living next door to him in the census records—and lived in Hall's old slave cabin with the black Fergusons. It occurred to me that Bettie Ferguson could have been his older sister, but the census taker did sometimes indicate the relation by writing "brother-in-law" to head of household, and he did not in Edward's case.

If Edward was indentured, he would have had to labor until he was twenty-one, and the possibility of obtaining whatever kind of education he might have heard about in 1865 was likely gone. White farmers had black contractees arrested for going to school, and sometimes roped them like cattle and dragged them back to work. When Pittsylvania freedman Edward Weir ran away from his contract in December of 1866, the employer, Beverly Lindsey, who had owned fifteen people in 1860, placed a "runaway" advertisement for Weir in the paper, just as he would have done during slavery.

Rather than becoming a scholar or running away, Edward Jackson

Mountain View, mansion built in 1842 for Thomas Jones, Tightsqueeze, Pittsylvania County, Virginia.

joined the labor force as a domestic servant alongside a lot of black teenagers in the Ringgold and Laurel Grove post area. Quite a few black girls rendered domestic service, and six colored males under the age of nineteen carried on this work also, including Collin Beavers, Abner Stevens, Harry Vauhn, Keen Leroy, John Blanks, and James Lindsey. Abner Stevens, one of two mulattoes (Lindsey was the other), probably worked at Beaver's Tavern, the community's local watering hole, which later became the town of Blairs.

Edward's jobs as a fifteen-year-old also would have included a lot of work outdoors, like wood chopping and water carrying and livestock feeding. It strikes me that the majority of the work he did would have been of that sort. Pittsylvania had some impressive homes, such as Windsor, Samuel Wilson's 1862 Georgian-style mansion, gaslit and finished in an Italianate style. Wilson even had brick dwellings for his bondpeople, but the house was in the western portion of the county. Closer to Edward Jackson was Mountain View, the more restrained, three-story, Federal-style mansion completed for Thomas Jones in 1842. Mountain View boasted an extravagant garden and a lane skirted by cedar trees. The estate sat five miles south of Chatham, just west of today's Route 29, near

The Guardian Angel.

Hotel worker. From Edward
King, *The Great South* (1875).

the town of Tightsqueeze. But the brick estates of the superwealthy were not typical. The gentry that the slaves and common whites alike would have trembled before lived in wooden houses, like Virginia statesman Patrick Henry's cousin John, who by the early 1820s had built Woodlawn Manor, one-and-a-half-story whitewashed dwelling near Sandy Creek, close to the border of Halifax County.[15] And even the luster of the Henry family plantation easily outmatched the area. Off the tobacco roads of Ringgold, Laurel Grove, and Spring Garden, few houses hired a duster.

So, as best as I could piece his life together from the scanty records of the time, my grandfather's father, Edward Jackson, was born into American chattel slavery around 1855, apparently in Pittsylvania County, Virginia, fairly close to the famed antebellum tobacco-manufacturing town of Danville. In the middle of spring in the year he thought he was born, a fire ruined Danville's Main Street, between the toll bridge and Craighead Street. My great-grandfather was probably born some distance away from the town, but Pittsylvania's Southsiders would have remembered that fire. He shared local origins with Nancy Langhorne, who became Viscountess Astor, the first woman to sit in the British Parliament. My great-grandfather's birthday was a year before that of James Bland, the famous black minstrel born free in New York who graduated in one of Howard University's earliest classes. Bland's minstrel shenanigans produced what became the official Virginia state song between 1940 and 1997, "Carry Me Back to Old Virginny," "where this old darkey's heart am longed to go."

Though black minstrels like Bland, films like *Gone with the Wind*, and apologists like Thomas Nelson Page seemed certain, I doubt quite strongly that Edward Jackson felt nostalgic about his enslaved past. From what I am finding out, he seems unacquainted with the bucolic Old Dominion life of ease and interracial harmony such as Page envisioned in 1897, when he wrote that young white squires mingled "with the little darkies as freely as any other young animals, and forming the associations which tempered slavery and made the relation one not to be understood save by those who saw it."[16] Since my ancestor did not merely "see" slavery but actually survived it, I think he deserves to be understood in a way that would be meaningful to him, which is to say, meaningful to me.

Considering the evidence, then, I can appreciate that my grandfather's father made a big jump. In the span of his lifetime he moved from Page's animal to his own man. Whatever else Edward Jackson did or did not do in his life, in which he may have never traveled farther than ten or twelve miles from the place he had been born, he passed on to many children a simple, stubborn, defiant feat, beyond survival, beyond memory, beyond future. This black man, whose children knew him as "Ned," passed on the feat of a jump, of a leap, what a geologist or scientist of evolution might call an interphyletic saltation. His jump out of slavery was, hands down, an evolutionary advance.

I guess it isn't really unique that my grandfather's father, not exactly a distant ancestor to me, was born enslaved. In fact, if you are a black American, it is the normal order of things and so well understood that it needs no explanation. Three generations back, and you might well be at a door of no return. But when I discovered the simple facts, witnessed the script on the census ledger, interpreted the hash marks in a column, the historical record took on another kind of life altogether. It seemed, well, the word I would use is *close*: uncomfortably present, not in the past, never safely tucked away at all. Indeed, to learn about Edward—and myself, his kin—I have to long jump too, and my leap to the future bounds into the past.

3 · The Dan River Betimes in the Morning

In Pittsylvania County beat the heart of the Virginia tobacco empire. My great-grandfather, always tethered to the same locale in census after census, spent his life in the Southside, a twelve-county area a hair east of the Piedmont in what some of the old maps called the Virginia Midland, between the fall line of the sandy Tidewater region to the east and the Blue Ridge Mountains to the west. With its clay soil and numerous low-lying hills, his was a populous region of Virginia in the decades before the Civil War, known for its low nitrogen-content soil, excellent for raising bright leaf tobacco. Tobacco was the mainstay of the Virginia agricultural economy from its earliest days as a colony, and it would continue to dominate the minds of the landowners even a generation after slavery. There was a common saying that "the man that ain't partial to the weed can't sleep sound even in a churchyard."[1]

Two rivers dominate Pittsylvania, the largest county in Virginia: the Staunton River to the north and the Dan River to the south. The Staunton undulates like a series of miniature bell curves, separating Pittsylvania from Bedford and Campbell Counties to the north. The Dan knifes along the southern edge of the county and nearly separates Virginia from North Carolina. A plethora of minor rivers and creeks spider their way like veins throughout the county and christen the area's neighborhoods: Sandy River, Pigg River, Stinking River, Banister River, Fall Creek, Sandy Creek, Cherrystone Creek, George's Creek, Whitehorn Creek, Bearskin Creek, Birch Creek, Cascade Creek, Tomahawk Creek, Turkeycock Creek, Cascade Creek, Strawberry Creek, and Stuart Creek.

Edward Jackson lived quite close to Sandy Creek, a waterway with three distinct branches. He married and raised a family by the main branch, which comes out from the Banister River and forks just north in Chestnut Level; the other branch is named for the early landowner Robert Sweeting. Sandy Creek, only a couple of feet at its regular depth and

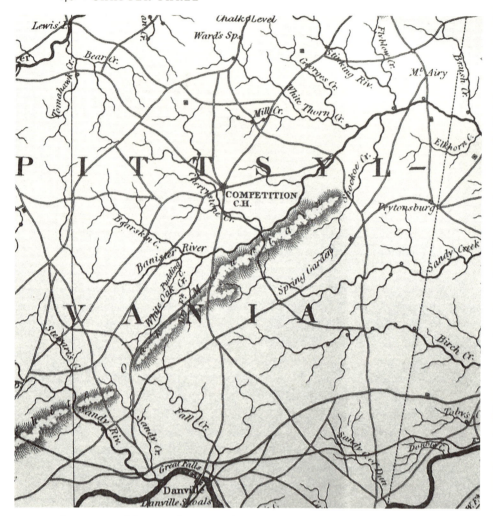

"A New Map of the State of Virginia Exhibiting Its Internal Improvements." James H. Young, 1852; Pittsylvania County detail. Photograph: Albert and Shirley Small Special Collections Library, University of Virginia.

roughly eight feet across, must have been important for bathing, household washing and laundry, perhaps some freshwater marine life, and certainly as a traditional reference point dividing landowners' holdings.

When Colonel William Byrd initially surveyed the county's southern border in 1728, he quoted the first verse from the twentieth chapter of the book of Judges, claiming that he had wended his way from "Dan to Beersheba," or the entirety of the ancient Kingdom of Israel.[2] He liked what he saw so well, the ample sturgeon leaping out of the river at Wynne's

Falls, that he called the county the Land of Eden, and he christened the river the Dan. Almost two generations later in 1767, Pittsylvania, taking its name from Great Britain's sitting prime minister William Pitt, broke off from Halifax County. At that time, there were 271 enslaved people, likely second- and third-generation Creoles along with a score or two of "saltwater Negroes," Africans who had been landed at Bermuda Hundred and then marched south.[3] The widespread development of large-scale farming in the eighteenth and nineteenth centuries involved owning slaves, and the numbers of black people would expand. By 1840 Pittsylvania County contained ten thousand mostly African-descended people. Twenty years later, the combined northern and southern portions of the county included 14,340 blacks and mulattoes, almost half the county's population.[4]

The eighteenth-century history of tobacco cultivation is one of strife and instability brought about by declining crop prices and less-than-savory agricultural methods. An American Cicero such as Thomas Jefferson disliked the slash-and-burn practices of single-crop tobacco farming, which he called a "culture productive of great wretchedness." From his mountaintop home, Monticello, he observed that the tobacco farmers were "in a continual state of exertion beyond the power of nature to support. . . . Little food of any kind is raised by them: so men and animals on these farms are ill fed, and the earth is readily impoverished."[5] By the end of the eighteenth century, the Tidewater-area soil was exhausted and cultivation moved fully toward the Piedmont, on the other side of the fall line, ensuring the growth of the region. It is inevitable that this migration from the exhausted eighteenth-century Tidewater soils to the nineteenth-century Piedmont land that proved such a good host for tobacco forms the saga of several generations of my family in America.

Half a century after Byrd's early survey, Pittsylvania citizens petitioned the state to "make the convenience of Inspection more serviceable" in regard to tobacco. Their request initiated the growth of a town on the Dan River called Danville.[6] Small farmers resisted the various Inspection Acts that were designed to regulate crop quality and foil the practice of packing the hogsheads with sand and trash to inflate their weight. Yet larger Pittsylvania growers, including John Wilson and John and George Sutherlin, naturally wanted to have their tobacco officially inspected and sealed before it made its way by wagon or hogshead to market. Thus, the idea of a Southside tobacco manufacturing town took off. In Danville, the manufacturers began a system of warehouse storage and loose-leaf inspection of the crop that helped the town secure a foothold. Even-

Tobacco sale bugler. From Edward King, *The Great South* (1875).

tually, loose-leaf tobacco from the nearby fields would be auctioned to tobacco buyers from wagons in the streets and then straightaway sent to manufacture. It was a revolution in the market. At the beginning of each trading day, black men would play three-foot bugles to announce the auction.

The Dan River was navigable down to the lower parts of North Carolina and capable of supporting flatboats, fifty-four-foot-long but narrow bateaux that could carry seven or eight full hogsheads at a time. Cured tobacco leaf was transported after it was packed tightly, or "prized," into a hogshead, an enormous wooden cylinder outfitted with shafts that attached to a team of oxen. At the time of the American Revolution, a hogshead weighed about thirteen hundred pounds. Smaller sizes included a tierce, or one-third of a hogshead, and a barrel, which was about one-half. Two hogsheads made a ton, and the barrels, with their empty weight branded on the side, were regulated at four feet high and thirty inches across. The customary route to the tobacco market was by teamster-driven wagon up the tobacco road to Lynchburg, and then by boat down the Appomattox River and into the Chesapeake Bay. The canal that was cut through the Dismal Swamp in 1819 gave access from the Roanoke River estuary, which includes the Staunton, Banister, and Dan Rivers, to the seaport Norfolk, the Chesapeake Bay, and the Atlantic shipping lanes. Fifteen years before the Civil War, a new variety of tobacco, "Bright

Hogshead on axle rolling to market. From Edward King, *The Great South* (1875).

Leaf," was introduced, an especially fragrant and sweet-scented yellow leaf that could be used as both wrapper and filler, reviving the market fortunes. Pittsylvania's soil, with its low nitrogen levels, proved excellent for the strand when it was cured.

Tobacco planters were artists. As the historian Nannie Tilley said, "No other agricultural product grown in the U.S. requires as much skill, knowledge, and accuracy in the matter of classing or sorting as tobacco."[7] It has also been supposed that transplanted West Africans, people such as the Wolof and the Mandingo, may have brought with them to the Chesapeake area advanced knowledge about tobacco cultivation in the later seventeenth and early eighteenth centuries: tobacco had been planted, harvested, cured, and smoked widely throughout Senegambia.[8] The farm economy for Virginia tobacco production enabled some remarkable bondmen to move from the laboring to the artisan class. They might have become the coopers who made the hogsheads, and the sawyers and carpenters who built the barns in which the tobacco leaves were cured before being packed and shipped. But most of the enslaved worked in the fields, and suffered great pains for the crop. Ex-slave Henrietta Perry offered a metaphor for the process: "Us black people had to look after that tobacco like it was gold."[9]

Cultivation of the plant was popular because tobacco could be grown profitably on small sections of land as well as on large tracts. But while major investments in money and land were unnecessary, the crop required as much skilled labor as humanity could provide. It was said that preparation of the tobacco seedbeds for the "Bright Leaf" or "Sweet-Scented" yellow-leaf variety that was the staple of Southside farmers required the same delicacy as that needed to make pillow lace. (The other tobacco variety, the Oronoco, with its heartier and less subtle fragrance, was easier to cultivate.) If it was a fine crop, it also demanded exhausting labor; the cycle from seed to market required eighteen months. Before the Civil War, an enslaved "full" hand could cultivate twenty thousand plants on four or five acres, though the epicures believed by 1867 that "that is too much to manage nicely."[10]

The onerous growth schedule conformed to a twelve-month calendar. In January, the plant beds were burned, broken by plow, and hoed. February's work demanded sowing the seed into cold frames, the giant opening act in which each of thousands of plants received individual attention. March continued the seedbed work: protecting the individual seedbeds with foraged brush. April brought on the agricultural work that became synonymous with the enslaved African: using a hoe to make "hills," or cones of soil in which the seedling would be placed later in the season. (Masters believed that plows and carts spoiled the slaves and made the work too easy.) One writer estimated the process to have required bending over four thousand or five thousand times per day. Perhaps it's unsurprising that an insurance company at the time offered "lives of slaves insured on favorable terms."[11]

The weather broke by May, and now plaster or manure was applied to the cones, and flies and insects swarmed and had to be fought in earnest. By June it was time to take the inches-high seedlings from the beds and plant them in the fields. Later in July, the young plants had grown for five weeks in full sun and warmth, and field hands were engaged in topping, cutting the blossoms off the top of each plant and pruning the bottom leaves so that the middle of the plant would develop more fully. In August the worms had moved to attack the delicate leaves, and they had to be collected by hand from the plants. The accepted practice was to have workers bite the heads off of whichever worms they had failed to remove from the leaves. The topped portions of the plant were also suckered, repaired. By September the tobacco leaves were ready to be cut, each

Worming tobacco plants. From Edward King, *The Great South* (1875).

stalk carefully and individually, and the black gummy tar that oozed from the stalks was thick enough to stick a person's fingers together. The black men could tell that a planter had tried to sow tobacco in nitrogen-rich soil if they identified the leaves as "greasy green." More than anything, to grow fine, high-grade tobacco required a feeling.

Part of the feel had to do with deciding the right time for cutting the plants. Too early or too late ruined the taste. After the stalks were halved with a tobacco knife and laid by, laborers skewered the leaves on sticks and scaffolded them for a couple of days until they had yellowed. Then they went to the special tobacco barns equipped with flues to achieve high temperatures so that the weed could cure, a process, depending on dampness, that could take a week or more. As a freedman remarked in the popular 1880 novel *Bricks without Straw*, "Ther ain't a minit from the time yer plant the seed-bed till ye sell the leaf, that ye kin take yer finger offen it widout resk ob losin' all yer wuk."[12] In November the hands

"Prizing" a tobacco hogshead. From Edward King, *The Great South* (1875).

stripped the individual leaves, now a deeper yellow—or dangerously brown if the process had gone awry—and tied them in "hands" of five leaves. Twenty-five acres would have produced perhaps two hundred thousand hands of fairly high-quality tobacco. The final activity in the sequence occurred in December, which was devoted to packing the hogsheads with the aged tobacco and getting them to the shipyards.

This work rhythm dominated the lives of black and white people in Pittsylvania. A farmer like Levi Hall, a man who must have been known to my ancestor Edward Jackson, planted tobacco crops along the land between the Birch and Sandy Creeks in the portion of the county east of the White Oak Mountain range. Driving his people hard, Hall might have been able to cultivate twelve good acres of tobacco in a year. That much land could have supported eighty thousand plants, which might have yielded about twice the number of "hands," or tied bundles of tobacco. Perhaps this could have become roughly eight thousand pounds of cured tobacco leaf, which would have been transported in roughly four to six hogsheads, which by that time tipped the scales at two thousand pounds apiece.

In the year before Civil War began, Pittsylvania County, Virginia, with a total population, black and white, of 32,267, alone exported more than 7 million pounds of tobacco.[13] Pittsylvania ranked second in the state for tobacco production that year, a million and a half pounds behind neighboring Halifax County. There were about 8,572 enslaved, and 9,893 whites and freedmen living in the southern half of the county where Ned Jackson lived. There were famously rich men named Sutherlin, Hairston, and Wilson owning scores of African descendants, but middling-fair planters like Levi Hall and his wife, who owned mostly black children, had been the economic mainstay of the Southside Piedmont.

Pittsylvania County continued to produce tobacco after the Civil War, as it had since its founding in 1767, but the immediate postwar years saw production fall by nearly half. In 1870 it led the state, but produced only 4,282,511 pounds. However, before the end of the decade, the county rebounded and grew more tobacco than ever before: 12 million pounds.[14]

That momentum, from 214 pounds of tobacco per person in 1860 to 263 pounds per person in the more populous county in 1880, was like an electric current modulating the pace, the warp and woof, of my great-grandfather's life. I imagine Edward Jackson was only vaguely familiar with the Gregorian calendar. My great-grandfather would have kept track of time and recorded events according to the tobacco cycle: hoeing time, or spring; worming time, or summer; and chopping time, or early fall. He never paid taxes on a clock, which he probably never had a need for. And although he would have been only a ten-year-old boy during the final year of slavery, likely too young to have performed regular work in the fields, and his career as a teenage butler notwithstanding, I would eventually find him among the many freedmen working in the corn and tobacco fields. Whether it was during slavery or after emancipation, tobacco farming and the terms under which it was conducted never really changed. And if he had any experience on larger plantations, he would have thought of agricultural work relative to his gang, his work unit: plow gang, hoe gang, and trash gang were the typical groupings for the laborers making their sweep of the furrows.

Pundits have argued that slaves were unable to do fine work and would not exhaust themselves in labor. New York chronicler and cityscape designer Frederick Law Olmsted, who toured the Virginia Southside by way of tobacco-flush Mecklenburg County in the decade before the Civil War, encountered a wealthy Tidewater master saying that black slaves "could not be made to work hard: they never would lay out their strength freely, and it was impossible to make them do it." This made sense to Olmsted, who agreed with little else that most Southerners believed in earnest. "This is just what I have thought when I have seen slaves at work—they seem to go through the motions of labour without putting strength into them. They keep their powers in reserve for their own use at night, perhaps."[15]

For the 189 planters in Pittsylvania, people who owned twenty or more African Americans, the night life of the enslaved was another kind of gold mine, a crop beyond the tobacco field. After 1775, the North American colonists began dubbing the Africans a "prolifick people," because, in spite of enslavement's tough pre- and postnatal conditions, blacks apparently were able to augment their numbers by natural increase. By the end of the eighteenth century, the gender preference of the slave trade, which originally had involved some calculus of the life expectancy of a young male captured from the West African savannah, forest, or river zone, turned on its head. Planters with an eye toward the future hoped to fill their estates "in Negroe Wenches or Girls" capable of "breed[ing] like sows," to ensure future wealth.[16] As early as 1769, advertisements for "fine breeding women" were appearing. Fifty years later, the reproduction of a most profitable industrial-era crop was common knowledge. In 1820 the former US president Thomas Jefferson, who owned hundreds of people, would write John Eppes and remind him that "a woman who brings a child every two years is more profitable than the best man on the farm."[17]

Ex-slave Joseph Holmes, who was born west of Danville, told a white interviewer that slavery in Virginia was awfully mild. I suspect the interviewer was white, because Holmes's dialect is as exaggerated as it is possible to make it, and this dialect persists despite Holmes's making a point of telling the interviewer he had been to school. "If anybody tells you that white was mean to their niggers, they never come from Virginia," Holmes said. But if telling white interviewers that slavery was mild was almost a literary conceit during the 1930s when the Federal Writers' Project collected the large body of ex-slave interviews, Holmes drove home another, less pleasant consideration: "Us was near to free states, and I'se already tole you they raised niggers to sell and they kept em in good condition."[18] Holmes thereby confirmed the traditional wisdom in the historiography of slavery—Virginia blacks received mild treatment—but he also undercut the theory with his determination to recount the spectacle of breeding plantations.

The "breeding" of black America, especially in Virginia, the great homeland of the black American past, will ever be a kind of beehive. How did black Americans, as a body, reach the hue of the Hershey's bar of milk chocolate? I believe part of the reason that black families have done such a good job at erasing the past of enslavement, such a commendable disposal of the entire nineteenth century—in which I include my own unfamiliarity with my own kin, even—has something to do with this swamp of race, sex, childrearing, and the financial health of border states in the forty years before the Civil War. The difficult points are these:

First, slavery was, more or less, a death sentence for any African who ever wore a chain or received a brand. A bare majority of Africans survived the violent warfare that resulted in their capture, the overland coffle—a train of strangers knotted together—through a dangerous and unfamiliar forest, and a lengthy spell confined to a barracoon on the coast, topped off by a Middle Passage in a putrid ship's hold for ten weeks. Nor was this the end of their ordeal. This slim majority of survivors suffered gruesomely high mortality rates in the Americas. One in four died during their first year in North America, and typically the number of deaths peaked in March, at the end of the first winter.[19] In other words, if you started with one hundred people taken one hundred miles overland to a coastal port in what is modern-day Nigeria, in twenty-four months you would have about thirty-five or forty survivors planting crops on a Virginia farm.

This death toll is the gist of Toni Morrison's "Sixty million or more" dedication at the beginning of her famous novel *Beloved*. If more than 12 million people were in condition to be resold after crossing the Atlantic, and yet three of five did not survive long enough to leave Africa, 15 to 20 percent died on the boats, and another 50 percent of those sold did not live more than a year or two on New World soil, the total black mortality certainly needs to be configured on a different scale.

For several hundred years, the Africans who survived the slave trade assembled a cultural tradition that prepared their people for death. It could have been sudden and violent or lingering and sore, but it was a certain dishonorable termination of life that would not have been conducted with anything like appropriate rituals commemorating the ultimate farewell. That intimacy with death that was not even remembered shapes the character and emotion of a people and makes them uneasy and remote. If anybody knew how they were dying, it was they, and that foreboding sense of doom and gallows humor were a giant part of what the kidnapped Africans conveyed to their descendants. "'Ma fr'en'? He ma fr'en'?'" questions a black passerby in a muddy Atlanta street in James Weldon Johnson's *The Autobiography of an Ex-Colored Man*. "'Man! I'd go to his funeral jes' de same as I'd go to a minstrel show.'"[20]

Second, the "prolificking" among black people could not be accounted for by the amorous gusto of underfed, freezing, emotionally scrambled, and short-lived African men. African abolitionist Olauduh Equiano, who had endured the Middle Passage himself, described the "constant practice" of whites in the Caribbean "to commit violent depredations on the chastity of the female slaves," some of them "not ten years old."[21] The working-class Englishmen in North America were the same as those in the Caribbean, just exponentially more numerous. While the historians remain convinced that black population growth in North America was due to allowing black mothers an additional three or four weeks to nurse their newborns, it strikes me that black survival had something to do as well with the assignations between black females and much better-fed and more energetic white men. The colonists had mythic New World dreams of extraordinary fecundity and the end of restraint. Educated and propertied white men saw themselves as biblical patriarchs and Roman gods, and they acted with that sense of cosmic entitlement (and paranoia) from a young age.

What accounts for the ability among people of African descent, after a generation or two, to withstand European disease, to walk barefoot in snow, and to reconstitute their diet around pork and corn, yet gain in stature and heft and achieve a robustness unknown to their African forebears? In a fairly short epoch, the hundred years from the mid-eighteenth through the mid-nineteenth century, a goodly portion of European and Native American genes made their way into a people in the process of becoming American African.

Third, the choices that women and men made for survival in the eighteenth century were greatly different from the ones that presented themselves after the invention of the cotton gin in 1796. Casual breeding evolved into systematic breeding. In 1790, half of American slaves had lived in Virginia,[22] but by the time of the Civil War only about one-eighth of bondmen would reside there. What happened was a Great Migration that is only now being given attention in the annals of history. Before even the Revolution, some of Virginia's planters could see the Tidewater and then even the largely unsettled Piedmont slowing in their agricultural fertility, as well as the end of the trade with Africa for men and women. American westward expansion occurred because of the development of cotton empires in the Deep South and Southwest, and it was a preponderance of Chesapeake slaves who chopped down the forests, built the roads and houses and barns, fenced in the land, cultivated the livestock and crops, and picked the cotton. Cotton comprised half the total US exports in 1860.

Not too far into the nineteenth century, the planters of the border

states Maryland, Virginia, and Kentucky stopped regarding their enslaved people as merely potential value and started cashing in on the
market. They sold "surplus" or "excess" to Mississippi, Alabama, Georgia,
Louisiana, Arkansas, and Texas, the great cotton lands that created the
national wealth. By the middle of the nineteenth century, it must have
been difficult to find a farmer who did not at least consider the premium
on human "production." Any of them must have regarded their prime
source of wealth with at least the attention they gave thoroughbred
horses, breeds of dogs, types of cows and pigs. In the personal property
tax records of the 1840s, these were the first three categories of taxation:
"Slaves above 12 years of age," "Horses and Mares [No.| Dolls.| Cents],"
and "Stud Horses." Animal husbandry was at the center of the taxonomic
logic of the American government in the nineteenth century. There were
sad repercussions for the enslaved who embraced what it meant to be
American. One ex-slave, a man named Elige Davison, proudly bragged
he was a stud and had fathered more than one hundred children.[23] The
sociologist, statesman, and historian W. E. B. Du Bois, who apparently
wrestled with this issue for decades, finally believed that the "deliberate
breeding of a strong, big field-hand stock" took place in Virginia, and the
result for African American families was "sexual chaos."[24]

Finally, in this circle of hell, insult was added to injury. American Africans began to embrace a standard of beauty that did not really include
us. We started to see light skin among us, what had been a mark of rape,
conquest, or disallowed family ties, as something else: as a sign of favor.
Because certainly one of the queerest parts of the forced-breeding problem is the evolved preference among blacks for light skin, particularly in
mulatto women, the "fancy gals," a peculiarity that fueled Jefferson's rac-
ist commentary in *Notes on the State of Virginia*: "Their own judgment in
favour of the whites, declared by their preference of them, as uniformly
as is the preference of the Oranootan for the black women over those of
his own species."[25]

And that was in 1784. My great-grandfather, my grandfather, and my
father all married and had children with women who would have been
termed mulatto by Pittsylvania census taker Drury Blair in 1860, and the
men would all have been termed black. Is theirs an example of deliberate
bias, proximate availability, or deep-seated conditioning? In my favorite
film, *Chameleon Street*, a character explains his preference for "girls with
that light complexion." "I'm a victim of four hundred years of conditioning," he smirks. "The man has programmed my conditioning. Even my
conditioning has been conditioned."

Death and fatalism. Systematic rape. Industrial reproduction as a commodity. Self-hate and admiration of a corrupt order. That's a hell of an inheritance.

◆   ◆   ◆

When I uncovered the fact that a young Edward Jackson was living with Isaac and Bettie Ferguson in 1870, I immediately expected the worst and presumed that his parents had been sold during slavery. Had a master put his folks "in his pocket," and sold them to the prominent Pittsylvania slave trader Philip Thomas? Maybe his parents had been sold in the early 1860s, when Virginia planters, fearing being overrun by Yankee troops, force-marched more than ninety-seven thousand American Africans out to Texas?[26] That march would have been three times as large as the infamous Trail of Tears, the forced relocation of the Creek and Cherokee Indian nations. And sixteen hundred enslaved African Americans marched that trail too.[27]

An 1849 advertisement for an estate sale in neighboring Campbell County that appeared in the *Danville Register* seemed to drive home the civility of slave trading in the Southside. The "Negroes," the advertisement read, "have been well raised and treated, and are valuable both for character and physical qualities. They will be sold as far as practicable, in families, so as to avoid the separation of husbands and wives, parents and children."[28] But closer to the Civil War, there were Southside advertisements for "30 or 40 Likely Negroes" from the estate of one James Peatross, with valued house servants and factory hands featured, but no mention of the intention to keep families together.[29]

Perhaps the genteel public conscience sometimes reflected in Pittsylvania's newspapers formed the top half of a slave culture that was embarrassed by what it needed to do to remain economically solvent: sell the enslaved to the highest bidder. In 1860 one speculator for the "Southern market" simply put in the paper in bold type, "Notice $50,000 Worth of Negroes WANTED," which suggests a hungry market, salivating at the prospects of putting enslaved people up on the block in Virginia and taking them down in Mississippi.

The very sight of the slave coffles, twin ranks of chained men followed by women and children stirring dust along the county roads, was so powerful that it captivated the imagination of ex-slave Lorenzo Ivy for the rest of his life. He had been enslaved near Competition. "I've seen droves of Negroes brought in here on foot goin South to be sole," Ivy recalled

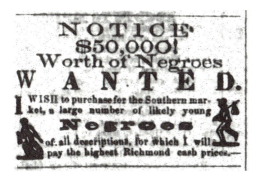

"WANTED: $50,000 worth of Negroes." Advertisement, *Danville (VA) Register and Bee*, July 7, 1860.

in 1937. "Each one have an old tow sack on his back with everythin he's got in it. Over hills they come in lines reachin as far as you can see. They walk in double lines chained together in twos. They walk em here to the railroad an ship em South like cattle."[30] When Ivy gave his account to interviewer Claude Anderson, he added—paraphrasing a Bible passage favored among African Americans, in which the Queen of Sheba gets Solomon right—"Truly, son, the half has never been tole."

The goodly portion of "the half" that Ivy believed was absent from the historical record is slavery in the industrial age, slaves in steel industries, gangs of black men, women, and children clambering aboard boxcars so that steam-driven engines and ships could carry them to the frontiers of the appetitive and expanding American empire.

The emotional toll on the family members was excruciating. After seeing his wife and children join the coffle headed to the Southern cotton fields, a man named Brown who worked in the Richmond tobacco factories sealed himself in a box about thirty inches by thirty inches, and had himself shipped by railroad to Philadelphia. At one point during the escapade, workmen ignored the instructions on the box and left Brown upside down—he felt his "eyes swelling as if they would burst from their sockets."[31] Surely there were others driven by the same troubles but without Brown's desperate ingenuity and courage, people who responded in a manner less daring and more obviously suicidal.

One afternoon in a private library in Durham, North Carolina, I came across an account of one of these forced marches to the cotton states that had originated in 1834 in Pittsylvania. Professional slave trader George Mitchell departed Virginia on October 18, 1834, and returned February 13, 1835. He kept an account, which he titled "The Expence of Travelin [*sic*] with negroes from VA to Miss and Returning home Commenced the 18 of October 1834 and continued to the 13th of Febuary [*sic*] 1835."[32]

Mitchell usually paid between two and three dollars a day for provisions for his coffle, and every week or so he bought about ten dollars' worth of bacon and cornmeal. With probably more than one hundred pounds of cured pork and cornbread, he was able to feed forty-eight blacks, himself, and two other white men. In addition, he had to account for the cost of loading the people aboard a ferry to cross a river, or sometimes paying the toll on a bridge, usually between three and four dollars. When the weather turned genuinely cold in December, Mitchell bought medicine—whisky—and warm clothes. To attend to bondmen Isaac Carter and Moses Fidler, he paid a physician a dollar and a half.

The gang made ten miles a day. Mitchell, the surrogate owner and figure of power, rode on horseback. In the rear, a carryall wagon pulled by some kind of dray animal toted the supplies while the coffle of the enslaved hoofed by foot. They quickly passed from Virginia to North Carolina, crossed the New River, and then made their way over the mountains and into Tennessee. By November 5, two weeks into the trip, they crossed the Clinch River beyond Knoxville. Almost three weeks later, on November 23, the weary Virginia natives crossed the Mississippi line.

Mitchell, called a "soul driver" by his enslaved,[33] sold the black Americans seemingly in two ways: individually, for the highest price he could command, and then in a lot, when more than a score fell to the gavel. Jordan Jackson sold as an individual for $375; Caly Toler fetched $400; Isaac Carter, Essex Shelton, Green Childress, Odneck H, and Daniel Woodrey were young and healthy, and Mississippi planters paid $800 apiece for them; Lewis Muse was obviously slightly older or younger than the other men and went for less; Mary and Moses Carter managed the unlikely and brought $1,550 as a couple; Martha Bundron was valuated to the last dollar and fetched $688; Jess Cook was bought for $625; but women Pochance Clemens, Marier Finney, Marier Stone, and January Talifaro brought the customary $600. Mitchell accounted for thirty-one of the Pittsylvanians, whose first and last names he wrote down, as "sold all together in one lot for $18,040." To sell that many slaves at that price, Henry Wiencek surmises that Mitchell must have been selling off people's children in a bunch.[34] The Pittsylvanians found themselves, apparently, working on plantations near Natchez in Jefferson County, and near Vicksburg. The dreaded fate had befallen them. They had been sold "downriver" to the cotton fields, and with the trauma of acclimating themselves to the local disease environment and facing thirty full years of grueling toil ahead of them, it is likely as not that none of them ever saw the other side of bondage.[35]

When Mitchell arrived in Mississippi and very rapidly started to sell off the black people, he recorded in his ledger first and last names for the enslaved. Curiously enough, their sale is the original instance in which black Americans needed surnames. Perhaps this was Mitchell's duty as a factor returning monies to his employer, but it made his entire trek seem conducted almost by a collection of business prospectors, moving from one place that had become commercially stagnant in search of a new market. I think this is the odd contradiction about bondage that still shadows black American life. The enslaved worked, often with scrupulousness, as commerce agents for their owners, yet against their best interest. For example, Mary and Moses Carter must have gone to some rhetorical lengths to convince Mitchell or their prospective owners that they should be sold as a pair. Their main bargaining chip was loyalty to the regime that was keeping them in bondage, the same framework of categories and hierarchies and meaning that perpetually threatened them with separation.

The nature of tobacco farming, slave reproduction, and sale south were crucial features affecting the lives of all the enslaved in Virginia. But my ancestor who remained in the county did not understand himself as a Virginian. He was groomed by a specific experience near Ringgold—a community named by failed gold prospectors with a sense of irony. The miners had dug but never found gold enough to make even a ring. I initially assumed that Edward and the Fergusons lived somewhere off Ringgold Church Road, which runs north to south five miles east of Danville, and slides into the Dan River at the Carolina border. As it meanders north, the road maneuvers a bit east and bends into Laurel Grove Road at the neighborhood of Laurel Grove. Laurel Grove itself lies between two later nineteenth-century hamlets, Keeling and Sutherlin. Ringgold was the first place in Pittsylvania to be connected by the Southern railroad to Richmond, which occurred a year or perhaps just a few months after Edward Jackson was born. The Ringgold station opened in February 1856, and by May the rail lines had extended another five miles to Danville.[36] Old Richmond Road runs through the heart of Keeling, which got its name near the end of the nineteenth century; it must have been one of the routes for the overland coffles headed from Richmond to points south and west, and out of the state of Virginia. If Edward Jackson was born close to Levi Hall's neighborhood, his earliest years must have included witnessing the half that Lorenzo Ivy said did not get told: the train taking miserable people away; the marchers loaded with children as small as himself, raising clouds of dust along the road.

Railroad depot in 1873–74 rural Virginia. From Edward King, *The Great South* (1875).

Several of the people who had profited the most from the internal slave trade and the sale of tobacco lived near Edward Jackson's neighborhood in 1870. The nearby town of Sutherlin must have been named for the family of the prominent tobacco manufacturer William T. Sutherlin, born on a farm two miles east of Danville in 1822. Sutherlin became a wealthy man before the Civil War. He was the first president of the Bank of Danville, and town mayor in 1855. In 1860, thirty-eight-year-old Sutherlin, a professional "tobacconist" because he manufactured the weed into plug tobacco suitable for chewing, owned land valued at $53,000 and controlled a personal estate of more than $102,000.[37] At that time Sutherlin kept at least thirty-nine human beings in bondage, a large number, and unlike some other slave owners, he did not own families. Rather, his lot was a group of "prime" or working-age hands capable of a full day's work in his urban factory.

Sutherlin owned only four black women of working age. Additionally, fifteen of the people he owned were between seventeen and twenty years of age—the most expensive enslaved people of African descent in the labor market.[38] The young hands alone probably accounted for more than thirty thousand dollars of Sutherlin's holdings. In the running of his tobacco manufacturing business, he had to lease an additional ninety slaves.[39] Since Sutherlin regularly contracted with blacks, he would be prepared for the change in labor relations after the Civil War that most of his peers were reluctant to embrace. Yet he was equipped for the shift from slavery to the machine age in another way. An early Southern industrialist, Sutherlin had steam and hydraulic presses at work in his tobacco factories.

To flaunt his wealth, Sutherlin built a mansion on Main Street in downtown Danville. After he died, the building became the town's public library, but that use of the rarified old home did not survive integration. Today it is the privately operated Danville Museum.

An even wealthier man named Levi Holbrook, born in Connecticut, had sold Sutherlin four acres of choice land downtown for Sutherlin to build his city estate, but on the unusual condition that Sutherlin provide a number of rooms for him to live in. (Holbrook himself had $281,000 worth of wealth and owned eight male slaves, seven of them in their thirties, which might suggest they also were skilled tobacco industry workers.)

Just before the Civil War, when it had come time for states in the South to secede from the Union, Sutherlin had revealed himself to be more of a manager than a fire-eater. He resigned as mayor to attend the first Virginia state convention of April 2, 1861, and voted against secession. At the bitter end at the second convention, he did cast his vote in favor of secession, but with regret.[40] Of course, any of the manumission schemes tendered by the Northern Republicans with their heavy industries would have ruined him. Sutherlin said he was voting with his state, but actually voted with his pocketbook when the time came. After the war and emancipation, he would continue to wield a powerful influence on the Southside and the state.

Sutherlin might have secured renown as a founder of Virginia Polytechnic; but in the antebellum era his wealth fell well below the mark set by Samuel Hairston, in 1860 a seventy-one-year-old farmer who, along with his mother-in-law, Ruth Hairston, operated several multifarm plantations. (The widow of a Wilson, another extra-prominent slave-holding family, Ruth had married Samuel's brother, a move orchestrated by the elder Peter Hairston, to keep land and slaves in the family. Samuel himself had married his own first cousin Agnes.[41]) The two Hairstons' combined holdings in land and bondpeople amounted to over $1.1 million.[42]

Apparently by the time of the Civil War, Hairston's holdings had de-

clined. In January 1855, *DeBow's Review*, the Southern agricultural report, had declared Sam Hairston "now the wealthiest man in the Union."
"William B. Astor is only worth about $4,000,000, and the estates of city
people are vastly overrated," sang out the anonymous booster, "while
Mr. Hairston can show the property that will bring the cash at any moment." His ready cash was in the persons of the 3,000 black people
whom he owned or controlled, and who were worth several million dollars. "They increase at the rate of nearly 100 every year . . . a fortune of
itself."[43] Toward the end of his life in 1860 in Pittsylvania, Hairston had 17
slaves in two houses on the Oak Hill Plantation; 85 in twenty houses at
his Homestead; 44 in four houses at the Goode Pond Plantation; and 39
at the Bries Field Plantation. That was just in Pittsylvania County. Other
farms and plantations he owned formed a halo encompassing Pittsylvania County, adjacent Henry County to the west and North Carolina to
the south.

So if Sutherlin was a giant in tobacco manufacture, Hairston must
have been something of a god, a man known to control the absolute des-
tiny of the nearly 200 black people he had working in his fields, and some
2,800 others over the course of the 1840s and 1850s.

Running afoul of an element of the discipline of one of the great planters must have guaranteed a one-way trip on the coffle to Mississippi. It
seems possible that the larger estates set the pace and tenor of black work
life for the county. In the state of Virginia in 1860, most enslaved people
lived on farms where the median holding was about nineteen, which is to
say that there were equal numbers of farms with fewer and greater numbers of people held in slavery.[44] The average slaveholder, however, had
fewer than five slaves. Pittsylvania was a slave society, where slaveholding was a way of life and a key measure of the owner's standing among
the other citizens. When the households in the town of Danville were ex-
cluded, almost 65 percent of rural landholding white Pittsylvanians held
slaves.[45]

Nearly 100 slaveholders in the county, out of a total 1,413 in 1860, held
somewhere between 30 and 100 people in chains apiece; Sam and Ruth
Hairston held more than 100. In 1860 in Edward Jackson's part of the
county, the southern district, 96 men and women enslaved more than 20
people apiece. In the same district, Alexander Cunningham, E. D. Walter, A. S. Walters, Elizah Williamson, David Logan, Jacob Coles, Rolley
White, Samuel Fitzgerald, George Wilson, John Wilson, William Wood-
ing, Sutton Smith, and Robert Wilson owned more than 50 African-
descended people. In the smaller northern half of the county, 79 people

owned more than 20, and 16 of them owned more than 50.[46] In the Piedmont, where bright leaf tobacco flourished, a historian reminds us that "ownership of the land was concentrated into the hands of the great planters to a degree that was only exceeded in the rice and sugar countries of the Gulf states."[47] Pittsylvania was home to large estates, and to own land meant to own slaves.

The rule of thumb has always been the larger the farm, the more impersonal the management, with human imperatives subordinate to the financial ledger. This was the case on plantations in the Caribbean, where the slavery was so pitiless that the African people could not replenish themselves. Pittsylvania County, Virginia, was also home to plantations of scale and the application of force. The drivers, overseers, estate managers, and owners regularly inflicted punishment—*correction* and *chastisement* were the universal terms for it—in pursuit of the highest commercial yields. In the southern portion of the county, there was roughly one overseer, a corrector, for every fortieth man, woman, and child, one for every single page of the US census. For white men in Pittsylvania, it was the most common occupation following farmhand.

I wonder: what kind of people my father and grandfather might have been, had they been reared in Alexandria or Richmond, or Washington, D.C., with their reputations for comparatively charitable slavery, or at least fewer overseers? Perhaps my father would have been more open and trusting? I can recall being "corrected" at three years old for peccadilloes that I would be reluctant—or unable—to chastise my own children for. My father also called the event of giving a spanking a "tanning," as in to tan a hide, to wear the hair and membrane off an animal skin before reaching leather. And he was a mild spanker compared with our neighbors, who overwhelmingly had Virginia and North Carolina tobacco-country pasts.

Some advantages are thought to have balanced the rigors of life on large plantations: chiefly a degree of autonomy that was impossible if you worked side by side with your slave master. Supposedly, when they had some distance from their owners and some time, the enslaved were able to sustain communal life, even to the point of keeping alive African traditions. The literal size of the slave villages would seem to have something to do with it. On Martha Womack's farm in Riceville, just northeast of Competition, for example, thirty-seven bondpeople kept themselves in eleven houses. The high number of dwellings suggests that each family could occupy its own private household space, and there may have been individual housing for people whose spouses lived abroad on other farms.[48] Eleven cabins might have been spacious, self-sufficient accommodation that granted a place for everybody by the fire on a cold night, and numerous places to convene unobserved. On the other hand, Henry Emmerson's twenty-six enslaved peoples in Whitmell, the majority of them children, surely must have been cramped and susceptible to disease in their mere two dwellings that Emmerson could easily patrol.

Of course, if you were enslaved on a farm where you had to live in the same dwelling as your owner, a close relationship of some kind would have developed. Those relationships with decent whites simply must have been advantageous after the Civil War, and might have even enabled freedom before the war began. Generally, it seems to have always paid to know and be known by the master. Maryland bondman Frederick Douglass recalled in his 1845 *Narrative* the misfortune of blacks who did not know their owner, Colonel Lloyd, by sight, and truthfully answered questions put to them by whites, namely, did they have enough to eat. For telling the master to his face that they were hungry, Lloyd's hands were sometimes sold down to Georgia.

Miscellaneous accounts and records from Pittsylvania County emphasize the basic decency of white slaveholders. But in 1839 an owner named William Walton deliberately killed a teenager whom he owned. Walton whipped an enslaved boy named Frederick thirty-nine times with a cat-o'-nine tails. This particular scourge, from which the saying "let the cat out of the bag" comes, is a flail containing nine individual lengths of leather or corded rope with lacerating barbs sewn into the strips. After Frederick's back was cut open, his master had a blacksmith chain him to a heavy log, and then the boy was required to do a day's work in the field. Frederick died in Walton's furrow, and the owner conducted a hasty burial to avoid prying eyes.

The local court had no jurisdiction over a master chastising a slave and then putting him to work, particularly since thirty-nine lashes was the legal limit. However, Walton's church, the Upper Banister Baptist, composed an investigating committee headed by Moses Hutchings, an act which implied community opprobrium of one kind or another. The Baptist gentlemen issued a report and concluded, "The said Walton acknowledged that he was sorry for having put the chain on his Negro—Whereupon the Church excused him and held him in fellowship."[49] As for the enslaved, they kept a healthy distance between themselves and Christianity: estimates suggest that as few as one-sixth professed Christianity before 1865.[50]

A particularly sadistic account of the penalty for slavery in Pittsylvania was transcribed in 1937. Punishment occurred not merely for failing to recognize the face of authority but also for having no face recognizable to authority. In May of 1937, a black woman named Roberta "Bird" Walton recalled a situation that was not unknown in Virginia between the wealthy planters and their chattel. When she was growing up, Mrs. Walton lived in the same part of the county as my great-grandfather. Her story involved Robert Wilson, who was one of Danville's richest men. With an estimated wealth of roughly $170,000 in 1860, Wilson was peer to the likes of Hairston, Holbrook, and Sutherlin.[51] His father was John Wilson, the patriarch of the town of Danville and a Virginian who had known both George Washington and Thomas Jefferson. Robert Wilson was the living embodiment of the American gentry. And he did not know his seventy-five bondmen by sight. Mrs. Walton remembered not a wise governor but a terrible man.

> Ole Bob Wilson use to get on his hoss and ride down the road. One day he seed a black man comin his way in the field. He stop him and say:
> "Hey you! Whose nigger is you?"
> Nigger say, "Ise yo nigger, Marse Wilson."
> Bob Wilson say, "You is, is you? Must a run away, cause I don't recollect ever whuppin you. Get that shirt off."
> An ole Bob Wilson rode up close to that black man and gave him thirty-nine lashes across the bare back just cause he ain't remember ever whuppin that one before.[52]

Thirty-nine lashes "well laid on" was the customary chastisement meted out by the sheriff of the county court, and was considered a hard punishment.

Walton was telling her story to Claude Anderson, a black Hampton Institute professor working in the 1930s for the Federal Writers' Project. The circumstance of Walton's interview was unique because generally, unemployed white Southerners conducted the more than 2,200 interviews with ex-slaves collected by the project. A formerly enslaved man named Ishrael Massie once told a black interviewer, "Lord chile, if you start me I can tell you a mess about Reb times, but I ain't telling white folk nothing cause I scared to make enemies."[53] Often the blacks censored themselves, but not this time.

For one thing, the Virginia Federal Writers' Project employed a number of African Americans, and it was organized by a Hampton chemistry professor named Roscoe Harris, a man with writerly pretensions. Claude Anderson worked under Harris. Anderson was an indefatigable man who scoured the Virginia countryside in pursuit of authentic slave stories. Over a couple of weeks in the spring of 1937, he collected all the extant interviews of enslaved African Americans then living in Pittsylvania County. He did not find Celestia or Edward Jackson and record their stories, but he did find a woman who probably knew them.

The tale that Bird Walton told the solicitous and well-dressed Anderson was one she had recited many times before. It was rehearsed and stylized, and she gave Anderson two versions of the same story. Since she had spent only her earliest years enslaved, she could not have witnessed this incident; likely no one in her immediate family had either. But the story had been told to her in the same way by the blacks in the community she had grown up in, the area bounded by Sandy Creek, where her family owned land next to where Edward Jackson lived. When an educated black stranger asked her about the horrors of slavery, she had reproduced a collective story that an entire community had carefully chosen to characterize the experience of bondage. Of the handful of direct accounts of enslaved life in Pittsylvania, this is one of the most startling, an account of a specific, easily identifiable historical figure.

This was the story that Mrs. Walton's parents thought important for her to know concerning the experience of enslavement in Pittsylvania. Here was the transmission of a legacy of wisdom they wished to pass on to her.

During her own lifetime, the white laboring class was much better known as the perpetrator of regular violence against blacks, but her family and community wanted Bird to know that Southside masters were the direct source of the brutality. During slavery itself, planters had employed black drivers, who set the work pace and were responsible for the minute-by-minute labor of the slave gang. But in the recollections, the enslaved tended to focus their criticisms on the owners and the white overseers.

Robert Wilson retained Samuel Hardy to coerce his people in the field. Samuel Hairston employed Absalom Shackelford and Joseph Walters as overseers, and Hairston was so wealthy that these men had their own dwellings on his and his mother-in-law's property. In the county, overseers outnumbered carpenters, and in only a few instances did these whip-wielding men own anything of value. On occasion a farmer would bring a son up to learn planting by whip-managing the labor, and every now and then a man like B. C. Hughes or William Slater might become owner of a woman of childbearing age and try to breed his way into the planting class. And in Whitmell there was one Daniel Freeman, a literate, free, forty-five-year-old black man without a stated occupation who lived with a professional overseer named Zacharia Owen and his family.

But the overall impression was that overseers tended to be poor, hard drinking, and bloodthirsty, and Virginia slaves made regular reference to that fact. Frederick Law Olmsted called the overseers "coarse, brutal, licentious; drinking men, wholly unfitted for the responsibility imposed on them."[54] Solomon Northup, a New York black man who was kidnapped and sold into slavery in Louisiana, said that the "requisite qualifications in an overseer are utter heartlessness, brutality and cruelty."[55] Of course, the fundamental point about slavery—unceasing labor—should never be lost sight of. US president and slave owner George Washington laid out the basic labor exploitation that drove the peculiar institution: "the presumption being that every labourer (male or female) does as much in the 24 hours as their strength without endangering the health, or constitution will allow of."[56] To coerce unceasing labor that did not profit the laborer required an instrument of force.

But black people became adept at uncovering the inner workings of power. Slavery was not quite life beneath the underdog for everyone. It was actually life, but under hard, sometimes perpetually hard circumstances. And sometimes, an enslaved person had as much freedom and autonomy as he or she could stand up for.

They scratched out their freedom by direct confrontation and sometimes gained autonomy by revenge. In Pittsylvania in the decade before slavery ended, a black woman named Narcissa was convicted of grinding glass into the food of Judith Gilbert, and a blacksmith named Cromwell attacked a white man named James Hall.[57] More spectacularly, between the general insurrection of 1800 plotted by Gabriel Prosser in Richmond and the 1831 Nat Turner uprising in Southampton, three Pittsylvania bondmen owned by Nathaniel Crenshaw—Shadrack, Joe, and Squire—plotted to kill their owner. Squire carried out the deed, assaulting Crenshaw with a rock and then shooting him.[58] Their legendary act of resistance would have been retold in hushed tones among blacks circled around a fire. After slavery ended, these same stories must have contributed to the thinking of self-proclaimed brigands like Kit Hubbard, John Jackson, and Sam White, when in the summer of 1870 they apparently robbed and murdered Joseph E. Anderson in Spring Garden.[59] Hubbard and Jackson were hanged by the sheriff for the crime.

Black women who cultivated the habit of violent resistance had more practical purposes than revenge—like self-preservation. They combated the sexual abuse that may have been their common lot. Attempting to strong-arm black women had its limitations in an era when women commonly were set to the same laboring tasks as men. Up in Petersburg by the James River, a young girl named Fannie tussled, knocked over chairs, and "scratched his face all to pieces" when a "poor white man" tried "to throw" her.[60] At least one Southside farmer got his hind parts scalded by a kettle of boiling water when, trying to throw down a big, strapping cook named Sukie, he got took instead.[61]

If some American Africans were coping with the problem of enslavement and its immediate aftermath by resorting to violence, others merely threatened to use force. Tim Thornton, who apparently spent much of his young manhood enslaved on a farm near Cascade, in the western portion of the county reputedly settled by Pennsylvanians and working-class Scotch-Irish, offered an account of a kind of freedom within slavery. He recalled his own father, a tanner so renowned for his physical power that local legends held he could slap a man to death. "My father was such a big man everybody was afraid of him," he told an interviewer, "so it was just like he was free."[62] Certainly the amazing bondperson was admired and revered in these rural communities in a manner similar to the accord placed on amateur and professional black athletes in the United States today.

To aid in disputes, African Americans attempted to gain the ear of sympathetic whites, owners or their kin; and often these rescues took advantage of the wide gulf between well-off slave owners and poor overseers. In September of 1858, a Pittsylvania tobacco-factory hand named Richard, owned by the father of John Carrington, returned to his home and convinced his owner's son that he had been unjustly chastised. "I expect the overseer was in a passion and did whip the boy unjustly," Carrington wrote to manager J. M. Sutherlin on his father's behalf, recommending that the matter be investigated. Convinced that the overseer had acted without cause and had violated a "a very timid boy," Carrington made two suggestions. First, he declared that "if upon investigation you find that the overseer behaved unjustly, I shall expect you to see that justice be done," which must have meant either fining or firing the criminal. On the other hand, if Sutherlin believed the enslaved male Richard had violated protocol by appealing to his owner rather than the white man he was hired out to for the year and hence merited new punishment, "stand by and see it done yourself."[63] Carrington perhaps believed that the gore accompanying correction, if witnessed by a member of the elite, would deter abuse.

Again, Bird Walton from Ringgold and Laurel Grove provided the lengthiest tale of a ritualistic encounter between the enslaved and the enforcer of the slave regime. She recalled her father, Paschal Price, reacting with anger to the child of the overseer and doing this in the overseer's presence. The overseer's son had persisted in landing a whip close to the adult Price, who verbally throttled this child eager to take on adult white male privilege.

> The kid say, "You got to take it. You got to take it."
> Pa said, "Who's a going give it to me?"
> The boy said, "Pa is. He done said so."
> Pa said, "If yo pa put his hand on me, I'll break his goddamn neck. I just wish he would lay his hand on me."
> All the time, the overseer standing right there. Ole marser was sitting on the porch when the fuss started. He got up and went in the house to keep from hearing a nigger lay a white man out.[64]

George Fowlkes of Pleasant Gap, sixty-two years old in 1860, owned Mrs. Walton's mother, Jane, while her father, Paschal (the 1870 census taker wrote "Paskel"), was owned probably by George Price or his son John R. Price of Danville. Together, the Prices owned a twenty-eight-year-old man and a thirty-year-old man, and they had almost $200,000 in land and personal property.[65] These affluent local tin- and coppersmiths seem to have had a home in town and a farm outside the city. Their overseer was named George Sutherlin.

In the confrontation recalled by his daughter—a confrontation she did not witness but had been told about, over and over again—Paschal Price was helping to hang hog meat in a smokehouse. Hogs were routinely slaughtered, salted, and smoke-cured at the first frost of winter, when it seemed the weather would be cold enough for a couple of days to keep the meat from spoiling. If he was skilled and worked at the Prices', Paschal Price may have calculated his own worth to be greater than that of the overseer, who inevitably would have been something of a ruffian from among the lowest class of whites, and threatened the rich planters as much as the blacks. Throughout the confrontation with the overseer through the child, Paschal Price demanded respect. In the rather complicated protocol of the South—whereby a gentleman slave owner did not desire to witness an act of "sauce," or impudence, against white supremacy, but might certainly encourage blacks he owned and who were personally loyal to him to put the rambunctious white striving class in its place—Price had power to assert himself.

Whites, of course, were not of a single mind in their relations to blacks or in their feelings about what the rebellion against the Union had meant. During the early years of the war, a nephew of the 1860 census taker Drury Blair expressed a sentiment common among the slightly educated, small slaveholders. John Booker criticized the practice of paid substitutes taking the place of drafted men. "I say put every one on equal foottin for this is a rich mans war an a por mans fight, I be leave thare are some of the men that have but in substitute are dooen a great deal of good but the most of them are doo en more harm than good they are just speculaten on the poor people, an soldiers."[66] After the Civil War, a Richmond man on the street responded to a Northern reporter's question about the fate of Jefferson Davis, the symbol of the Confederacy. Davis, of course, was not just the president of the Confederacy but also one of its wealthy men. The white loafer in Richmond said, "I know what I'd like to do with him: I'd hang him as quick as I would a mad dog!"[67] If slavery taught anything, it taught blacks to understand precisely the seams and divisions of power, the exact places where non-slave-holding whites and the wealthy slaveholders had divided interests. Paschal Price apparently understood these fissures quite well.

Price continued to be a thorn in the side of more than one white man after slavery ended. He may have had an even more considerable reputation as an opponent to the slavery regime than even his righteous debate with the overseer's son suggests. Price lived in the same neighborhood as my ancestor, Ringgold and Laurel Grove, and some of its defining features were the numerous mills on Sandy Creek; a few were notorious. According to one local legend, on Christmas Eve 1840, to escape disgrace on his wedding day, James Lanier, heir to one of the county's more prominent mills, used an axe to split open the heads of his black mistress, their two children, and her mother.[68] He then fled west.

Another mill as prominent as Lanier's stood on Sandy Creek and was also enshrouded in mysterious rumor. In December 1873, Paschal Price was the last person listed by mill owner George Fowlkes in a will that granted equal shares to four other African Americans. The grant was large: "my mill and Blacksmith Shop including all machinery and tools in, and attached to each, and fifty acres of land around and also enough land so as to embrace all the land covered or damaged by the mill pond."[69] Fowlkes left only scraps to his own white family, who claimed he had been conjured or poisoned by "Dr. Cherokee," an herbalist known to the local freedman. The will was appealed to the Virginia Supreme Court, and Price was the only person listed in the lawsuit who seems not ever to have been owned by Fowlkes. In his lifetime, the unusual man Paschal Price was at the center of more than one dispute about race and power.

Price's curious vernacular victories reminded me that there was much more to my family story in Pittsylvania than rape, overwork, and sale. Edward Jackson undoubtedly knew some adversaries in his leap from slavery to freedom. But he could tap into the wisdom from the quarters, the remedies of black rebels and herb-conjuring artisans, or just his neighbors, like Paschal Price, who was all three.

4 · Make Do

Between 1861 and 1865, Danville served as the munitions depot and quartermaster stores for the Army of Northern Virginia, and had one other bona-fide claim to Civil War fame. Jefferson Davis, the president of the confederation of states in rebellion, sought refuge there after General Ulysses S. Grant took Petersburg on April 2, 1865, and caused the evacuation of Richmond. For several days in April, Davis was a guest at William T. Sutherlin's mansion on Main Street. From there he took a stagecoach on April 9 to North Carolina to evade General George Stoneman's four-thousand-strong Union cavalry, onrushing from Tennessee. Danville, Virginia, was the last capital of the Confederate government.

It's difficult to draw a line from the appearance of Union troops to the formal end of slavery. It's more difficult to know what Pittsylvania's ex-bondmen thought about it all. The official occupation of Danville began when Colonel Thomas Hyde's Third Brigade, Second Division of the Federal Sixth Corps entered the city on April 27, 1865. Among other things, the Union soldiers published the newspaper *Sixth Corps* for at least several weeks. The Federal army news conveyed to the locals the general orders made by the military government. By May 6, 1865, Major General Wright had issued "General Order No. 13," which mandated that to bring in the crop that year, "Negroes will therefore remain at the homes and plantations to which they belong, attending to their work as usual."[1] General Wright hoped to turn back the clots of freedmen flooding the town, a clustering that took place throughout the South, as bondmen tried to test out physically their new freedom and, under the protective umbrella of Federal soldiers, plot a course for their new lives.

Some former slave owners were convinced that the freedpeople would resume the relationships of the slavery era if briefly indulged and petted. "A striking fact respecting the negroes in Virginia is their cat-like attachment to places," wrote a white Southside mother to her daughter in January of 1866. "The passion for change once gratified," she continued, referring to the widespread drifting of black Americans to collect their families after the war ended, "and themselves satisfied of the ability of the change in their condition by leaving their homes, they seem to desire to return at least to the neighborhood and their old associations."[2]

Ex-slave owners' sense of self-interest and the paternal benevolence they insisted was at the core of bondage went even further. Few Virginians were more committed to slavery and the Confederacy than the diarist, legislator, and early soil conservationist Edmund Ruffin. Ruffin had seen John Brown hang and had pulled the lanyard to fire the opening shot against Fort Sumter. In the weeks after the war's end, and while living on a farm along the course of the railroad between Danville and Richmond, Ruffin described the technical transition from slavery to freedom that must have unloosed many a young adolescent from his kinfolk.

> Even as to negroes, though no one doubts the speedy enforcement of complete emancipation, the former proprietors, & still retainers of the slaves, are under still greater disadvantage than their total loss in their present possession. They might make arrangements with their negroes, heretofore their slaves, to hire the labor of the able, & be remunerated for the support of the helpless and expensive, when a family was constituted of suitable and proportionate members of both classes. But, when expensive members are in excess of the laboring & aged or infirm seniors, the former proprietors must either continue to furnish maintenance, without any prospect of remuneration, or turn out helpless children to starve.[3]

After having benefited from the work-without-pay of this class for decades, Ruffin now debated whether or not to push them outdoors. He was so emotionally embroiled over the Southern defeat and black freedom that in short order he would wrap himself in the Stars and Bars and put the contents of a rifle through the roof of his mouth. He killed himself over the major tension in the years following the end of slavery: what relation would the freedmen bear to their former owners, whose chief interest was now in securing labor and saving money?

Most disconcertingly to some whites, black women and girls were leaving their former places of enslavement for better opportunities. An unhappy *Danville Daily News* recorded the controversy, and quickly appointed a scapegoat. By May of 1865, "servants," "especially females," had left their former owners and were ensnared by "the unaccountable influence of certain persons who, being acquainted with their good qualities are doing everything in their power to retain them." The newspaper, and the town by extension, convinced themselves that "after a short trial in their new mode of life," these "poor, deluded creatures" "would willingly return to their former homes." But some local devils of "sinister motives" and "unworthy of a place in respectable society" were interfering with the class of recently emancipated black servants. The threat tendered by the whites in position to enjoy service was not veiled but explicit. "We mean just what we say, and if certain people that we wot of do not take hint, we intend to say a good deal more, and be less guarded in our expression."[4]

The editorial concluded on an ominous note: "Better look out." In the mysterious communication I can't exactly figure out who was meant as the target: Black men? Northerners? Or scalawags, that ingenious designation for inferior cattle that became the sobriquet for native Southern white men who admitted that blacks were as good as whites? Mainly the article conveyed the determination to keep a prone serving class.

By the fall of 1865, Pittsylvania's freedmen found, over and again, the mixed blessing of their new mobility and a martial Federal bureaucracy unequipped to rewrite 250 years of Virginia history. In November of that year, the Philadelphia Quaker newsletter *The Freedman's Friend* offered a sad report on the general condition of black people in Danville:

> You have no idea of the amount of misery and suffering; of the great destitution among the colored people . . . driven from their homes by their masters, who having got all the work for fall done, crops gathered and wheat sown, send them away without anything . . . just as winter is coming on. In some cases, the Freedmen's Bureau drives them back and they are obliged to stay under the old slavery conditions.[5]

Perhaps one kind of slavery ended only for a new but similarly strict order to take its place.

The transition to the new way of life after slavery ended was a kind of Middle Passage: disorienting, wearying, emotionally painful, lethal, and indiscriminately cruel. The bands of freedmen who left the countryside in 1865 for Danville faced a smallpox and typhoid epidemic. There were too many people and not enough clean cups for water or plates for eating. Edward Jackson seems to have welcomed his nominal freedom in the countryside and not in the incorporated city of Danville or the county seat of Competition, and that decision would have brought at least the tangible benefit of health in the months after the end of hostilities.

Typhoid, caused by feces coming in contact with drinking water or food, was a regular bane of life in the nineteenth century, especially for American Africans, who regularly lived in close, banked quarters. To stay healthy, the youngsters Edward Jackson and Celestia Hundley had their work cut out for them. A Northern reporter was told by a farmer living just south of the county courthouse at Competition, "I hear they're dying, heaps of 'em, in Danville."[6] By "them," the farmer meant freedmen.

Weather conspired against the new day for many consecutive years. Conditions were bad in 1866, and by January 1867 exceptionally cold weather added to the misery and brought death by simple privation. In 1868 a Philadelphia Quaker schoolmistress named Eunice Congdon consoled a mother who had just lost her child due to the combination of summer drought, which had ruined the crop, and another frosty winter. "It has been very sickly here," she said. A devoted white woman who had braved the rebels and ran the school in downtown Danville since 1865, Congdon had unimpeachable social capital among the freedmen. However, the ex-slave woman corrected her words. "No," the woman said. "Deathly, nothing but death."[7]

Communicable disease and inclement weather were acts of God, but there were acts of man to contend with as well. The end of the war returned white Confederate soldiers home to Pittsylvania County, furious in defeat. Local attitudes were notable enough to catch the attention of Freedmen's Bureau executives, who tossed off memoranda to one another in June of 1865. "The people throughout the county are feeling bitterly towards the colored people," one observed, "and are determined to make their freedom more intolerable than slavery."[8] The Southern laborers and artisans—the foot soldiers in the Civil War—obviously had not supervised the course of American slavery. Now, however, they became contestants in a struggle beyond rifles, a conflict of belief, myth, rumor, and ideology. Well-to-do Southerners who had been involved in slaveholding for generations had evolved a near theology of paternalism regarding the operation of slavery, a kind of religion that had at its heart a guarantee of care for blacks in return for their submissiveness. This paternal care was often more fiction than fact, and it could do little to check the attitudes of the majority of the South's whites, who had not held slaves and who, after 1865, had to compete with freedmen and mechanical engines for their bread.

Americans had the opportunity to read about the nearly half a million Virginia freedmen and their former owners in newspapers, magazines, and books. The *Nation*, a brand-new magazine founded by the likes of Frederick Law Olmsted and Wendell Phillips Garrison, son of the famous abolitionist William Lloyd Garrison, sent a twenty-six-year-old Harvard graduate and "special correspondent" to cover the Southern scene. John Dennett rode through Pittsylvania on horseback in late August of 1865, collecting evidence of racial strife.

Outside Competition, a tavern keeper's son told him, "I'd rather be in war ten years than pull fodder two days. D——n farming; it's enough to kill a horse; it's just fit for a nigger."[9] More than one Confederate veteran scorned the prospect of doing heavy manual labor. Modern industrial warfare and its techniques, and the mental adjustment needed to deal with the memory of carnage on the scale introduced by the war, had transformed these Southern men. For at least some of them, men who might have felt a kind of seigniorial tie toward area blacks, the war had ravaged them and cleaved their shared sense of belonging with freedmen. Their views toward blacks had hardened, and they would become capable of atrocities. Without a doubt, masterless African Americans were the prime symbol of not just their military defeat but the end of the way of life the Confederate veterans had known.

At Lynchburg, twenty-five miles north of the Pittsylvania county line, a corduroy road connected the tobacco towns, and ferries replaced the bridges destroyed by retreating Confederate soldiers. In that town a former owner of more than sixty African-descended people expressed a common estimate of freedmen: "Since mine were freed, they have become lazy, stubborn, and impudent. . . . I begin to believe that they are without gratitude." In a succinct manner that held widespread authority for a century, the former slave owner went on to characterize the immediate postwar "Reconstruction" era as an abject failure: "The troubles we have all grow out of the complete anarchy in which our Negro population now is."[10]

It was difficult to find a white man who thought that black freedom was anything other than regional catastrophe.

Close to Thanksgiving 1865, Byrd Ferrell, who was sixty-eight, wrote to his son Peter in Danville about the labor conditions. Ferrell lived in Halifax, bordering Pittsylvania, and his farm was near Birch Creek, which ran through the upper portion of Laurel Grove and bottomed into Spring Garden, just south of Sandy Creek. Thirty-five years old, Peter W. Ferrell had gone into the tobacco business with the town factor, William Sutherlin. "I suppose you have been informed before this time," the older man wrote to his well-connected son, "that my freed Negroes have all left me, they have all left me but Joshua and Lindy and her children, and I suppose they will leave between this time, and Christmas."[11] Ferrell groaned with displeasure in his letter:

Aaron and his family have set in with Rich. Henderson to make a crop at Mrs. Eldridges; Cornelius and Henry and Harrison to make a crop with R.Y. Eldridge, and Randolph to make a crop with G.W. Davis; their time expired with me the 28th of Oct. by mutual consent; them and me went to the Ct. House on that day, and layed our case before the provost Marshall, or the manager of These Negroes, and he gave them Wages, *Monthly*; and that was the end of our Misunderstanding.

Ferrell seems to have abhorred the idea of monthly pay to his former slaves, and as time wore on and he conformed to wage labor, he continued to express dissatisfaction with what was taking place. "Have lost my two ablest hands," he complained to his son at harvesttime in 1868. "One by begging off, to go to the West, and the other, Doctor Reves, *by dragging* off; he is a great Rascal; a considerable portion of My Tob. Is now ready for cutting and houseing; no fodder saved; and no force to take in and save my crop."[12] Ferrell was obliged to contract hands by the day and week, but none were available by month or to the end of the year. The old white farmer's disgust with the "great Rascal" "Doctor Reves" caught my attention because of a historical curiosity. Doctor was a popular and unusual name among black Americans in the Southside.

The local whites in Pittsylvania cultivated an easy intemperance toward freedmen. A remarkably steady opponent to blacks' new status was William Duncan, who lived in the western portion of the county by the Sandy River. In November of 1865 he wrote to Asa Holland, "The negroes give me some trouble. They do but little work. I think the sooner we can learn to do without them the better it will be for all of us."[13] Not quite two years later, in August of 1867, Duncan corresponded with his wife, readying himself to commit what the Freedmen's Bureau termed "outrages," or violent hate crimes.

> I am every day more fully convinced of the importance of getting rid of all the negroes. They are always destroying something on the plantation and about the house . . . Wife! The great mistake of your life is confidence in the negroes . . . There is not a negro on this plantation that cares a straw for you or more, or that would walk 10 yds to save anything that we have. And I am determined not to hire a single one another year. They treat me so badly. The old set of negroes that we have had around us all the time are the worst of all.[14]

When the census taker came to him three years later, Duncan owned no land and had about three hundred dollars' worth of a personal estate.

Times were hard enough that he put his own twelve-year-old son in the fields to work, about the same age that Africans in bondage were when they had been first set to adult tasks.[15]

I can only imagine that the attitude of a man like Duncan was embittered by the times, and that he had other old military buddies from various parts of the county who held the same view. Directly west of Pittsylvania in Franklin County, Betty Saunders of Bleak Hill expressed her sense of the poison of freedom in the months following the end of the Civil War.

> The absorbing subject with everyone now is the negroes. Ours have until lately behaved as well as possible but a good many of them now are becoming disconted [sic] and anxious to look out for homes for themselves. I believe the best plan is to get rid of our own and hire others from a distance. The foolish creatures do not seem to feel their freedom until they break loose entirely from their old Masters. Our house servants go on as usual, though they expect to leave us at Xmas.[16]

Industrious regional planners would take much of the lead in the adjustment from to wage labor from slavery. Forty-four years old in 1866, tobacconist William Sutherlin continued to wield a powerful voice, not just in Danville but in the state of Virginia as a whole, as an advocate of moderation and common sense to his peers. At the Virginia State Agricultural Society meeting of planters in Richmond in November 1866, he addressed the new problem of labor management. Mainly, Sutherlin encouraged "the settlement of negro laborers upon a place, and creating in their minds feelings of attachment and domiciliary influences."[17] In his personal life, this was apparently the case. At his mansion on Main Street, Sutherlin employed black workers—technically mulattoes in the eyes of the census taker—who drove his carriage, tended his garden, cooked his food, and cleaned his home. The carriage driver had even attached himself to the Sutherlin surname.

At the agricultural society meeting, Sutherlin insisted on the financial up-side to emancipation. "The abolition of slavery, much as we deplore it, has not only unlocked the labor of the country, and placed it within the reach of all who have energy, industry and intelligence, but it has also unlocked the broad acres of the country, and opened up their cultivation."[18] The trained managers with ties to factories, railways, and shipping were prepared to succeed the old landowning barons whose feudal-era gallantry had led the South into an unwinnable slaughter.

Not a year later, the *Southern Planter and Farmer* swung in Sutherlin's direction with an article tellingly titled "Let the Plow Be King and Cuffee His Prime Minister."[19] Sutherlin wanted the freedmen—Cuffee and Sambo were the famed generic names—to sustain a kind of permanent peasantry in the short term who would not impede economic growth by voting or owning land, but who as tenant farmers would work harder than ever before and lift an agricultural county like Pittsylvania beyond its rough patch of military defeat and economic devastation.

In the not really distant future, Sutherlin hoped for Danville to become a destination of heavy industry in the South. By 1868 he administered the dose of what Yankee victory meant to the advisors gathered at the Boarder Agricultural Fair. "We must learn the important truth that iron muscles require neither food nor clothing," he lectured them. "One man" equipped with "labor saving machines," he preached, "can do the work of five without them."[20] Sutherlin's grasp of the situation proved prophetic. In a little bit more than ten years, tobacco production would outstrip slave-era yields.

As Federal garrisons reduced in size, local whites evermore shifted blame to Cuffee for much of the tangible and shared hardship they were experiencing. In January of 1868, when Pittsylvania County changed the law requiring landowners to completely enclose their property, a point of particular concern because property owners were required to fence in lands that they rented, a letter to the newspaper praised the new law and offhandedly cast aspersion on freedmen. Foraging African Americans were held responsible for having "nearly completed the destruction of the hogs, sheep and cattle, of both the rich and the poor."[21] The penalty at the time for stealing a hog or a sheep was to be hung by the thumbs for two hours.[22]

But such standing punitive measures did not slow the momentum of white backlash against freedmen. The town of Danville had swiftly enacted a system of ordinances that tried to replace the summary justice of the whipping post, which emancipation had managed to abolish. In June of 1867, the Common Council passed ordinances "to Establish a Chain Gang," "Punish Breaches of the Peace and other Misdemeanors," and "to Allow Costs." The chain gang operated under the mayor and the city's jailer and could be employed in public works projects. Arrest for disturbing the peace was very much left to the discretion of "officers of the peace," and typical charges were intoxication or loud talking. But the last ordinance of 1867 was designed to introduce a new kind of relationship between the black poor, the state, and heavy industry.

A person convicted of a misdemeanor would be held in the town jail and then sent to work on the chain gang, where he would earn fifty cents per day as a laborer. But the convict also had to pay off his penalty, the fine that accompanied conviction, and all the "costs" connected to his arrest and adjudication:

> persons so convicted, in addition to fine or penalty under the ordinances, for fifty cents costs of arrests and ten cents costs of summoning, for each material witness summoned and examined in the case; the said costs are to go to the policemen to making the arrests.[23]

Under this arrangement, laws against vagrancy, changing employment without the previous employer's consent, moving off an employer's land, and the like corralled the freedmen back onto the farm. Before they had the opportunity to consider themselves wage laborers, they had become serfs.

The Pittsylvania resentment toward the Reconstruction years gave way to something else when it was picked up by the descendants of the last generation of slaveholders, the white children who went on to write the local and national histories. Pittsylvania's most meticulous historian to this day, Maud Carter Clement, was a member in good standing of the Daughters of the Confederacy. Indeed, as a young lass in 1899 she represented one of the Confederate states in the pageant held in Chatham to celebrate the twenty-year-long struggle to complete the Confederate war memorial. She took her own life's work from the inscription on the monument that read: "Go tell the listening world afar of those who died for truth and right."[24]

Clement referred to black Pittsylvanians in her masterwork *The History of Pittsylvania County* in only a single chapter, "The War 1861–1865," and she included blacks only to disparage the period between 1865 and 1877: the Reconstruction. For her, the problem was not my ancestors—whom she unfailingly described as docile and meek children, necessarily absent from the historical record—but the carpetbaggers, the huckstering, venal, cheap salesmen from the outside whose mercantile trademark was their ever-ready cloth valise.

> A man named Lehigh from Pennsylvania became Sheriff of Pittsylvania County. . . . A carpet bagger from Maine named Tucker was commonwealth's attorney and was very active inciting a spirit of resentment among the negroes toward the white people. These northern visitors had no kindly feeling for the colored people and never as slaves had they suffered anything like the cruelty meted out to them by Lehigh, the sheriff.[25]

In 1929, when the book was published, most Americans like Clement with a passion for Southern history accepted the view of Reconstruction written by William A. Dunning, a Columbia University historian, and his students. In 1940, when the Dunning school showed signs of collapse, a writer characterized its main assumptions as having been "that carpetbaggers and Southern white Republicans were wicked, that Negroes were illiterate incompetents, and that the whole white South owes a debt of gratitude to the restorers of 'white supremacy.'"[26] Dunning's basic line was that a "mass of barbarous freedmen" threatened civilization in the South until the Federal troops left in 1877 and white property owners regained control.[27]

In Dunning school accounts, the immediate postbellum world was filled with silly freedmen who did not know their place and ruined the Southern economy and legal system. For Clement, the hallmark occasion of black ignorance in Virginia was the referendum on the state constitution, and the clause in question would have disallowed ex-rebels from voting.

> The negroes under the leadership of the carpet baggers held nightly meetings, with much oratory. One old darkey was heard arguing in favor of the much talked of clauses along the following lines: "Cose I'se gwin ter vote for de claus. How de constitution gwin to hol' wid out claus? How kin 'er a cat climb er tree wid out claws."[28]

The "old darkey's" remark, describing black support for clauses that would disenfranchise the ex-Confederates, seems folksy, metaphorically rich, and witty to me. But the play on words was a source of scorn for Clement, whose comment, "Such logic seemed irrefutable to his hearers," is supposed to prove the low-grade mentality of the freedmen.

Clement's standard account of Pittsylvania history for the eighteenth and nineteenth centuries insisted that the gentry after the Civil War were Knights of the Roundtable protecting a battered Camelot. In her hands, black pursuit of the Fourteenth and Fifteenth Amendments to the US Constitution during Reconstruction was confined to two Chatham mob scenes. In the first, "one of the negroes had some trouble with a white man," and the "blacks grew very ugly and sullen." But then she introduced a valiant white man with a long pistol who "brought his gun down to aim on the approaching negroes," who then indecorously "began running in every direction." "The white people had no desire to hurt their former slaves," she explained. "When they saw danger threatening they met it coolly and thus averted it."[29]

Here's her final description of blacks and whites resolving political disagreements in the immediate aftermath of the Civil War:

> One day when there was no gathering of men at the courthouse—just the few town people who were residents being present—a large number of negroes were seen coming down the street. Three white men were sitting on the porch of Carter's Hotel, and when the negroes halted out in front of the hotel the white men arose, went to the edge of the porch and stood calmly waiting to see what the negroes intended doing. The crowd seemed to hesitate and after talking among themselves and repeatedly looking at the white men they dispersed. The next day one of the gentlemen who had been on the porch, meeting with one of the negroes, asked him what they were about the day before. The man replied that they had held a meeting and determined to come down town and demand some of their rights from the white folks, but when they saw him and those other two gentlemen standing there on the porch, just looking at them, they got afraid somebody might get hurt and they decided they had better go home.[30]

When I first read this account, I didn't have any name of an ancestor who might have been in the black legion at Carter's Hotel, but what's most immediately obvious about Clement's retelling of events is the extraordinary value that white men and women born after the Civil War put on creating "negroes" who completely lacked valor. The other thing that is abundantly clear in the passage is the precise reason why, after the Dunning school had been respectably overturned, people of reasonable conscience shunned the word *Negro*. In twentieth-century white Southern speech, it means even less than *nigger*; it means not cattle so much as it means specifically cow.

The view that Clement put into words was not extreme. Myrta Avary's 1906 *Dixie after the War* was a much better-known book, and in it she presented the belief shared by very many Americans, including a not inconsiderable number of African Americans. "Without decrying Hampton, Petersburg and Tuskegee, it can be said with truth that these institutions and many more in combination would be unable to do for a savage race what the old planters and the old plantation system of the South did for Africa's barbarians," wrote Avary.[31] Southern slaveholders were, in her eyes, sort of missionaries in reverse, bringing the animist cannibals home with them. But the messianic work went for naught. "With freedom," Avary warned, "the negro, *en masse*, relapsed promptly into the voodooism of Africa."[32] I imagine that the avoidance of the appearance of voodooism was something my father and perhaps even my grandfather paid quite a bit of attention to. Whether or not it was a concern of my great-grandfather's, I am unsure; I know that for certain that Edward Jackson's neighbor Paschal Price disregarded whites like Avary.

◆　◆　◆

Part of the rising antiblack spirit also must have stemmed from the simple fact that within the South itself, a sizable percentage of its inhabitants greeted the outcome of the war with jubilation. One black Virginia freed-woman, two or three times a week and for years following the end of the conflict, would lift her arms skyward and cry out in the street of her village, "Th-a-nk Je-e-sus I'se free-e! Ya-a-s my Je-esus I'se free-e!"[33] In Danville, the newly freed women and men held Emancipation Day parades every January first during the second half of the 1860s. Marching brass bands conveyed the earnest rejoicing through Main Street downtown, and attendees from the countryside must have swelled the well-known and heavily celebrated pageant. The merry, gaily dressed parades must have thronged Mountain Road and Ringgold Church Road near Edward Jackson as revelers trooped to and from town, gamboling unmolested. In the first years after slavery had ended, the ability to tread the public road, day or night, without a pass, must have been chief among the freedmen's new delights.

In 1868, the three-year-old Emancipation Day festival warranted braving snow and slush and merited two brass bands, complete with "treats of oratory" at the chapel on the hill in Danville.[34] In days of bondage, the first of January had been the occasion of "valuation," when the enslaved were typically hired out to new masters for the year or sometimes sold, and families were often split apart. Since it probably took a year or two to get the tradition going, January 1, 1868, must have seemed astonishing to ex-slaves insofar as the scope of transformation that it signaled. A day that had once sharply marked renewed slavery now brightly broadcast freedom.

Pittsylvania was home to a messy flux between violence and peace, possibility and frustration. The whites rightfully felt in the immediate aftermath of slavery that they were being punished for a system that the entire country had profited by. In 1870 the *Danville Register* reminded its readers that a 1760 Rhode Island newspaper was rife with "ancient documents, two of which would have been of interest in this latitude a few years ago, as showing that a certain reviled institution was not always confined to the Southern States of the Union."[35] Of course, it was talking about slave advertisements. Southern public sentiment continued to believe that the Federal garrisons were organized and successful plunderers who had imposed a regime of bankruptcy by ending slavery and then one of humiliation by treating blacks as US citizens, which we indeed became in 1867.

On the peace and possibility side of the ledger, there was the unique intermingling of the races. In the South, even after emancipation, whites and blacks continued to share households, for example. And while blacks, even with the presence of Federal troops, seem to have been pretty much at the mercy of whites in Danville and Competition, the relations simply could not have been exclusively mercenary. In Pittsylvania, a seventy-two-year-old white woman had living in her household a fifty-four-year-old black man; the pair lived by themselves. At the prosperous farmer John Keen's, alongside his wife, their three children, and a white domestic servant was an eleven-year-old black domestic named "Keen Leroy." The census taker seems to have reversed the name of the boy Leroy Keen to emphasize this distinction: he may have been part of a household, but perhaps he was not quite part of a family.[36] However, it stands to reason that the boy had made the jump from being called Keen's Leroy to having a name of his own. Perhaps there was harmony; perhaps only if everyone kept to their place.

The Bureau of Refugees, Freedmen, and Abandoned Lands, more commonly known as the Freedmen's Bureau, kept records of the times when harmony wasn't the norm. In 1868 the bureau reported "outrage[s]" in Pittsylvania in July, August, October, and November. This was the year that the Ku Klux Klan made its first appearance in Virginia. Near Competition, William Bobbett, a white man, stabbed Scott Coles, a black man who had gotten into a fight with Bobbett's father. In another incident, night riders rode up to Wesley Edwards's house, threatened his ill wife, then raped his daughter. In an additional outrage, E. H. Cook, obviously with some assistance, tied and then whipped black Milton Runnells.[37]

Whites who didn't respond affirmatively and with alacrity to the violent management of black citizens were also threatened. Reminding everyone that "we are many in number," anonymous gunmen left an ominous letter at Sam Hairston's Oak Hill house during the first week of October that year.

> The Negroes at the Royal Oak plantation must and shall leave this country or there will not be a house left standing upon the place. . . .
> Sutch a den of thieves cannot nor shall not go unmolested. . . .

If you can't moove them we can and everything else, so take warning. . . .
for this Den of Thieves shall go to flames if not Broken up & those vilons
that now live on the plantation shall be burnt to death.[38]

Naturally enough, blacks did not accommodate the abuse with uniform passivity. Morton Witcher, a black man working shares at white farmer Alex Dodson's, was accused of stealing and violating his contract. Dodson and his grown son rushed the Witcher cabin, called Mrs. Witcher a "bitch," and then flew at Morton Witcher with a stick. The result? Morton Witcher shot Alex Dodson for his pains.[39] The federally installed magistrate judge convicted Witcher of second-degree murder in the bureau-run court. Morton Witcher filed a petition for writ of error against the judgment. Later he formally petitioned Virginia's governor, H. H. Wells, seeking a pardon.

Pittsylvania was designated the Seventh District of the Freedmen's Bureau. Seventh District, in the southwestern portion of the state, was headquartered in Lynchburg, seventy miles north of Danville and in next-door Campbell County. The principal bureau agent in Lynchburg was Captain R. S. Lacey, who worked for Colonel Orlando Brown, the state commissioner. Yale educated, Brown had fought the South for four years as a Union soldier. However, his feeling toward blacks was not easily distinguishable from the position of an educated Southerner; they might charitably be termed paternalistic.

Brown addressed the freedmen in July of 1865, when he proposed "to teach you how to use that freedom you have so earnestly desired." He encouraged my Pittsylvania ancestor to "be industrious and frugal" and to remain "independent of charity and of government aid." He exhorted the root-hog-or-die Republican sermon: "It is feared that some will act from the mistaken notion that Freedom means liberty to be idle." If perchance the former top rung of the rail "fail to recognize your rights to equal freedom with white persons," Brown said, "you will find the Government through the agents of this Bureau as ready to secure to you, as to them, Liberty and Justice." He reminded the freedmen that work was scarce, and that the possibility of higher wages found after months of vagrancy was an illusion. "If you are in a location where work is to be obtained at fair wages, it is much better for you to remain than looking for something better."[40] I suppose I think "wisdom," yes, but "free labor," not quite.

The Freedmen's Bureau closed its doors by the end of the decade, before it had been able to get to what was arguably the most important element of Brown's address. "Schools, as far as possible, will be established among you, under the protection of the Government," he had promised.[41] Although several schools were operating in Lynchburg, Pittsylvania had only three schools that made it into the bureau's records. In Competition, Mrs. Ann Benedict, a Virginia-born white woman who was fifty-five when the war ended, and a man named Herbert Vickers were teachers. In another instance, an energetic, enterprising freedwoman ran a school out of her house that responded to the needs of eighty-four children and adults.[42]

The major educational effort for blacks took place twenty-five miles south of Competition on the other side of the Dan River, in Danville. The wooden building on Dan's Hill accommodated 522 pupils by January 1866 in a school headed by "Yankee teachers" Cara M. Young, Helen and Estelle Johnston, Annie McKissic, G. Galloway, M. Calloway, H. Inge, and J. Jackson. A Quaker organization called the Philadelphia Friends Association founded the Danville school; it leased a 45-by-120-foot building, described by Chaplain Ralza Morse Manly, state superintendent of Freedmen's Bureau education, as being in "not good" condition and worth about $800. By contrast, in Richmond, which had brick schools, the best, which was half the size of the Danville primary, was valued at the much more impressive $3000.[43] Initially, strong African American enthusiasm greeted the Northern teachers, but none of these instructors were recognized by the US census of 1870; perhaps five years of uplift had been enough.

By 1881 the Danville school had moved into a brick building on Holbrook Street and had a black principal, Reverend William Yancey. After Yancey, W. F. Gratsy, a black native of Danville, served a marathon tenure as school principal from 1888 until 1929.[44] Furthermore, despite the importance of the Northerners in developing the public school tradition for blacks, statewide, half the teachers were black. As well as I know, none of my relatives attended any of the nineteenth-century schools.

The school did not owe its growth to the enthusiasm of the area whites. The June 1866 report of the state school superintendent to Freedmen's Bureau commissioner Oliver Otis Howard reflected the reality on the ground in Virginia. Manly described a defeat by way of attitude.

> No appreciable amount of sympathy or assistance from citizens is to be looked for in the work of educating the freed men. Many of the better class of white citizens, in private conversation and in deliberate discourse favor the education and elevation of the Negro, while all the religious conversations of the state have endorsed the same idea. But the controlling classes

have neither the disposition nor the ability to undertake any part of the practical work beyond a very little in Sunday School.[45]

In Pittsylvania during the late 1860s, educational institutions were a battlefield. Two years after his first bleak assessment, Manly increasingly recognized the importance of education to the newly freed. "The whole colored population, with few exceptions, are calling for schools," he wrote to Oliver Otis Howard in Washington.

> Education seems to be regarded by them in a three fold light: First as a long denied *right* and therefore they demand it because it is *theirs* without reference to the uses of it when it shall be attained. Second as a badge of freedom and of manhood. Third as an element of power. Many see clearly that without education their political and social position as well as their material interests will never be advanced.[46]

My own family was part of this plaintive, pathetic, and exasperatingly incomplete pursuit of literacy, particularly those, like Edward Jackson, who had just gained their freedom. I believe one way that they expressed the frustrated pursuit of education was shame, a sentiment very familiar to me.

The gulf between the two sides on this issue was painful to witness and impossible to reconcile, it seems, without fighting the war again. Joe Anderson, a contemporary of Maud Carter Clement and a historian of the Shockoe Baptist Church near Chatham, seems to speak for his congregation when he belittled freedmen's attempts to advance themselves with education. "He can learn arithmetic and history and literature," admitted Anderson, but the skills were meaningless, because freedmen "will not learn morality."[47] Superintendent Manly of the Freedmen's Bureau countered that a courageous will and moral fiber were in evidence, citing the case of children walking seven and nine miles to get to schools. "I doubt if the history of education can present instances of greater sacrifice to secure the advantages of education than are furnished by colored children and youth all over the school."[48]

My family experience can only reinforce the suspicion that the freedmen's educational pursuit was stymied at every turn. My great-grandfather might have been born slightly closer to Danville than to Chatham, but I am not sure where he would have gotten the Booker T. Washington notion that literacy was eminently valuable and worth unbounded sacrifice. It isn't at all clear to me what he passed on to his son, or what his son passed on to my father. It certainly doesn't seem as if my grandfather attended school much.

My father, Nathaniel Jackson, 1985.

My dad, however, was a leaper in his own right. He would surpass his humble educational foundation and attend and finish college in 1958, well before the dawn of integrated tertiary education in the United States. He was a formally learned man with an official baccalaureate degree, and he conducted himself as a credentialed professional man in all the memories I have of him. He anticipated at least some of my own wonderings about racial ancestry and African heritage. When I was eighteen, he gave me the two-volume *The World's Great Men of Color* by West Indian historian Joel A. Rogers, which was precisely what I was searching for at that time: a vantage on a more distinguished past.

But I also recall my parents' struggle to supply me with suitable reading material as I moved from one threshold of learning and understanding to another. It's one thing to recount the glorious story of a child or an adult learning to read for the first time. But the process whereby parents deliberately or obliquely direct children away from the ambition to master more sophisticated elements of language and literature is a less-told but equally frequent story. In a ten- or twelve-hour car trip to visit my grandmother in Cleveland, after I'd run out of comic books and *Encyclopedia Brown* and begged them for something more to read, somehow a *Harper's* magazine short story fell into my lap. The story featured a disabled, shell-shocked Vietnam veteran, and the plot I remember had something to do with him racing up flights of stairs to a brothel to get his cane in the door in time for a throwdown. My parents were embarrassed by the incident, and I think they were relieved that I spent the next five or six years reading the history of military conflict and collecting miniature soldiers. Though they were well-read people relative to the folk in our neighborhood in Baltimore, they didn't have stores of books that were dense without being sexually explicit. The English professor in me recognizes that their literary palate did not include many of the masterpieces of the nineteenth century.

It occurs to me now that my parents' educations were bereft of Walter Scott, Stephen Crane, Mark Twain, Henry James, William Dean Howells, or Horatio Alger even. There were some deep gorges for us in regard to the nineteenth century, the distance between what my mother and father had been able to master in school and what traditions they had inherited from their own parents and teachers. Added to this, my father seemed to have had a lurking suspicion about education, a kind of reluctance to give himself over to it. I think he resisted because he thought education could wear away hardened belief or commonsense value.

Of course, in word and deed my parents praised education highly, but as soon as I got to know white families on my own, in junior high school, I noticed—embarrassingly but irrevocably—that we *esteemed* education in the way that one venerates an icon, and they *used* education like a hammer and nails. I think the difference I became aware of at the end of the 1970s was connected to the observations of amorality and sacrifice made by whites, such as the theologian Anderson and the government official Manly, when they tried to understand the educational tendencies of blacks in Pittsylvania after the war.

It was as if we who had been cut off from education showed our hostility toward that injustice by resisting conventional knowledge. That kind of willful ignorance was buttressed by the fact that few of the contributions of black people to their own freedom and uplift were celebrated. If we never heard Abraham Lincoln's observation that "without the military help of the black freedmen, the war against the South could not have been won," how would we know to look for Freedmen's Bureau executive Manly's acknowledgment of black Virginians' "great[er] sacrifice to secure the advantages of education"?[49] Booker T. Washington, who survived enslavement in the county next door to Edward Jackson, glowingly praised "that Christlike body of men and women who went into Negro schools at the close of the war by the hundreds to assist in lifting up my race."[50] But Washington's first chance to get a lesson was from a veteran of the United States Colored Troops, a fellow African American, and an inspiring learning example he shared with many other black Virginians. Where did that tradition go, that sense of education coming from within our own resources and believing in our own dramatic capacity to change our circumstance?

Contrary to the lore about the Freedmen's Bureau ruining the postwar economy, Pittsylvania's schools did not receive much government support. The county's difficulty in paying teacher salaries and providing books, heat, and light for public schools probably had everything to do with Oliver Otis Howard, the Washington commissioner of the bureau nationwide, and Samuel Armstrong, a Union officer setting up high school and college departments in Washington and Hampton Roads, Virginia, before the end of the 1860s. Their schools became Eastern Seaboard leaders Howard University and Hampton Institute. But private enterprise, even when self-sacrificing and altruistic, did little to adjust the economic and social realities of a century.

My grandfather Nathaniel Henry Jackson, Edward's seventh child and born in 1895, may have never really learned to read and write, at least not in a school. It's hard to tell where he would have had the opportunity. A mile or so due south of the creek and mill where my grandfather seems to have lived was a place noted on a 1918 soil conservation map as "Union School," which might have meant there was a school there or one had been there. It's a mystery, since the map itself shows a building with a cross, the topographical symbol for a church, not one with an isosceles flag, the symbol for a school.[51] Whatever the case, I have great reason to doubt the accuracy of the popular wisdom expressed by the best-known novel set in latter nineteenth-century Pittsylvania. A quid-chewing character from *The Deliverance* says he "watched the nigger children traipsin' by to the Yankee woman's school" while white children were at the plow.[52]

Pittsylvania's educational offerings for freedmen's children seem hardly so robust. In the town of Chatham proper in 1910, there was probably only one teacher, a twenty-three-year-old African American woman named Celeste Carper. She was a preacher's daughter.[53] From the place where my Jackson kin farmed, they would have had to walk the Old Richmond and Malmaison Roads three miles west and then a good fourteen miles up the public road to reach Chatham. In 1902 Virginia made education compulsory for children between the ages of eight and twelve, but with a couple of caveats. Children could be excused "for cause by the district trustees," and Section 140 of Article Nine of the state code carried even heavier weight: "White and colored children shall not be taught in the same school."[54] In the US census in April of 1910, my fourteen-year-old grandfather, now a full-time farm laborer, was actually enumerated as being able to read and write. But it seems this was literacy of a different kind, considering his older brother, Berkeley, and his younger brother, Hugh, were not similarly equipped.[55] It's hard to know what happened. The story my father regularly told me that reflected Grandpa Jackson's position on education was this: "Juneya," my grandfather told his son, "get you a Cadillac so everybody know you got education." I guess he meant that a cat does indeed climb a tree with its claws.

5 · The Names of Guinea Roads

A fifty-five-year-old mulatto man named Granville Hundley was plowing fields on a tract of land within shouting distance of Edward Jackson in 1870. The great forward leap had happened for Hundley too. His fifty-year-old wife, Charity, no longer chopped the corn, wheat, and tobacco crops but was "keeping house." Charity Hundley had made, in fact, two leaps: one from enslavement, the other from the not female/not male omnigender role that human bondage forced on black women, who were and reproduced the labor force. Undoubtedly Charity Hundley's liberation from common field labor was envied by black women like Mary Ladeper, twenty-three; Febbie Gaults, thirty; and eighteen-year-old Hildy Oliver, who yet worked full-time in the field. The Hundleys are significant to my own story because in 1870 their oldest child living with them was a daughter named Celestia. The couple thought or knew her to have been eleven in that year, and at some point before 1880, she and my great-grandfather married.

Celestia would have a son, Charles, around 1877, and she would continue having children into the twentieth century. Thus, the first free generation began in their family the same year that Federal troops left the South and the relationship between the formerly enslaved blacks and the former rebellious whites, low and high, resumed its previous paramount importance. In places where my ancestors lived, such as Danville, there were violent struggles between whites and blacks over labor contracts, voting, and access to public places that culminated in a massacre of blacks in downtown Danville in 1883, ending the work of the multiracial Readjuster political party. But before that wild and anxiety-filled time, Edward Jackson and Celestia Hundley grew up as neighbors, perhaps even within the same cluster of cabins. They shared at least a portion of childhood and adolescence together, and then they were married.

My grandfather knew his parents' names to be Ned and Less, as he had written on my father's birth certificate, but I found so much dignity in Edward and Celestia. I have tastes like my own father, and they lay a foundational sensibility always at odds with the multiple truths that construct the past. For example, the less formal names my grandfather used for his own ex-slave parents exemplify the naming practices of the Creole generations, trying to hold on to some sense of their African parents' unique identities. A prominent historian of colonial Virginia calls the informal naming an example of the "tenacious retention and later adaptation of some African ways."[1] These naming practices helped black Virginians endure in a world in which death and despair were a great part of their lives. The names that the ex-slaves gave themselves on the 1870 census knit together a good deal of the black Virginia story.

Next door to my great-great-grandparents lived a man called Nathaniel Hutchings. He and his wife had a nine-year-old boy named Granville. Celestia would one day have a son named Nathaniel, who had a son named Nathaniel, who had a son who named his son Nathaniel. This was everyone's first chance to make a community after outright bondage had passed, and whether they were kin or just neighbors, the two families seem to have been close-knit.

Granville Hundley, a farmer prosperous enough to employ and house a 23-year-old black man named Preston Cole, lived in a neighborhood that contained other moderately prosperous freedmen. Thirty-nine-year-old Alexander Boswell, a blacksmith, had a personal estate worth $125. This makes sense, considering that Boswell needed to own an anvil, tongs, hammers, mallets, punches, chisels, a forge, and a bellows. In the aftermath of the war, this amounted to almost as much in personal estate as one of the local physicians. Fifty-five-year-old Hundley declared himself a farmer to the US census taker, although he didn't own land; he could make the assertion hold water because his personal estate was valued at $100. In that rural land where people bought little from stores, he owned valuable goods that set him apart from the majority of destitute freedmen.

With their comparative wealth, both Alexander Boswell and Granville Hundley belonged to a rare class of men who had emerged from bondage with something more than abject poverty. A few other neighbors joined them in that distinction. The freedmen of Laurel Grove could boast of William Night, a sixty-six-year-old black farmer with a personal estate of $150, and Frank Cunningham, a mulatto-looking carpenter whose holdings amounted to $130, probably, like the blacksmith, in tools. William

Night was uncommonly vigorous. Born at the turn of the nineteenth century during the final heyday of the Atlantic slave trade, he had a two-year-old child in 1870; his wife was fifty.

But these men who seemingly contended with bondage and freedom could neither read nor write. During slavery, some bondmen had been taught to read, though nearly all were actively discouraged by law and by custom from learning how to write.[2] A slave who could write could, of course, make passes for other blacks, which would allow them virtually unlimited travel throughout the United States; consequently, slave owners strictly enforced the mandate against enslaved persons writing.

Frederick Douglass, who left detailed accounts of nineteenth-century American slavery, glossed over the point of his decade-long labor at the copybook, at one point or other probably a cloth-covered McGuffey's Reader, by saying, "Thus, after a long, tedious effort for years, I finally succeeded in learning how to write."[3] The difference in chronological time between young Frederick's earliest instruction and his remark in the narrative about putting writing to use is roughly ten years. The advent of Douglass's literacy in Maryland occurred during an era of general alarm. Virginia's 1819 code prohibited "slaves or free Negroes, or mulattoes mixing and associating with such slaves at any meeting house or houses in the night; or at any school or schools for teaching them reading or writing either in the day or night under whatsoever pretext."[4] After Nat Turner's 1831 rebellion, it was illegal even for free Negroes or mulattoes to assemble to learn to read. The punishment for teaching a slave to read was twenty lashes, though masters were known to remove portions of fingers for writing. So for the middle-aged elites among the freedmen, writing would ever remain a distant hope.

◆　◆　◆

Often during my research, I had imagined, perhaps sentimentally, that Granville and his wife, Charity, had been working together on the same farm during slavery. After all, several white Hundleys were living in Pittsylvania County over the years and owning slaves. I had assumed that William B. Hundley of Sandy River, about fifteen miles west of Danville and on the opposite side of the county from Ringgold, owned my forebears. Hundley was fifty-two in 1860, and he owned six thousand dollars' worth of real estate and roughly twelve thousand dollars' worth of black people. Just before the Civil War, Southside Piedmont land was valued at about $12.70 per acre.[5] On five hundred acres, Hundley could have cultivated a decent tobacco crop, along with other staples like corn and wheat. He owned eleven people, and he listed a man at thirty-five, a woman at thirty-two, and most important, a one-year-old girl. Those would be fairly rough approximations for the ages of my family members. Of course, such a connection hinges on the premise that my forebears all lived on the same farm in 1860—everybody together—and survived slavery in a coherent family unit.

But slavery wasn't like that. So-called marriages for blacks tended to take place at a distance, and the relationships flourished during the seasonal breaks of the intense labor system.[6] Slave masters arrogated the term *family* to include people they owned, which perhaps made the "family" of a white slave master, a black woman, and her children a symbolically complete unit. Families might have taken the same name, but even after slavery they must have been composed most regularly of half-relations. Marriage had been a man and a woman periodically sharing a cabin with children whom they had had with other people along the way; perhaps the group included a new child they had together. The phenomenon of the half-relation sibling and foster parent would account for what seemed a queer language practice among precocious children during my youth: we would call each other "cuz," a deliberately abbreviated form of *cousin*, and there was always a hint of mockery. The term could be used to address absolute strangers as well as legitimate cousins. Family was a sought-for boon as much as a question of likely probability that spilled over with haunting gaps.

So I revised one of my hopeful dreams and tried to limit my search to facts: neighborhood, names, and ages. Maybe the district neighborhood along Ringgold and Laurel Grove was the glue that brought Granville and Charity together? Was the age that Granville Hundley gave the census taker in 1870, fifty-five, accurate? I had minimized his reported age for any number of reasons. One factor undercutting the likelihood of his being exactly fifty-five was the slave owners' practice of estimating the enslaveds' ages at five-year intervals. In the US census of 1860, for example, once the slaves had passed the prime age of twenty-five, the owners overwhelmingly lumped them into age cohorts: 30, 35, 40, 45, and 50 years old. There were no appreciable numbers of the enslaved past 50, which was quite near to the end of their capacity for the hard farmwork lasting from betimes in the morning to late at night.

Of course, Hundley might easily have over- or underestimated his own age. According to Lorenzo Ivy, who grew up near Competition and graduated Hampton Institute with Booker T. Washington's class in 1875,

"White folks was spose to keep the ages of slaves in order to know when they was spose to start payin taxes on em. Guess you can see why they weren't so anxious bout keepin close track of the ages of niggers."[7] Most farmers would have kept the age of the enslaved in a simple ledger or commonplace book.

It would have been necessary to have accurate farm book records of slave ages, because physical appearance was not a real gauge. If the photographs of American presidents like Lincoln and Obama tell an accurate story, physical appearance and aging are greatly connected to the caliber of day-to-day stress. Enslavement appears to have been quite stressful and was capable of causing premature aging. Frederick Law Olmsted noticed this miserable phenomenon during his 1853 travels through Southside Virginia. Making his way through Mecklenburg County, Olmsted needed directions, and he asked "an old servant." On a brief journey together, Olmsted inquired of the black man the age of a forest they crossed. "The most accurate information he could give me was, that he reckoned such a field (in which the pines were now some sixty feet high) had been planted with tobacco the year his old master bought him. He thought he was about twenty years old then, and that now was forty. He had every appearance of being seventy."[8]

Masters had little reason to miscalculate the age of their mature bondmen on the US census, but the survivors of slavery always troubled after an accurate account of their years. Frederick Douglass obsessively pursued information about his biological age, and engaged in correspondence with his former owners throughout his maturity to arrive at a satisfactory conclusion. For Douglass, the lack of fundamental knowledge about his birthday or his mother and father was the prime iniquity of bondage, and his query resonated for my grandfather's parents. When Edward and Celestia Jackson were in their forties at the census of 1900, after years of variation, they synchronized their birthdates to 1859.

Considering all this, I decided there was a better choice among the plentiful Hundleys of Pittsylvania for Granville's slave owner in 1860. One man named Hundley lived quite close by Sandy Creek and Mountain Road, somewhere in the vague quadrangle of Chatham and Danville and White Oak Mountain and the eastern hamlet of Keeling, the place my grandfather had identified as being close to his home on a 1917 selective service registration form. Old Tidewater planters and their sons fleeing soil devastation reputedly settled the eastern portion of Pittsylvania, so the slave owner I was looking at was perhaps not a vigorous Simon Legree setting out to build a fortune. The candidate I identified, in fact, was a lonely descendant of one of the pioneer families, seventy-two-year-old John Hundley, who owned one person in 1860, a forty-five-year-old man described as mulatto-looking. John Hundley was the uncle to William B. Hundley in Sandy River, whose father, Caleb Hundley Jr., was fifteen years or so older than his youngest brother, John.

When the 1860 census taker Drury Blair took his slave schedule census on August 24, he counted fifteen people in four houses at the property of Sarah and James Lanier, then John Hundley's one mulatto man living in his own cabin, then Levi Hall's nine people (including six children) in one house. Hundley and Hall were close neighbors, and Granville Hundley was quite close to Hall's property ten years later, in 1870. I know that Edward was more or less living on Hall's land with the Fergusons, I assume in the old slave cabin.

Three other slave owners lived between Levi Hall and Mary Shelton, the mother-in-law who shared the house with Hall in 1860 and perhaps had her two laboring-age women cultivating his five thousand dollars' worth of land. A. E. Blanks owned ten slaves, perhaps six in prime condition; Royal King owned six and probably had them all in the field, since families worked together and ten-year-old children could work; and the physician Edward Williams owned eight slaves and probably sent out seven, perhaps exempting a man thought to be eighty.

John Hundley was not a regular tobacco farmer, though it certainly seems that Lanier, Blanks, King, and Hall all cultivated that leafy coin of the realm. He was the youngest son of a large family, the many descendants of Phillip Hundley Sr. who had emigrated from England to Gloucester County, Virginia, in 1634. Phillip Sr. named his oldest son for himself. Phillip Hundley Jr.'s second son, Ambrose, was John Hundley's grandfather. Ambrose Hundley lost his life in a hotheaded dispute with the shoemaker James Blaxton in 1777 in Charlotte County, after he sent his bondman to fetch a pair of shoes and was informed that he owed three shillings. When he bragged to his friends that he "expected to have the son of a bitch to whip," and then later struck Blaxton with a switch, Hundley got this throat cut in the bargain.[9] Ambrose's wife remarried, and his son Caleb moved to Pittsylvania, married Sarah Walker in February 1778, and embarked on his own large family. In 1782 Caleb Hundley, about twenty-five years old, purchased 191 acres in the vicinity of the Pigg River and Potters and Harpen Creeks, roughly in the center of the county and near a town that would later be called Gretna.[10] Sarah and Caleb had twelve children; the first was named Ambrose, whom they called Granville, and the last was named John, born in the mid-1790s.

SCHEDULE 2—Slave Inhabitants in *The Southern District* in the County of *Pittsylvania* State of *Virginia*, enumerated by me, on the *24* day of *August*, 1860. *Drury Blair* Ass't Marshal.

	NAMES OF SLAVE OWNERS	No. of Slaves	Age	Sex	Color	Fugitives from the State	No. manumitted	Deaf & dumb, blind, insane, or idiotic.	No. of Slave houses.	NAMES OF SLAVE OWNERS	No. of Slaves	Age	Sex	Color	Fugitives from the State	No. manumitted	Deaf & dumb, blind, insane, or idiotic.	No. of Slave houses.
1		1	24	m	B	1					1	7	m	B				
2		1	22	m	B						1	6	F	B				
3		1	22	m	B						1	4	F	B				
4		1	20	m	B						1	2	F	B				
5		1	17	m	B						1	¾	m	B				
6		1	16	F	B					A. E. Blanks	1	65	m	B	1			2
7		1	12	m	B						1	33	m	M				
8		1	11	m	B						1	32	F	B				
9		1	4	m	B						1	23	m	B				
10		1	2	m	B						1	18	m	B				
11		1	90	F	B						1	16	m	B				
12	Harrison L. Hodges	1	38	m	m	1		2			1	14	F	B				
13		1	20	m	m						1	10	m	m				
14		1	33	F	B						1	7	m	B				
15		1	15	F	m						1	4	F	B				
16		1	14	F	m						1	2	F	B				
17		1	12	m	m					Royal King	1	41	m	B	1			1
18		1	11	F	m						1	21	m	m				
19		1	4	F	m						1	18	F	B				
20	James A. Lanier	1	33	F	B	1		4			1	16	m	B				
21		1	20	F	B						1	13	m	m				
22		1	18	m	B						1	10	F	B				
23		1	17	m	B					Edward William	1	80	m	B	1			1
24		1	15	F	B						1	68	F	B				
25		1	13	F	B						1	26	m	m				
26		1	11	m	B						1	26	m	B				
27		1	16	F	B						1	18	F	B				
28		1	1	F	B						1	16	F	B				
29	Sarah Lanier	1	70	F	B	1					1	16	F	B				
30		1	50	m	B						1	14	m	B				
31		1	65	m	B					Mary Shelton	1	65	F	B	1			1
32		1	25	F	B						1	35	F	B				
33		1	5	F	B						1	35	F	m				
34		1	4	m	B						1	9	F	B				
35		1	2	F	B						1	7	F	B				
36	John Hundley	1	15	m	m	1		1			1	5	F	B				
37	Levi Hall	1	25	F	B	1		1			1	3	F	B				
38		1	21	m	B						1	1	m	B				
39		1	21	m	m					William Hall	1	64	F	B	1			1
40		1	21	F	B						1	36	m	B				

No. of owners, _____	No. of male slaves, 44		No. of fugitives, _____	No. deaf and dumb, _____	No. insane, _____
No. of houses, _____	No. of female slaves, 46		No. manumitted, _____	No. blind, _____	No. idiotic, _____
	Total slaves, 84				

1860 US Census, Schedule 2, Slave Schedule, Pittsylvania County, Virginia; shows holdings of Harrison L. Hodges, James A. Lanier, Sarah Lanier, John Hundley, Levi Hall, A. E. Blanks, Royal King, Edward Williams, Mary Shelton, and William Hall.

Caleb Hundley wasn't a large farm owner, but he did own slaves, and probably more than those who had lived with him and were evaluated with his estate after his death in 1841. At that time he owned a very old woman named Dinah; an old man Adam; Brunswick, Bartlett, and Cinda, who were in their prime; and the boys Dennis, Arthur, and William.[11] Seven years earlier, in 1834, he had paid taxes on at least six black people over the age of sixteen, but by the end of his life he was keeping only four.[12] In 1819 he sold 150 acres to his youngest son, John, who never married and seemed to have a knack for land deals.[13] John paid a dollar an acre for a tract of land near Turkey Cock Creek. To a favored son, like the third boy, Charles, Caleb generously gave outright 332 acres by the waters of Sandy Creek in June of 1831.[14]

John Hundley liked the Sandy Creek land himself, and in 1840 he paid $300 to Nancy and Johnson King for 150 acres of it by a branch called Echols Spring, and in 1845 he purchased another 107 Sandy Creek acres from planter Griffith Dickenson Jr. for $538.[15] There were three Sandy Creeks, but the significant one for the eastern portion of Pittsylvania County seemed to have stemmed from the Banister River and spent itself just short of Courthouse Road between Danville and Competition. The soil around the creek in the Spring Garden area was a fine sandy loam, acidic, and appropriate for cultivation. John Hundley never owned any slaves until 1844–45, when he paid taxes on one person over the age of sixteen, and then by 1848 he paid taxes on two men. In the US census of 1850, Hundley was shown as owning two men, one mulatto and one black, ten years apart in age.[16] In 1860 he owned only one person, a forty-five-year-old mulatto man.

The intelligent thing, for a person in the Virginia Piedmont who owned slaves by the mid-nineteenth century, was to train the males in some kind of artisanal craft, put them to work on improvements around the property or hire them out, and then set the women and children to work raising tobacco.[17] If the enslaved were treated tolerably well, it stands to reason that deep and complex emotional ties could have resulted, especially from the relationships between enslaved artisans and their owners. Perhaps my ancestor Granville Hundley thought well enough of his owner to keep his name; or perhaps it never occurred to him at all to choose a different way of calling himself.

If John Hundley owned my ancestor Granville Hundley in the vicinity of Spring Garden or Chestnut Level in 1860, forty-year-old Charity and one-year-old Celestia may have been anywhere in the area, lost in the same formless web of possibility as Edward Jackson. Here's what I mean.

In 1860 Levi Hall's mother-in-law, Mary Shelton, held a thirty-five-year-old female, thought to be mulatto-looking, and a three-year-old female black child, along with two other women and four other children.[18] Hall himself had a twenty-five-year-old black woman and also a two-year-old black girl. The owners might have known these ages precisely, "guesstimated" on secondhand slaves, or dissembled to avoid paying taxes on them. Maybe Charity was a proven breeder who had had several older children sold, and her owner wanted to make her attractive to prospective buyers; then he rehearsed his lies by reducing her age with the census taker.

As father to my own little Southside descendants, I can admit to feeling a remarkable sense of vulnerability about infant Celestia, born in 1859 or so, with so many years to survive being "smothered" (the catch-all term that registered much of black infant mortality), the slave trade, illness, starvation, marauding secessionist troops, and the like before she could live long enough to have my grandfather.

Because the specific connections to my family are so lean, the community of people who remained in the households near Sandy Creek in 1870 began to claim more and more of my attention. One black woman named Cindy Keesee lived in Mary Shelton's house. Because it is such an odd surname, I imagine she was related to a man or a woman who had a son named John Kesee, the same John Kesee who was married to my great-aunt Mary. My grandfather lived with his younger sister Mary, a twin, and her invalid husband, John. They were relatives I had visited in my childhood and then found their house thirty years or more later, when I went back to Danville. At the house of Samuel Anderson, a white farmer who had four hundred dollars in land and a personal estate valued at to hundred dollars, lived forty-year-old Ann Kesee and three-year-old Anna. Ann Kesee worked as a seamstress; it was quite rare for a black woman in Pittsylvania to have an artisanal occupation.

Even more intriguing to me was that in the house of seventy-two-year-old William Hall, a white man, were two women who had the surname Shelton. Nancy Shelton was white, in her fifties, and had no occupation. But black Aniky Shelton was seventy-five years old and still trudging along as a domestic servant. She probably had survived slavery and remained with the family of the person who had owned her. Though advanced in age, she was still working, and perhaps doing hard work; she repulsed the stereotype of the aged and "expensive" black former slaves whom Edmund Ruffin had been concerned about. In some way, this was a privilege, as the white farmers had turned their backs on many blacks after the Civil War. Some of the labor contracts explicitly forbade the provisioning of young or old relatives who were not directly laboring; if everyone didn't carry their weight, even the contracted workers would be fired.[19] But two other noteworthy facts from the census caught my attention.

The first is age. Aniky Shelton would have been born about 1795, or thirteen years before Britain outlawed its involvement in the transatlantic slave trade and suppressed the shipment of slaves from major portions of the western coast of Africa. Before the ban, more Africans had landed alive in the New World than ever before. Literally hundreds of thousands of human beings were mutilated and scrotomized, and then parceled out to remote farms in a densely forested wilderness. They were exchanged with the amount of reflection we would give to a transaction at a pet store.

The mountainous history of Africans in Virginia has so many nooks and crevices that it was hard for me to catch hold all of it. In reference to the period before 1680, Virginia's colonial governor Edmund Jennings wrote, "It was very rare to have a Negro ship come to this Country directly from Africa." But this was not true twenty years later. Between 1700 and 1775, Virginia imported roughly 75,000 Africans and enslaved them, and perhaps as many as 63,000 came directly from Africa.[20] The others were "seasoned," or acculturated, in the Caribbean, so it is more difficult to determine what their African points of embarkation might have been. During the 1760s, Pittsylvania's founding decade, 7,645 fresh Africans, known as "New Negroes," "Outlandish Negroes," or "Saltwater Geechees," arrived in Virginia. In fact, since African men fresh off the boat were set to work clearing forests in uncultivated areas, more African-born blacks were living in the Piedmont region by the second half of the eighteenth century than in the Tidewater, closer to the coast. Also, by the end of the eighteenth century, there were far more females among the native African population in the Piedmont, enabling the resumption of family life and the practical rudiments of handing down traditions.[21]

Virginia already had ended its African imports in the revolutionary time of 1778, when the British ships stopped unloading Africans at Bermuda Hundred, the historic inland slave port for Virginia where the James and Rappahannock Rivers converged. So by the aftermath of the Civil War, genuine eighteenth-century American Africans were increasingly rare. Their memories of black life as it had been in Africa, then in eighteenth-century colonial Virginia, and then in the Jackson-era United States of America, dramatically countered the reality of the industrial-scale manufacture of tobacco and the sale of lots of human beings for the cotton farms of the Southwest. They had also lived through the accultur- ation of West African folkways into American folkways, principally those having to do with language and food. And in the Piedmont, where they had numbers, their older traditions would have resonated.

The second and related curiosity about this senior working woman was her name, Aniky. I once had a friend named Aniké. She was a Ni- gerian woman from Onitsha Province in the Niger delta, just north of the old slave ports Calabar and Port Harcourt. While that is the only other time I have ever heard the name, I found out that the name Aniké is well known among the Igbo, who come from the same region in Nigeria. Perhaps Aniky Shelton from Edward Jackson's Sandy Creek neighbor- hood was a very old woman who had survived Middle Passage and the First Winter and then held on to some semblance of her original African name? Perhaps she kept the name of a parent, relative, or revered person who came from the land of the Igbo? She definitely was one of the oldest black people in the district, and undoubtedly freedpeople knew and re- spected this woman who possibly had a profoundly different philosophy of time, God, and the afterlife.

If her name indicated some preservation of an Igbo naming pattern, Aniky Shelton was not one of a kind. In 1870 there were three families with male children named Doctor living in Ringgold and Laurel Grove alone. At first I had thought the name was designed only to ensure that the child received adequate respect in a time and place disinclined to grant a black boy very much. But there was more to it than that, I learned. To name a boy Doctor was an old Igbo practice, and it identified a per- son who was destined to be familiar with herbs and who could "doctor," or practice *dibia* or *obia*, the sacred science of the ancient Igbo religion.[22] The outstanding ethnicity of eighteenth-century Piedmont Africans was Igbo, and the figures show that some 37,500 Africans sold to Virginia between 1716 and 1755, the height of the slave trade to the colony, de- parted from Biafra in the Niger delta, the home region of the Igbo.[23] One such-named boy, "Doctor Day," was born in 1867 to parents in their early twenties, and they lived only a dozen or so households away from Ed- ward Jackson and the Hundleys.[24]

In fact, a singularly compelling feature of my great-grandfather's part of the county, the 2,880 people, couple thousand acres, and few hundred households found within the scissors-shaped area from Whitmell to Laurel Grove, was its pattern of African names. Considering the injunction of famous Tidewater slaveholder Robert "King" Carter to his overseer in 1727—"take care that the negros both men and women I sent you up last always go by ye names we gave them"—these names represent a rebellion all their own.[25]

In 1864 a Laurel Grove black couple named Judy and George Walton, who must have realized that the Civil War was nearing its end, decided to name their son "Cuffee." Judy was about thirty-four, and George was past fifty; they wanted to mark their boy in a particularly African manner, and I could only assume for someone whom the middle-aged couple knew. The Waltons lived a few households away from Chestnut Level physician Edward Williams. There was an older freedman on the Danville side of the county born in 1800, who called himself Cuffee Macko; judging from his surname, he may have traced his origins to Congo-Angola.[26] Everybody knew what these names meant when they came from black people: pride in themselves and remembrance of their ancestors.

Every now and then, whites in Pittsylvania too acknowledged an older history to black Americans than one of bondage and servitude. In September of 1857, Sarah E. Cabell, a slave owner, reported to Langhorne Scruggs, the county clerk in Chatham, that a seventy-year-old enslaved person, entry number 1194, had died. Under the category where the owner was invited to report the "given" name of the deceased, either Cabell or the clerk decided to record simply "African." Scruggs regularly recorded the deaths of enslaved human beings anonymously, but to report that person as African was unique. It suggests to us that here was a person who might have noticeably resisted the pattern of acculturation and submission to European American folkways, to Christianity, or to the English language itself.

Hostility toward African culture in the United States often has been systematic, other times unconscious and eerily powerful, but I suppose its origins were simple: animus toward things African served to reinforce the helplessness of the slave population. And yet, many African customs survived and found their way into everyday life both during slavery and after it ended. The persistence of elements of these customs was illustrated, for example, when the vanquished rebels walked back to their homes from Appomattox in April 1865. They took the turnpike between Lynchburg and Danville on their way south, bringing thousands of them through Competition, the center of Pittsylvania. According to the genteel history of Maude Carter Clement, one afternoon a well-to-do white woman named Lucy Lanier Carter "determined to offer them refreshment,"

... although her pantry contained nothing but several bushels of black eyed peas and some corn meal. Large iron pots were placed out in the yard, fires built and all the peas cooked, while the meal was baked into small pones—a few faithful slaves assisting in the preparations.[27]

The narrator Clement switched into the passive voice at this point in her story—"pots were placed . . . fires [were] built"—because her Southern belle heroine did not, perhaps could not, do any of this heavy and imaginative work herself. Build the fires, hang the heavy cast-iron pots and load them with water, prepare the largest skillets, and figure out how short rations could feed a mob—all this work was being done, not by "faithful slaves," but rather by loyal, physically robust, and resourceful free black women. It's even more fascinating to link their pots of food back to African cooking techniques that had been passed down to them through generations of enslaved women.

In Nigeria, there is a well-known and highly regarded dish that uses black-eyed peas and turns them into pone. It is called *moi-moi*, and it is a cross between a dumpling and a loaf. In America, corn was grown expressly to feed livestock and the enslaved; whites would have known they were a member of the better class if they had wheat meal ground at the mill for bread made from wheat and baked with yeast. Eating corn-bread and corn pone, field peas, black-eyed peas, hush puppies, crackling, maws, and chitterlings would have signaled a white man's flinty table and his own embarrassing proximity to the enslaved. What did it mean for the rebel soldiers to eat an African American staple from African American women's hands, and for an ancient black memory, however imperfectly or improvisationally recalled, to save them? How had the strong African American women understood their duty and their own determination to preserve particular ways of preparing food, especially single-pot stews?

Preserving names and keeping alive the elements of African foods and preparation styles could take place within the confines of slavery, but of course the champion attribute conveying the strength of the enslaved's African identity was the manner in which they responded directly to their bondage.

According to US census taker Drury Blair, who tallied Schedule 2—the Slave Schedule—for the slave owners around Sandy Creek on August 24, 1860, none of Pittsylvania's black Southern inhabitants had stolen themselves away and thus had to be reported at-large (see illustration p. 100). The "Slave Inhabitants" section of the census was crucial because of its impact in apportioning congressional representation. Although no enslaved person was listed by name, the enslaved were all individually tabulated, from oldest to youngest. The document contained nine points of basic information, such as the owner's name; the number of slaves; the enslaved's age, sex, and skin color; the number manumitted, "Deaf & dumb, blind, insane, or idiotic"; and the number of slave houses. On one occasion, category eight, "Deaf & dumb, blind, insane, or idiotic," proved the most chilling. Pittsylvanian Nannie Echols admitted ownership of a distraught sixty-year-old black woman who had become "Insane [by] grief."[28] Undoubtedly the tragic circumstances of one black woman were so well known among black and white, even the census recorder grieved.

Blair, who was also a slaveholder, made some other curious notations when he completed the slave schedules for 1860. Next to each slaveholder's name and at the top of the entry on every page, he placed a faint check beside box number six, "Fugitive from the state." He made it seem as if the slaveholders were nearly missing their oldest hands. The US census takers had regional peculiarities when it came to enumerating enslaved populations: in upcountry South Carolina, for example, the Spartanburg enumerator put his faint check in 1860 by the entry of each mulatto. Which category was more dangerous or needed closer accounting: black, mulatto, or fugitive?

But if Blair seems to have accounted for no person who actually had escaped from Virginia, flight itself was common. Better known as "running off to the woods," maroonage was the time-honored manner of arbitrating disputes over labor and severity of treatment. Black slaves ran off to the woods for hours or days or even weeks to object to unfair work conditions. The former slave Lorenzo Ivy recalled in an interview that there were "two kinds of runaways—them what hid in the woods and them what ran away to free land. Most slaves just runaways and hide in the woods for a week or two and then come on back." And then Ivy recalled a third type, a permanent maroon: "My grandmother lived in the woods."[29] He believed his relative had to escape the plantation and disliked slave owners, the "mean masters" like Robert Wilson and the town road-builder and court clerk William Tunstall. Maroons lived lives of never-ending rebellion, remaining near to slavery's grasp but refusing to acquiesce.

The handful of advertisements from Danville's irregularly preserved newspapers offer an account of flight around the time of the Civil War that was closer to maroonage than it was to the trajectory of escape that would lead a bondperson to everlasting liberty in Canada.

Escaped off the South-Side Railroad at Prospect depot, Sunday morning March 1st, two negro men, one named AMOS, very black, five and a half feet high, 20 or 22 years old, very powerfully made, weighs about 175 lbs.; the other named ALFRED, brown skin, about same height, 22 years old, small whiskers, weight about 160 lbs., also stoutly built. They were both clad in light colored clothes, very much soiled from lying in jail.

Said negroes were raised by WM. May of Pitt Co. N.C., and it is believed will attempt to get back that way. A reward of one hundred dollars will be paid for both or fifty dollars for either one of them.[30]

I typically do not consider that people escaping during the year of the Emancipation Proclamation would have made their way further south. But those stout young men must have known something of the world and how to get around in it.

The next year and in the same fashion, J. Motley, who lived seven miles south of Danville, advertised for other young runaway men of medium height: Madison, "very black and likely," and Abram, "very black and heavy built." "They are probably gone to Richmond or to the neighborhood immediately in the fork of the Dan and Stanton Rivers."[31] Well, in that time and place, "likely" meant that a person was capable and attractive, and where the pair probably was headed was not a utopia where they planned to escape slavery forever. But the freedom offered at the river-way crossroads or in an urban Richmond neighborhood snuggled beside the James River was a particularly black cosmopolitan kind of life. The two young men could look forward to pleasure and opportunity along the swift river, in the ample free black communities, and in the world of traveling black artisans, sailors, and musicians, as well as in the reality of public and private places where most people were black. Even the man who owned them understood that the young men were prepared to accept a life of turpitude on the outskirts of the law and proper society that might at any time exact violent revenge. In their youth, Madison and Abram embraced a life of nonstop contending.

I am pleased by the idea that male friendships, such as those Frederick Douglass described when he planned a group escape in rural Maryland around Easter 1836, provided hearty sustenance and affirmation. If African American culture began aboard the slave ship, the cultural foundation was the union of the shipmates chained side by side, the "sippi" in the pidgin.[32] It's certain that the rogues Madison and Abram weren't trying to get North, and they may not have even been looking for their families. That fork at the "Dan and Stanton" that attracted the rascals must have been a hell of a neighborhood, the briar patch where Brer Rabbit turned into Stagolee.

♦ ♦ ♦

Not every route to freedom required risking life and limb. In the encompassment of Ringgold, Laurel Grove, and Spring Garden that the census taker might have described as the contiguous portion of the county my ancestors seem to have occupied in 1860, I found a spellbinding pattern of African American freedpeople. Their lives must have been some kind of measure for what a general emancipation would have resembled at the dawn of the Civil War. Of something like 2,200 free white and black inhabitants living in those areas, 114 were black or mulatto, or a bit more than 5 percent.[33] Where Edward Jackson wound up at the dawn of his freedom is within a rough neighborhood of several of the notorious black freedpeople, and nowhere else in Ringgold, Laurel Grove, or Spring Garden were there consecutive households with an equally large number of free black adults. Without a doubt, freedpeople, especially consecutive households of them, turned the farms of enslavement in the southeastern portion of the county into zones of freedom where life beyond slavery could be more than just imagined, it could be observed.

I believe my great-grandfather spent his days in a legendary Pittsylvania briar patch, this minor outpost of free blacks. To the enslaved, free blacks made the complicated future real. In 1860 three consecutive households of free American Africans lived somewhere between Birch and Sandy Creek and Mountain Road. First, there was John Foreman, a thirty-two-year-old blacksmith; his twenty-five-year-old wife, Sarah; and the children Eliza, Rosa, and Ellis. Fifty-year-old farm laborer Willis Gie lived next door, with Sallie, also fifty; Atlas, a twenty-one-year-old bricklayer who may have been reputed for his strength; ten-year-old Sallie; and five-year-old William. Drury Blair thought that the elder Sallie and Atlas looked black, and that Willis and the younger children looked mulatto. Since Blair was a slave owner and a regular county official, he would have had commonly shared ideas about a black American's appearance. Foreman and Gie are illuminating surname choices for freedpeople. The foreman was, of course, the labor gang leader, and "gie," or more usually "gee"—as the Missouri-born, Mississippi-bred African American novelist Chester Himes reminds us in his novel *A Case of Rape*— was the call to the mule, heard ubiquitously in farming zones, to pull left.

Sixty-year-old Sokey Henderick (a slight variant of the more common "Sukey") headed the third house of free people. She had living with her Martha Henderick, seventeen; Martha's nine-month-old baby, Anna; twenty-year-old William Anderson; and Charlotte Davis, a young woman variously listed as fifteen or twenty-five between the Free Negro Register and the US census, respectively. (Of all the bunched freedpeople noted by the census, only Charlotte Davis, five foot four and with a brown complexion, would, in 1864, register her free status with the county clerk.)

The given name Sukey was not West African in the way that Aniky, the name of two women in the county, or Yaraky, the name of a woman south of Chatham, probably were. Sukey—or "sukey, sukey"—had been a popular cry for bringing in the cows and penning the pigs in the early nineteenth century. Nearly at the same time, it became a choice name for enslaved African American women, and it certainly may have been a homonymic reference to wet-nursing. Thirty-one black women named Sukey lived in Virginia in 1870, which might not seem all that many, though the fact that small-town Bryan, Georgia, was able to support fourteen women so named reflects the broad power of the tribe. One of the clan, fifty-five-year-old Sukey Wilson, lived in Danville, several Sukies lived nearby, and of course Sokey Henderick was the neighbor to my ancestors.[34] Sukey was a name that white women might have gone by as a pet name or informally, but not usually on some formal occasion like the US census. Sukey seems to bear some relation to the other name that was used almost exclusively by black women: Franky, which also bore a connection to hog pens and hog fattening. (A sixty-year-old black woman named Franky Pritchett lived near Ms. Henderick.) But naming children Sukey, like naming a black Danville woman Still Easter, did continue a tradition among freedpeople of purposely differentiating themselves from white Americans, the "tenacious retention and adaptation" of a different, African past.

The Sukey name has retained its cachet into the twenty-first century. Today "sukey, sukey" is a kind of bon mot uttered by glitzy women of the African American peasantry. A paraphrase of the immortal lyrics from the soul group First Choice's smash hit "Let No Man Put Asunder" captures well the spirit in which "sukey, sukey" would be uttered today. During the break, when the bass fiddle and the drums are pounding holes in the floor, the singer moans to the man she desires: "Come out and get you some more." "Sukey, sukey."

Turning a pig call into a matriarch's christening name expressed a defiant creativity, a unique African American resourcefulness. With spirit and pride we continued for decades after slavery to name ourselves Sukey, and Morning, hopefully—or woefully.

◆ ◆ ◆

Sukey Henderick was an older woman herself, but she lived with two women and a man who were in their laboring prime. However, the census taker, Drury Blair, noted the occupation of only one of them, William Anderson, whose real estate property was accorded the astounding value of $1500. That might have been 185 acres, or perhaps, more incredibly, he owned a building of some kind. Anderson, identified as a mulatto born in North Carolina, was said to hold the occupation of a "hosetelen," which I assume was an innkeeper and not a stable boy, so perhaps somehow he had managed to become the proprietor of a remarkably well-built and appointed tavern. In 1860 there was another free black person living in the southern half of the county with significant holdings, the sixty-year-old tanner Jesse Booker of Whitmell, whose real estate value was also $1500 and who had $280 in personal estate.[35] A wizard of commerce, Booker had been emancipated as an infant around 1799 in the Sussex County will of Caleb Ellis.[36]

Two households seem to have been traditional families. Perhaps the blacksmith John Foreman had married a free woman and been industrious enough at the forge to buy himself out from slavery with the help of a fair master. Perhaps he had worked as the "foreman" or driver of a gang of enslaved men and women and received emancipation for his pains? It certainly seems impossible that someone who had no personal estate of value would have been able to purchase multiple people out from slavery. The Gie household seems more complicated because of the thirty-year gap between parents and the oldest child, followed by a ten-year gap between children. Twenty-one-year-old Atlas Gie probably had siblings closer to his own age, one would think.[37] Under the condition of slavery, it's hard to know whether or not the birth of a child was a moment of joy or another chain to the world of inherited bondage. But the freedmen clustered along a road must have been a tangible and hopeful sign to the enslaved, and the memory of so many freedmen living close together must have endured in the minds of the residents in spite of the upheaval that came with the war.

Virginia had more freedmen than any state other than Maryland, and throughout the nineteenth century it had sought to tighten its control over them. Most of Virginia's 58,042 freedmen in 1860 were direct descendants of Africans manumitted during the Revolutionary rights-of-man era.[38] Women were manumitted more frequently than men, and some of them had sexual, even romantic ties to slaveholders. It may not have been exactly frequent, but it was not unknown for a slave master to acknowledge a consanguinal tie with an enslaved offspring and arrange some sort of compact or covenant with the mother for freedom, hers or the children's. Exceptionally industrious, motivated, and powerfully constituted grown women and men could have worked their way out, with the help of a considerate master. But it's difficult to conceive how entire families—two parents and children—could have outmaneuvered slavery. Probably they could not.

There was little broad social encouragement to accomplish something so hard and requiring so much sacrifice. The general view held by the wealthy was to refer to the free Negroes as the "drones and pests" of society.[39] Pesky freedmen were seen as bad examples to the large majority of enslaved blacks. In response to the Gabriel Prosser conspiracy of 1800, Virginia passed an 1806 legislative act requiring freed slaves to emigrate from the state after twelve months, or face re-enslavement. According to the act, "If any slave hereafter emancipated shall remain within this Commonwealth more than twelve months after his freedom, he shall forfeit such right, and may be sold by the overseers for the benefit of the poor."[40] Ex-slaves needed special permission from the county court to remain as a permanent resident of the state. While the emigration and registration laws were not strictly enforced, they hung like a sword of Damocles. Freedpeople were closely watched and sought to remain in the good graces of the local white community.

Pittsylvania had one grand example of manumission on a large scale. John Ward Sr. left provisions in his 1826 will for the emancipation of perhaps 136 enslaved Pittsylvanians, very many of them in families. Between January and April of 1827, County Clerk William Tunstall recorded the manumission of dozens of African Americans. Ward was affectionate in the will, providing cash prizes for everyone over the age fifteen, and he left his favored servants, the siblings Dave and Nancy, $150 apiece, along with horses and cows. When the pair went to the county courthouse to petition to remain in the state, however, the judge denied them permission.[41] The provision Ward made in his will for this dismal but easily anticipated refusal was that the enslaved might "have the privilege of choosing their master."[42] That is, they could willingly re-enslave themselves and thereby remain in Virginia. This sort of scheme made sense, unless the white master chosen for his kindness died suddenly and in debt, which left any enslaved people on the auction block.

Because the court records needed juridically worthy descriptions to be able to identify the free black Americans, the Pittsylvania freedmen registers contain the most elaborate descriptions of black Americans living in the county at the time of the Civil War. There are two striking phenomena about these registers, and one is the large number of freed black people of mixed race. County Clerk Tunstall used a color scale for distinguishing African Americans that was nearly as exhaustive as the famed French Code Noire. He began at a very dark color that needed no refining until he arrived at designations of people who must have been impossible to distinguish from those deemed legally white. His scale included these designations: "very black," "black," "dark complexion," "dark Mulatto," "Mulatto," "light complexion," "rather light complexion," "bright mulatto," "bright complexion," "rather bright complexion," "very bright," and apparently even an albino, one Henry Dudley "of the white negro appearance, yellow eyes."[43] Of the 136 people freed in the Ward will, seventy-two of them were considered "dark mulatto" or lighter in color, with "light complexion" being about the average. In the nineteenth century, the term *mulatto* was often applied to people of mixed African, Native American, and European ancestry, and several of the women were noted as having the long, braided black hair common among Native Americans.

Tunstall also noted distinguishing marks with care. Many women and children bore distinctive scars from burns. I assumed this was the result of the onerous nature of nineteenth-century open-fire cooking with iron kettles. For that matter, the mud-and-stick chimneys of the slave cabins were prone to collapse, creating more of a peril than touching the heated metal of a cook pot. Men, on the other hand, had prominent nicks on their fingers, hands, and wrists, I assumed from chopping wood and clearing regular brush. And then several people seemed to have lost toes as the result of exposure, frostbite. I can only imagine that these losses happened with some regularity; after all, people were known to die of exposure. In March 1854, the *Danville Republican* carried this notice, which contained elements of the sentimental, the pastoral, and the fatalistic:

A negro man was found dead last Sunday Morning, in "Thompson Grove" in the Corporation [the incorporated City of Danville]. He died in Saturday night, and as the night was very cold, it was thought, he might have drunk too much liquor and frozen to death, but it seems more probable from the evidence that the negro died of a congestive chill. He was sick that night, as several testified, before starting home. He had, also, made himself a bed of leaves before lying down, which was a precaution a drunken man would scarcely have adopted.[44]

The man must have been either free or so old that, if he was missing, his owner reported no property loss. It occurs to me that an older black man, single and impoverished, free or enslaved, in the past or in the present, might have a difficult time. Many times on the streets of old Southern towns such as Chapel Hill's Franklin Street, when I have encountered older black men sleeping in doorways or on iron benches, I think I am looking directly into the wounds of the past.

Among Pittsylvania's registered freedpeople were several cohorts who shared a common family name; they may have been related by blood, or they may have been freed by the same master. Though there was probably no fee to register, the ceremonial trip to the courthouse at Competition certainly must have been a solemn occasion. The county marshal was not in the habit of summoning freedpeople if they had an out-of-date registration; the rare danger would have been a nasty disagreement breaking out with a vindictive or powerful white person, who then could threaten an unregistered freedperson with sale. Common surnames for blacks who renewed their registrations in Pittsylvania County as freed persons, a sign of their knowing and observing the letter of the law, included Bowman, Cole, Davis, Gee, Going, Hendricks, Mason, Reynolds, Stephens, and Valentine.

However, numerous freedpeople accounted for in the US census of 1860 as well as in the 1864 Confederate conscription muster never seemed to have registered at all. Several of them had the same surnames as known freedpeople who probably had had an ancestor who registered at some point. Two adults, George and Nancy Burnett, registered on November 11, 1857, but none of their children, Pamelia, Monroe, Sally, or George, ever signed up at the courthouse. Perhaps county officials, slave patrols, and the freedpeople themselves shared an unspoken agreement that the registration of one person conveyed a semiofficial certificate for the entire family. It always pays to know your white folks.

The slice of southeastern Pittsylvania that census takers called Ringgold and Laurel Grove surely must have been known also for its free black matriarchs. Mary Ann Stephens of Ringgold, who apparently had a twin, Martha, headed a household that included Willy, Mary, Martha, Jenie,

Charles, Sarisa, and Melia, in all probability related to the other people living next door. On one side of Mary Ann Stephens lived Joe, Morning, Abner, and Missouri Stephens, and another woman called Mary Stephens resided on the other flank. Mary Ann Stephens was born free in Pittsylvania in the 1820s. Her mother was probably a woman named Wilmoth Stephens; her grandmother Catherine Stephens had been freed as a young woman by the June 17, 1799, deed of an explicitly conscientious Sandy Creek–area landowner named John Terry, who said he was carrying out what had been in his father's will. James Terry, a county surveyor and property owner from the 1760s, had gobbled up land on "both sides of the main branch of the Sandy Creek" in 1766.[45] Subsequently, Terry freed Catherine, a condition she then passed on to children Agnes, Silva, Nancy, William, Wilmoth, and Phillis. Mary Ann Stephens was a third-generation freedwoman living on land she had owned for more than sixty years.

None of the women ever seem to have lived with a free male during the last sixty years of chattel slavery. The logic of the peculiar institution *partus sequitur ventrum*—that which comes forth follows the womb— allowed the women to have enslaved men for husbands or lovers and to pass on freedom to their children. Logically enough, then, the freedwomen's maiden names, not the children's fathers', were, like many of today's African American families, the key passport to status and social standing. In any case, the Sandy Creek freedpeople and the enslaved men and women who lived nearby would have had deep and enduring relations.

The other important freedwoman living in Laurel Grove and Spring Garden was the forty-two-year-old farmer Susan Richerson (probably Richardson), who had fifty dollars of useful property and ten children. Both Richerson and Mary Ann Stephens may well have been married to enslaved men. And they only sporadically appear on the official registers of freedpeople. Mary Stephens registered herself and her oldest daughters, but neither of the women tried to register all the children, and Susan Richerson herself apparently did not register. One reason it occurred to me that they must have set some kind of example is that my grandfather had twin sisters named Mary and Martha. These were common biblical names, of course, but the local twins who had exercised freedom for themselves and so many children in the era of bondage must have shined brightly some horizon of possibility that the people close by the banks of Sandy Creek would have long cherished.

6 · To the Courthouse in June

On a Monday morning late in June of 2008, I drove my family to Chatham, the county seat of Pittsylvania. Rechristened from its antebellum name Competition, Chatham is the location of the county courthouse and the repository of ancient county records. I had lumbered along the same route, more or less, four and a half years earlier on my tramp from Durham, North Carolina, to Blairs, Virginia, to find my grandfather's house by the railroad tracks. Now I was in search of the ancestors, the people I'd never even heard of, people whose names probably hadn't been uttered in more than a generation. My earlier trip had been in December, with its wintry bare landscape, but this was the first week of summer, and a luster was on the terrain; the ground and the trees were lush and verdant; even the sky was cracking with crystal light. When I struck out on this campaign four years earlier, I had been expecting my first child. I couldn't have imagined then that another little Jackson boy would come to spend his years with my wife and me, and ours with him. My new son, C. Mitchell, was a butterball and "chocolate to the bone," as the saying goes. I remembered praying that curse to the Romans for my first son, Nathaniel, "Avum aethiopam regeneravit"—the Ethiopian grandfather returns— but Mitchell traveled into this world guarded by his own spirits.

Although the ostensible purpose of the trip was to hunt for property records at the courthouse, I also was picking up a scent from Edward Jackson's time. My sons were named for grandfathers and great-grandfathers. And unlike on my earlier trips to Danville on my father's birthday in 2001 and to Blairs in December 2003, I planned to search out the neighborhood where my grandfather was born, where *his* parents lived. I knew the place was unnamed but "near Keeling," a phrase my grandfather used on his 1917 selective service registration card, close by the junction of Keeling Drive and Malmaison Road. Five years ago I had driven to that point when I got lost and was trying to rescue my bearings.

I pulled off of Route 29 shortly after making the Virginia border. At first, I headed in the direction of South Boston, Halifax County, on the South Boston Highway, Route 58/360, which was supposed to roughly parallel the old railroad line. The trees and old buildings have been cleared out for hundreds of yards on either side of the state road, and only hints of the bygone era remain. My children clamored for the restroom and snacks, and I was on the verge of driving into the wrong county. On a lark, I left the highway at Melon Road and headed north at the border, just between Pittsylvania and Halifax Counties.

The heavy green stalks hugging the edges of both sides of the road indicated that the corn harvest was about due. The foliage was dense and the asphalt road immediately narrowed, with shade trees forming a tunnel that blocked out the sun. City people in the United States like myself do not often deal with the reality of rural agricultural production, or for that matter have the ability to know even exactly where "rural" begins. But rural Virginia was immediately beneath my turning rubber tires, and I was fully surrounded by the plants, the animals, the people, the past, and the story.

Up the road apiece, at a small, whitewashed country store, I observed three men engaged in painting the trim at the bottom of a cinderblock foundation. As I got closer, I noticed that it was one man cautiously at work while another man appeared to be supervising the labor, and a third was merely watching. The laborer and the supervisor were involved in an active discussion. I drove across the gravel and asked if I was near the town of Sutherlin.

"You in it," said the one with the paintbrush, a tall, glossy ebony man. His smile was filled with gold, and on his chest hung a nest of shimmering jewelry.

"I am looking, really, for Keeling," I confessed, trying to develop a conversation. The men seemed absorbed in the job, which made sense to me at first. Only, when I scrutinized what they were doing, I thought that I could paint more effectively than they. I told myself that I didn't come out here to pass judgment, and I certainly would not wish myself to be judged frivolous for meandering on a country road at midday.

Naturally, I was a foreigner of the first class. The door was open to my family's Japanese-made, economy-style minivan with its Georgia tags. My Haitian American wife was sitting stiffly in the car, absorbed in a textbook. I had no intentional design to repudiate my grandfather's standard of tangible success—perhaps a Cadillac Escalade, and a creamy siren for my spouse. But I admitted that I needed all black country people to be tolerant and good-natured, more good-natured than I am regularly, be-

House and tobacco fields, Pittsylvania County, Virginia, 2008. Photograph: Lawrence Jackson.

cause that attitude explains to me why and how they have been able to remain in the country. They are easy to get along with and not too demanding of the world. That it is their own powerful connection to the past that kept them there never crossed my mind. I did not want the men to imagine I had lost my ties and was not too sure about how to get them back. The painter told me to proceed west at the crossroads to wind up where I wanted to be.

Not a mile away, I turned left at the crossroads and slipped back in time. Small wooden structures dotted the burnt-sienna–colored, rutted mud roads. They were spaced at intervals rather than bunched together. These weren't cabins but rather nineteenth-century-vintage, two- and three-room framed houses made with planed wood and tin roofs. Cabins would have been architecturally more simple, probably some version of post-in-ground construction with rough-hewn logs or boards. Seas of bright-green leafy tobacco framed all the wooden structures.

After driving past a beautiful weather-beaten house set high on a hill with a winding wave of red earth in front of it, I backed the van up and, ignoring eight-month-old Mitchell's crying, started snapping away with my 70mm camera. Driving along the worn, shaded paths, I was stunned by the sight of a framed, sunken-roofed cabin in a clearing, sitting back a hundred yards from the red clay road sparkling with mineral depos-

Tobacco fields, Pittsylvania County, Virginia, 2008. Photograph: Lawrence Jackson.

its. The building, whether a house or a barn I could not tell, looked as though it could almost be from the era of enslavement. I stopped the car for a second time and bounded out to try a picture of the house from a distance of two hundred yards. After making the shot, I studied the maps to try to figure out precisely where I was. I could be photographing an ancestor's house, and I would have no way of knowing. But the dirt and gravel paths I was rambling over did not exist on the AAA Road Atlas or the Google Maps.

Moving west, I trolled the old lanes, lost in a kind of chasm of possibility, imagining the reality of enslavement and freedom for black people working this land. After an hour I saw a gang of men, fifteen deep and with limp black hair and skin more reddish than brown, tending the tobacco plants with hoes; a few minutes later I glimpsed a black man in a tractor preparing a part of his small acreage on Malmaison Road. By the time I had hit that familiar area, I decided to head on up Route 29 to Chatham, my original destination for the trip. In an hour of stop and go, I had rattled from Sutherlin to Blairs, from the southeastern edge of Pittsylvania to near center of the county. Now it was time to try for some lunch.

Chatham seemed curiously swept of black people that afternoon. We stopped the car downtown, and while my wife, Regine, kept the baby, I walked with my older boy, Nathaniel, to James Womack's tack shop on

House with new concrete-block chimney, Pittsylvania County, Virginia, 2008.
Photograph: Lawrence Jackson.

Center Street. Turning briefly away from the seat of a saddle he had been
working on, Womack tried to draw my three-year-old out from behind
me to show him a toy in the window. Of course, it was a winning gesture
to me. On his own, Nathaniel fingered the array of dusty bric-a-brac on
the window ledge. The plastic figures and ornaments were the kind of
stuff that you find in a place where no one ever throws anything away and
artifacts of fifty or one hundred years ago aren't yet antiques. Womack
was the rare working black male adult I encountered on my visit to uncover Pittsylvania County's history, and his personality seemed a model
of fierce understatement. On the way back to the car, Nathaniel became
bubbly and loquacious about all the new things he'd seen, and I promised
that we would ride a horse soon.

My family and I were spending two nights in an elegant-looking bed-
and-breakfast within walking distance from the Chatham Courthouse.
The B&B was in a historic house, the kind of home at which my father's
mother and my mother's parents would have cooked and cleaned and
served, and in whose fields my great-grandparents would have toiled. I
thought there was some poetic justice in my little family spending the
night there, but our accommodations turned out to be form without sub-
stance. For a fee that exceeded five hundred dollars for two nights' stay,
the host and hostess confidently sent us out into the world with nothing for breakfast but parfaits and mini-muffins. I had been anticipating
something tasty, ample, and fried. My grandmother Virginia, born in an

abode an hour's hike from the white-columned house where we lodged, always prepared hearty fare for our visits: Smithfield Ham, homegrown blood-red tomatoes, hominy grits, scrambled eggs, and scratch biscuits. This was the second experience I have had at a bed-and-breakfast that imposed skimpy morning meals in its dining room, and both times the town itself offered little by way of decent food. The other B&B was on Cape Cod.

◆   ◆   ◆

My errand to the Pittsylvania County Courthouse was exhilarating. I had gone into archives before on professional jobs, but never before on an assignment with heavy emotional stakes.

The county clerk's office sits in the basement of the courthouse on the main street going through Chatham; the courthouse was built in 1853 and would have been a familiar, maybe even fearsome landmark to all my father's ancestors. The door to the clerk's office opened into a heavily air-conditioned chamber, its counter only a full stride from the door. Behind the counter, five or six metal desks and file cabinets were huddled together, staffed by trim female deputies in their fifties. The deputy clerks wore jackets and sweaters to fight the air-conditioned chill. Twenty feet or more behind the desks was the county clerk's office itself. Seniority obviously was signaled by one's closeness to the clerk—an elected official, forever the fast friend and intimate of the county's sheriff—and by one's distance from the public. At a desk right outside the clerk's door sat a woman the color of fresh ginger, her salt-and-pepper gray hair pulled back into a tight bun. She seemed to engage the others and her work with a cheery dazzle. All the other deputy clerks were white. One of them near the counter got up when, after taking in the details of the place, I cautiously approached the desk.

After explaining what I was looking for, I was led to my left into the basement proper, perhaps a ten-foot-wide corridor, outfitted on one side with floor-to-ceiling metal shelves. Each shelf was made of half a dozen two-inch-diameter metal rods, to help citizens wheel the hefty volumes away from the stand. As a person whose research work had been confined mainly to the twentieth century, I was impressed by the dusty, leather-bound, embossed fifteen-by-twenty-four-inch legal volumes dating to Pittsylvania's founding in 1767. This is something about the United States that I genuinely admire: public access to records.

Each book seemed to weigh about the same as a gallon of water. In

Pittsylvania County Courthouse, Chatham, Virginia, 2009. Photograph: Lawrence Jackson.

the middle of the corridor was a long metal drafting table, angled at about thirty degrees and with a lip to catch the heavy volumes. Speaking through a cigarette smoker's rasp, the clerk identified the indexes for marriage, deed, and land records. Her hair was curled, blown, and dyed into a style that reminded me of the 1970s model Cheryl Tiegs. In a fashion that was professional and measured, she clarified the arrangement of the stacks, but already it was more information than I could put to long-term use. I wondered how she would respond when I had to ask for clarification again.

In my experience, certain white Americans put on a particular kind of armor when dealing with black American natives, or American Africans, as Toni Morrison says. It doesn't matter what we natives look like, nor does it matter if the whites had ancestors in the United States during slavery time. Some of our white American countrymen are defensive, even when they are solicitous, and I distrust that guilt-based defensiveness. Besides, I don't believe it anyway. I actually think that it is a mask concealing a sentiment closer to arrogance, an element of insult that rides underneath the hood of their remote eyes. These women seal their irises into a pale blue glaze, and the men narrow theirs into a serpentine fire. And this sentiment quickly becomes evident when the black people are asking questions about anything that can loosely be described as racial injustice, which is also known as American history.

Because I am black and know that all my ancestors were living in the United States in 1850, I don't feel that much difference between being in the North or being in the South. By now it has become a part of my own protective conditioning not to let a surveyor's lines confuse the shared reality of Harrisburg, PA, and Forsythe, GA, Meriden, Connecticut, and Meridian, Mississippi. Some black people I have known counter that look of remote defensiveness by making every interaction with whites a confrontation with the enemy. The author Richard Wright once wrote of another style, insistent and obsequious; but in my day, apart from courtrooms, welfare offices, hospitals, banks, and police stations, I have not seen black people kneel in fear and submission. I have, however, witnessed numerous occasions where I watched blacks zealously guarding white feelings. As for my approach, I style myself a spy in the enemy's country.

These thoughts occupied my mind as I set up my computer and pulled gadgets out of my pack that proclaimed my professional credentials and social class in a way that my diction and accent, dress, and carriage were unable to guarantee. In the side chamber, I noticed another deputy clerk's desk at a bend in the room, at the junction of another groove in this basement tunnel. She was a handsome African American woman, likely the same age as the others, but she looked younger. Her desk faced the wall and abutted a door leading into the contemporary deed office. On the desk were photographs of children, an ashtray, and light-hearted mementos. I exchanged pleasantries with her, noted her complete suit of jacket and pants, and wished I had chosen better attire than shorts.

I began my search for my known ancestors with the marriage records. I was looking to see how far back the names of the brides' and grooms' parents could help me travel. Among the nearly fifteen thousand black people held in bondage in Pittsylvania in 1860, these ancestors might have had surnames more distinctive than my own. Perhaps one of their owners had made a will, or had their estate inventoried before 1865, which would result in the enslaved being listed by name. If I could connect that dot, then I would have some of the best proof known to exist concerning the whereabouts of an enslaved forebear. But I knew from some experience that any such records, if they hadn't been misfiled, misplaced, or misnamed, could be in any of dozens of places within this narrow and chilly basement. Really, I needed to sit down and read all the volumes and master the story of the entire county, and probably those adjacent to it, to get a handle on the Jackson saga. My procedure could be likened to two ancient crafts. First, as a stonecutter I was chipping off blocks of neighborhood history from the quarry of the county's legal records. Second, as a mason, I was attempting economically to size the blocks and gussy them into a pattern to fit a family's life.

The famous line in the most official of the enslaved's marriage ceremonies was "until death or distance do us part." Despite the assumption embedded in this vow that a husband and wife could be sold away from each other, some records had been kept that formally recognized the marriages that black people were allowed to have under slavery. I had heard of a magical and storied federal government account book, taken down in 1865 and 1866 and called the *Register of Colored Persons* _____ *County, State of Virginia, cohabiting together as Husband and Wife.* While the record proved espousement, it also gave the name of the former slave owner. I knew, however, that like many of Virginia's ninety-five counties, Pittsylvania did not keep its great Yankee book of black marriage records for posterity.

In the middle of the stacks closest to the street were the massive volumes indexing the county's marriage certificates and deed books between 1767 and 1889. I began looking up the marriage records, maneuvering the weighty leather-bound volumes off the rods with alacrity and rushing them three feet over to the examination table before I could feel their heft. Lawyers must have been as strong as farmers at one time, or maybe they were all the same people.

The subject of marriage during and immediately after slavery takes on special significance when it is juxtaposed to the weakness of marriage in contemporary American life, where more than 50 percent of all the nation's newlyweds will land in divorce court, and where more than 50 percent of African American children never live in a household of their own married parents. The chief impact on the children is poverty. In the 1950s and 1960s, historians and social psychologists pointed to slavery as the culprit for high out-of-wedlock birth rates among African Americans. In the 1970s much of this thinking was revised, particularly on account of Herbert Guttman's book about black marriage, *The Black Family in Slavery and Freedom, 1750–1925.* The era of enslavement, when marriage was esteemed and widely practiced, instead became viewed as a time of comparative health for the black family. No one can miss the doleful irony that black family life has been purported to be stronger and more enduring in the last generation of slavery and its aftermath than it is today.

As for the recently freed, I think that marriage was one straightforward way of asserting equality to whites after bondage. What was more important—and as anyone who has ever walked a distance to a spring to bathe, wash clothes, and tote water knows—in a rural economy that twined all wages to seasonal crops, it was vital to have two people working hard every day to ensure family survival. In their world without disposable diapers, I could imagine that boiling rags might take on an outrageous importance. Yet the postbellum marriage logic for these black farmers would change, irrevocably, once they moved to cities with indoor plumbing and heat, and where women could earn as much cleaning houses as men could earn cutting grass and sweeping the streets.

◆　◆　◆

I thought it foolish to expect any magic, but rather quickly I found the evidence for my father's mother's side. In my own family's history, birth certificates are an archival phenomenon that begins with my parent's generation in the 1930s. None of my grandparents have official birth records, and they were all born at home when the US flag contained only forty-five stars and the country was still largely rural. My grandmother, the former Virginia Jefferson, was born in 1907, twelve years after my grandfather, and I found the certificate issued for her own grandparents Richard Waller and Sally Breedlove, who married on March 25, 1875. Except that it seems like maybe they were her great-grandparents.

Richard Waller and Sally Breedlove got their marriage license three days before the ceremony took place, and they received it from the county clerk himself, Langhorne Scruggs. Richard and Sally both said they were twenty-one on the marriage certificate, which struck me as an unusual coincidence. What is more likely is that neither of them knew their true age for sure. They both had been born enslaved, so the written record of their birth would have been nothing more than a farmer's notation in a journal, if the owner kept written records of his crops. Men had to be twenty-one to marry, so it makes sense that Richard gave that age; perhaps Sally thought that age was a good bet too.

The groom, however, was not sure where he had been born, so Scruggs wrote "Not Known" in that space on the certificate. It certainly did not occur to me that Richard could have been born in Africa, though the last slave ship, *Clotilde*, reached Mobile in the fall of 1859, and *The Wanderer* reached Jekyll Island, Georgia, in 1858, so it is at least a technical possibility. Richard Waller was sure about who his parents were, Lewis and Eliza Waller, and his wedding ceremony took place at their house.

In antebellum Pittsylvania County, several slaveholders were named Waller. Chalk Level and Green Hill were home to numerous Waller clans in 1860, when my ancestor Richard would have been of school age, or else old enough to carry a water bucket to a thirsty gang of field hands. But I found census records for neighboring Henry County to the west—in an area called Horse Pasture, on the west side of the town of Martinsville and perhaps thirty miles from Danville—listing a white man who was sixty-seven in 1860, with land worth $10,000 and slaves worth $20,000. George Waller owned eleven working adults and children over twelve— the age at which full-time fieldwork was mandatory, because slave owners began paying taxes on blacks at age twelve—and ten small children.[1] The adults, all under forty, would have been evaluated collectively at more than one thousand dollars apiece, and the children at less than that. Three of the black men—aged fifteen, twenty-one, and twenty-seven— would have commanded the highest prices of the lot. Three of the adults were childbearing-age women. What was most significant to me, however, was that George Waller owned three very young boys, one of them four years old and two of them six years old. Richard Waller thought he was six in 1860, on the eve of the Civil War. Perhaps he was born in Henry County and then moved over to Pittsylvania—indeed, perhaps his family had run away when he was a small child, in a manner clandestine or ruthless and such that he could never be certain about where he had been born.

In the space where Sally Breedlove's father's name should go, Langhorne Scruggs substituted a squiggly line. The squiggly line in fact begins the entry "Names of wife's parents." I suppose if you got Booker T. Washington's marriage certificate, or Frederick Douglass's, they too would have squiggly lines in place of their father's name. How does the fact of their unknown fathers make these African American heroes different from men like my enslaved ancestor, Richard Waller, who was not famous, not even completely literate, but who would have had a fundamentally different sense about his human connection to the past? His father was not a squiggly line but a black man like himself. It's the same way for me, for Howard University's chairman of African American studies, Greg Carr, and for my sons. We knew our fathers.

My dad's mother was born in Dry Fork, a crossroads at a creek that

MARRIAGE LICENSE.

VIRGINIA, PITTSYLVANIA COUNTY, TO WIT:

TO ANY PERSON LICENSED TO CELEBRATE MARRIAGES:

You are hereby authorized to join together in the Holy State of Matrimony, according to the rites and ceremonies of your Church, or religious denomination, and the laws of the Commonwealth of Virginia, *Richard Waller* and *Sally Breedlove*

Given under my hand, as Clerk of the County Court of Pittsylvania, this 22nd day *March* 1875

S. Scruggs .... Clerk.

CERTIFICATE TO OBTAIN A MARRIAGE LICENSE.

To be Annexed the License, required by Acts passed 15th March, 1861, and February 27th, 1860.

Time of Marriage *25th March 1875*
Place of Marriage
Full Names of Parties Married *Richard Waller and Sally Breedlove*
Color
Age of Husband *21*
Age of Wife *21*
Condition of Husband (widowed or single) *Single*
Condition of Wife (widowed or single)
Place of Husband's Birth *Not Known*
Place of Wife's Birth *Pittsn*
Place of Husband's Residence "
Place of Wife's Residence " "
Names of Husband's Parents *Lewis & Eliza Waller*
Names of Wife's Parents *— & Dicey Breedlove*
Occupation of Husband *Farmer*

Given under my hand this *22nd* day of *March* 1875

S. Scruggs .... Clerk.

MINISTER'S RETURN OF MARRIAGE.

I Certify, That on the *25th* day of *March* 1875 at .... I united in Marriage the above-named and described parties, under authority of the annexed License.

D. F. Hodges

☞ The Minister celebrating a marriage, is required within TEN days thereafter, to return the license to the Office of the Clerk who issued the same, with an endorsement thereon of the FACT of such marriage, and of the TIME and PLACE of celebrating the same.

Richard Waller and Sally Breedlove, 1875 marriage license. Pittsylvania County, Virginia. Clerk's Office, Pittsylvania County, VA.

branched off the Banister River, just south and a bit west of Chatham; I assume that her grandparents Richard and Dicey lived around there too. Sally Breedlove was a county native, and her mother's name was Dicey Breedlove.

This surname has been made famous by the Nobel laureate novelist Toni Morrison. In her novel *The Bluest Eye*, set in 1930s Ohio, a young girl named Pecola Breedlove wishes to be white with blond hair and blue eyes, and she is raped by her own father for her trouble. In Morrison's hands, Breedlove is rawly analogous to Ralph Ellison's incestuous farmer Jim Trueblood from *Invisible Man*. Dicey was a popular name in the county, and it seems the name of a classic femme fatale, along with Trixy and Foxy. But to me, these are my folks, not literary archetypes.

I showed the handsome clerk the marriage index with my ancestors' surnames as I prepared to request the official marriage certificates. I noticed that the clerk's last name was Breedlove. Staffing a post that protects access to Accounts, Current Inventories 1770–Present, Final Decrees, 1926–1948, Miscellaneous civil and criminal records, Chancery and law records, Civil records, and a few early Miscellaneous records, she believed we were certainly kin, four generations removed. From that point on in the day, she adopted me and tried to assist in every way she knew how.

Breedloves lived in the southern portion of the county, near the Dan River, especially at Whitmell, due west of Blairs. Richard Breedlove, a fifty-five-year-old farmer, owned a personal estate of $2,100, which of course suggests he wasn't a wealthy slaveholder. Not four miles northwest of Whitmell in Swansonville, sixty-two-year-old David W. Breedlove had the holdings of a small-scale planter. He planted no more than a few hundred acres, but in two dwellings he housed his fifteen people, seven of them adults and one a man nearly fifty. He estimated their value at $17,600.[2] David Breedlove owned two childbearing-age women, one of whom was fourteen in 1860, and one four-year-old black girl. A fourteen-year-old enslaved young woman certainly would have been required to take on full-fledged adult responsibility insofar as labor and sex reproduction were concerned. Could an adolescent barely a teenager have been the mother of a four-year-old child? I am not quite able to consider if motherhood had been forced on her at nine or ten years old. Whether such a thing is physically possible or was ethically permissible under the regime of bondage is something else.

This puzzle may have had something to do with the squiggly line that Sally Breedlove had in the place of a father's name fifteen years later. When US census taker G. W. Wells looked at Sally, he termed her a mulatto. Where Sally Breedlove came from and how she got to look the way she did is a question I might not be able to stomach the answer to. One could suppose that her father was a white man. Whether she did not know who the man was, or if she simply chose not to render his name, is a question of another order.

Five years after they were married, Richard and Sally had three children a year apart: William H., B. L., and Anne. Richard told the census taker in 1880 that he was about thirty years old, but Sally claimed the same age as the day she married. Reading these records, I worked the numbers backward, uncertain that Richard was actually six in 1860; if the 1880 census is accurate, he would have been a fifteen-year-old teenager at the end of the Civil War. Richard Waller could also read, and his wife was able to read and write. I can't imagine what they looked like, but my father had two pictures of my grandmother: one as a toddler and the other as a youthful divorcee. In the second picture my grandmother is beaming into the camera, her honey-colored oval face framed by a wreath of black hair.

The other marriage record I found was from the twentieth century, and it seemed to be that of my grandmother's parents. Here the fragmented oral history of my own family conflicted with the records. According to what I had been told, my grandmother's parents, who partly raised my father, were supposed to be Sarah and Arthur Joyce. But the marriage certificate that was connected to them proved confounding. On December 20, 1905, during the farmers' brief slack time, twenty-four-year-old Dicie Lee Waller married Lucius Jefferson, a twenty-one-year-old farmhand. They had gotten their license two days earlier from a clerk named S. S. Hurt. On the marriage license, Dicie Lee gave her mother's name as Sarah and left her father's name blank. Going by the records, it seemed that after my grandparents left Danville, moved to Roanoke, and then divorced, my father's great-grandmother, Sarah Joyce, had raised him. If the records are accurate and Sally Breedlove had a daughter after 1880 named Sarah who had a daughter after 1890 named Dicie Lee, then my grandfather was as close in age to my grandmother's parents as he was to my grandmother.

The Reverend Jeff Broadnax of the Primitive Baptist Church, a congregation whose land had been donated by John Hundley in the 1880s, performed the ceremony. The couple was married in Whitmell, I assume at Richard and Sally's house. Since my grandmother was definitely born in 1907, I assume that she must be Dicie (Young Dicie) Lee's daughter. But again, could Sarah Waller, who does not appear on the US census of

My grandmother, Virginia Jefferson Jackson, mid-1930s.

1880 (and the 1890 census was destroyed), have given birth to a child in 1892 or 1893, and then this daughter, Dicie Lee, herself have brought forth a child by 1907, my grandmother? Well, the simple answer is yes.

The evidence clearly proves that my grandmother Virginia Jefferson had more generations in her family between emancipation and World War I than Grandpa Jackson did. I imagined that the squiggly line on that 1875 certificate impacted some of the marital choices made by these women, and even if they were living, I am not sure that I would ask my grandmother or father about this tangled skein of family history. Perhaps it was a broad discomfort with what had happened to black families, their "prolificking," that sped my father's favorite admonition to me when I got to college. It was "Don't write about the family."

But write I do. In the second half of the afternoon, after I had whet my research skills, I went in pursuit of Edward Jackson, the key to my family name. I found my grandfather's parents, Edward and Celestia, indexed on the marriage register. Reading their names was simply glorious, as if a friendly portal to another time had opened up. It felt as if I had been rescued. My grandfather's parents married on December 19, 1878, after filing their marriage certificate the day before in the same clerk's office I was standing in that very moment.[3] The wedding occurred during the brief slack time in farming life at the end of December. The license itself had three portions: the "Marriage License"; a "Certificate to Obtain a Marriage License," which was an informative segment annexed to the license after the passage of state acts in 1861 and 1866; and a "Minister's Return of Marriage," which completed the form. I hope that 1878 was a good year for them. I hope that when Edward and Celestia stood in that office long ago in December, attesting to the facts, they didn't have to consider politics, they could just be young and in love.

The official conducting all this, the only formal state business that either Edward or Celestia ever engaged in, as far as I know, was a twenty-two-year-old deputy clerk named George Noell. Noell boarded in a rooming house in Danville with a lot of other single men, including his brother Charles.[4] He took a regular railroad train to Chatham, which must have been an extraordinary example of modern technology for Pittsylvanians, who would have been more accustomed to seeing that distance covered by the daily stagecoach between Danville and Lynchburg, which changed horses in Dry Fork and Chatham. Noell was too young to have served in the Civil War, which may have disposed him more to blacks needing his services at the courthouse. On the other hand, a child admiring Confederate martial legends could have evolved into a young adult seeking after conspicuous ways to show a commitment to a cause he had not shouldered a musket for.

American popular culture sought to give a young deputy clerk like Noell a third path: a chortle. Noell's view about the black Americans taking out marriage licenses might have been reflected by the folksy humor of postbellum editorials that sometimes entertained newspaper readers in the *Danville Register* and *Lynchburg News*.

"A CRUEL PARIENT"
A colored lady from Halifax county, ran off with her "lovyer" to North Carolina last week, where they were "spliced." The lassie, in reply to the question why she ran away to get married answered that "her mammy thook she wur too young to enter the matrimonical repersentertion, but she'd show de ole gal she weren't"—*Lyn. News.*[5]

The 1868 article is a stock "Zip Coon" caricature. In the depiction, the freedwoman performs a comic imitation of white class and elegance. Whites uniformly thought of these portraits as innocent fun. I say "uniformly," because I remember listening in 1995 to a National Public Radio commentator proclaim the innocence and harmlessness of the television show *Amos 'n Andy*, which was discontinued on account of vigorous protest by the NAACP, because he had anecdotal proof that black Americans admired it. The "Zip Coon" newspaper article was seventy-five years before *Amos 'n Andy* first took to the airwaves as a radio program, and Pittsylvania was a far cry from NPR. In my view of the church of the American religion, the caricatures, the derogatory types, the minstrelsy, and the vaudeville corn worked one side of the aisle, and lynch law, administered by the Klan, worked the other.

Before going out on his own into urban life at a Danville rooming house, George Noell was the oldest son of a farmer who lived in Ringgold. It wouldn't have been that unusual if he had seen or even interacted with Edward Jackson prior to the day of issuing the marriage certificate. Noell had grown up on a farm with enough to eat: his father owned two thousand dollars' worth of land in 1870 when the ground would have fetched five dollars an acre, and the elder Noell had about four hundred dollars in his personal estate, probably in horses, livestock, and a few household goods, now that the chattels personal were free. But for his time, young Noell wound up an extraordinarily literate man, the sort who had given up farming for town life. It seems there would have been little for the two men to have discussed: George Noell, the registrar moving to and fro with the aid of modern heavy industry, and Edward Jackson, whose life after marriage was set permanently in a fifty-year groove of farm labor and supporting children, making do for travel with his feet. Edward's early life in slavery fastened to him a gap: his chance in life would be different from the clerk's, a shortfall pinned to him as by a nail driven into a tree.

The Pittsylvania County clerk's office was a cliquish center of power. From 1767 to 1875, only four men had ever held the job, and three of them had the same first and last name: William Tunstall. The last of the four was Langhorne Scruggs, who held the post of Clerk of the County Court for a quarter century, and in the 1870s he boarded in his home another youngish deputy named Conway Whitte. Scruggs was prosperous, owning $4,100 worth of real estate and having personal goods valued at $900. He also came from a family capable of handling debates with wit, if they did not share some literary pretension. Consider this bit of correspondence that his cousin Jason Whitehead wrote to him in 1857 concerning the delicate subject of guerilla warfare on the border between Missouri and Kansas.

> Times have been very much changed here since I last wrote to you the clarion Sound of the warrior's trumpets is no longer heard from on the farm hills of Kansas. No longer is seen the glare of the midnight conflagration or companies of men women and children frantic with excitement fleeing the territory to haunt a more peaceful abode among the *Border Ruffians* of Missouri, but peace with all her attendant blessings has once more perched upon our Land how long it will continue remains to be Seen. I for one am satisfied that its character is a lasting one both fanatics and filibustering have principally left the land and the national Democrats have the ascendency here as well as in the Union and we expect no further trouble about Slavery here. If a majority of our population vote for a free state next June then we will have such an one.[6]

Scruggs's Democrat-sounding cousin took a balanced view toward the imminent conflict, and that he would consider the possibility of ending slavery in Missouri in a letter to his cousin suggests he anticipated an equally balanced reply from the county clerk. The clerk's office, after a fashion, might have been a nook of reasoned thinking in the county.

After the Civil War, clerking for the county was one of the few white-collar jobs in a still largely rural county; the other prominent clerk's posts were at Sutherlin's tobacco plant in Danville. But even if men like Noell and Scruggs were fair, I think that because of the rarity of schools and the complete absence of libraries, it must have been overwhelmingly intimidating for my great-grandparents Edward and Celestia to walk into the province of all those white men and legal volumes being unable to state their ages with complete accuracy, and being unable to read or write. When Noell turned the marriage ledger in their direction so that they could mark it, what was their endowment, to protect them in that moment? What was their storehouse of mother wit that guided them when they were asked questions in English, perhaps an English quite different from the one they used on the farms watered by Sandy Creek? How did they muster the wherewithal to cross the gap, to respond quickly and precisely to the questions, to pay the fee and make the correct change?

On the certificate, Edward claimed he was twenty-one, and Celestia believed she was nineteen; neither of them was ever completely sure, but from one census to the next, Celestia came closest to maintaining a consistent birth year. In subsequent years they would tell the census takers that they were both born in either 1859 or 1860. One piece of evidence from the form helped quite a bit. Both of my great-grandparents said that they had been born in Pittsylvania County, which eliminates my census flirtations with the Halifax County Jackson families. Edward might have worked as a "domestic servant" in 1870, when his age was recorded as fifteen, but by the time he got married he had left that career behind for the calluses of a full-fledged farmhand. That's what he did for the rest of his earthly life, which seems to have ended on November 17, 1944.[7]

A twenty-two-year-old white man of the cloth from Tunstall named E. B. Dillard married the couple. The ceremony itself took place at Celestia's parent's house, surely indoors because it was just before Christmas, and Dillard would have traveled something like fifteen miles on the Franklin turnpike and close to ten on Mountain Road to reach near Keeling, where the Hundleys farmed. Perhaps Dillard even stayed overnight. If religion had not gotten hold and made them teetotalers, maybe they had a frolic in celebration and served spirits. Did Edward's comrades chant at him during the dance? Did someone call to him the old way that blacks in Virginia's Piedmont did during a spirited hoedown, "Congo is a *scrouger*; he's up a gum, and no bug-eater I tell you; he carries a broad row, weeds out every thing—hoes de corn, and digs de taters"?[8]

In two days, Edward Jackson dealt with two white professional men who were either his exact same age or younger than he was, which gives the impression that Pittsylvania was not a country for old men. I imagine his relation to the two officials—neither of them in fields requiring physical development—had something to do with his own size or swagger. But certainly the minister, whom they had some choice in, would have been paid and predisposed to them; as for Noell it is ambiguous, and their contact was brief. Judging from my grandfather's build and that my great-grandfather's first job was domestic service, I doubt if he was a large man. I would guess that in his young adulthood Edward Jackson was about five foot seven and 140 pounds.

And here the remarkable record simultaneously gave me something and took something away. On the portion of the marriage certificate designated for her parents' names, Celestia had listed at least one of the same persons whom I had glimpsed through the census of 1870, Granville Hundley. The certificate listed her mother's name as Mourning, but the adult woman who lived in the Hundley household according to the census records was Charity. Of course, I had also hoped to uncover the generation before my great-grandfather, and tease out where the Jacksons began. For his own parents' names, Edward had Noell write that his mother and father were Jennie and Sandy Dickerson. The names of these great-great-grandparents bewildered me. In 1870 Edward had been living with the Fergusons over by the former slave owner and Fall Level tobacco farmer Levi Hall. Under what circumstances could he have been named Jackson but his parents were named Dickerson, and then at fifteen he was living with the Fergusons? I had meddlesome information that I couldn't get a grip on.

In 1870 a fifty-year-old African American blacksmith named Sandy Dickerson resided in the postal delivery area called Chatham, which you would think was no more than an hour's walk in any direction from the courthouse door, and probably not that far. He was a man who could have been known to Chatham's local officials, such as deputy clerk George Noell. He might, indeed, have participated in that civil rights march to Carter's Hotel in the later 1860s that was so roundly scorned by Maud Carter Clement. The community was small, grouped around the lone "Public" or "Court House" road north–south, today's US 29, which paralleled the track of the Southern railroad. The public road was bisected east or west at the center of Competition, and another east–west route ran a bit south of the town at Tightsqueeze. Generally, houses, two room-cabins of squared timbers with yards overrun by towering prince's feather plants, were placed five hundred or six hundred yards apart. If Dickerson had lived south, in the two and a half miles between Chatham and Tightsqueeze, there were, by 1917, about fifty households, with the Banister River as their boundary. North of Chatham to Whittles Depot

MARRIAGE LICENSE.

VIRGINIA, PITTSYLVANIA COUNTY, TO-WIT:

TO ANY PERSON LICENSED TO CELEBRATE MARRIAGES:

You are hereby authorized to join in the Holy State of Matrimony, according to the rites and ceremonies of your Church, or religious denomination, and the laws of the Commonwealth of Virginia _Edward Jackson & Celestia Hundley_

Given under my hand, as _Deputy_ Clerk of the County Court of Pittsylvania this _18_ day of _Decbr_ 18_78_

Geo L Noell D Clerk.

CERTIFICATE TO OBTAIN A MARRIAGE LICENSE.

To be annexed to the License required by Acts passed 15th March, 1861, and February 27th, 1866.

Time of Marriage _19 Dec 1878_

Place of Marriage _Pitts a_

Full Names of Parties Married _Edward Jackson & Celestia Hundley_

Color _(Colds)_

Age of Husband _21 yrs_

Age of Wife _19 "_

Condition of Husband (widowed or single,) _Single_

Condition of Wife (widowed or single) _"_

Place of Husband's Birth _Pitts a_

Place of Wife's Birth _"_

Place of Husband's Residence _"_

Place of Wife's Residence _"_

Names of Husband's Parents _Saudy & Jennie Dickerson_

Name of Wife's Parents _Granville & Mourning Hundley_

Occupation of Husband _Farmer_

Given under my hand this _18_ day of _December_ 1878

Geo L Noell D Clerk.

MINISTER'S RETURN OF MARRIAGE.

I Certify, That on the _19th_ day of _Dec_ 18_78_, at _Granville Hundleys_ I united in Marriage the above-named and described parties, under authority of the annexed License

Rev E B Dillard

The Minister celebrating a marriage, is required within TEN days thereafter to return the license to the Office of the Clerk who issued the same, with an endorsement thereof of the FACT of such marriage, and of the TIME and PLACE of celebrating the same.

Edward Jackson and Celestia Hundley, 1878 marriage license. Pittsylvania County, Virginia.

was another pretzel of roads duplicating the southern pattern, following the railroad north to Lynchburg and being guided east and west by Cherrystone Creek. About forty households were in town.[9]

Five years after freedom came, Sandy Dickerson was married to a woman named Eliza who was thirty-one, and three young boys under the age of twelve lived with them; one of them too was called Sandy. In fact, six houses away lived a young man, eighteen, a farm laborer and yet a third Sandy Dickerson. Under my search, Jennie Dickerson does not exist on county census records in 1870. Why would Edward Jackson have called these people his parents when they had a different surname and lived some distance away from him?

I know that human beings can look far away for something when an obvious answer is close at hand. I have a teenage stepdaughter who lives with me and does not share my last name. I thought about possible situations when she might put down my name and my wife's name as her parents, Regine and Lawrence Jackson. We do this on her school records, for one. How will she fill out the information for her college applications? By that same logic, what if the names Edward wrote on the official certificate were those of his "natural" mother and his stepfather?

I had to tease out another confusing element here; this one was geographic. I had been thinking about my relatives as residents of Danville, on the border of North Carolina. I never had any idea about why my grandfather, Aunt Mary and Uncle John, and Aunt Sally all lived in Blairs, which is between Danville and Chatham. But if Edward Jackson was related in some way to Sandy Dickerson, then I had been spending too much time looking in the southern portion of the county, in the area of Ringgold. Where I should have been looking is just south of Chatham in a neighborhood called Spring Garden and a smaller community just underneath it, called Chestnut Level. In the back of the courthouse is a county map from the 1930s that shows where the county's census enumerators divided Pittsylvania in half, into southern and northern portions. I had looked exhaustively at the southern half of the county, especially Danville and vicinity, but the dividing line is just south of Chestnut Level.

I knew that before my great-grandparents Edward and Celestia were married, they lived near each other, somewhere between John Hundley's Sandy Creek properties (some purchased from Griffith Dickenson) and the tobacco farm of Levi Hall, where Edward most likely worked. Celestia's father, Granville Hundley, was in a position to observe the teenage Edward Jackson reaching young adulthood. And it's also quite probable that Granville had met Sandy Dickerson, a man of some accomplishment and purpose and close to his own age. Sandy was certainly owned in 1860 by Vincent Dickenson,[10] and may have been owned by Baptist minister Griffith Dickenson twenty years before that. Granville Hundley was almost certainly owned by the land speculator John Hundley, who seems never to have made regular crops. John Hundley probably hired his one man out, and it is a certainty that one of his favorite business partners was Griffith Dickenson Jr., who served as either witness, third party, or executor to at least four of Hundley's indentures for debt in 1840, 1841, and 1845.[11]

But on my first afternoon at the courthouse records, the Sandy Dickerson connection baffled me. I knew then only that in the aftermath of slavery, black people reconstituted themselves mightily. We tried, to the extent we were able, to remake our families and renew old alliances, to fill in the gaps of damage, pain, and shame. It seemed odd to me that Edward would hold on to those people who, if they were not his biological parents, should have at least known his biological parents, but not take their name. I thought that maybe he was making a dramatic statement. I allowed that perhaps he did not know his parents, but, refusing to put squiggly lines on the form, he inserted the names of some local people he admired.

There is another wrinkle. Celestia and Edward Jackson got hitched in December 1878, but the US census of 1880 listed my great-grandparents with a child, four-year-old Charles Jackson. Charles would have been at the wedding, since Celestia was around seventeen in 1876 when she seems to have had him, and she didn't get married until just two weeks before 1879. This circumstance remains not uncommon and falls well within my own personal experience.

Naturally, I considered that perhaps Charles was not Edward's child. Granville Hundley's daughters Fanny, Harriet, and Adelaide married quickly and left home; by 1870 only the youngest, Celestia, was living with him. If Celestia had carried a pregnancy to term sometime in 1875 or 1876 while living in her parents' house, maybe they had become acutely desirous of finding her a mate. And Granville Hundley was working on a plan to purchase some land, enough to stake a young family.

I also can't dismiss the chance that Celestia may have been victimized during the long tumult after the Civil War. Her neighbor Nathaniel Hutchings had a daughter Celestia's exact age who, by the time she was eleven in 1870, was working as a "domestic servant." There would have been enormous pressure for Celestia to begin working by the age of twelve, especially in the years leading up to her father's purchasing his own land, when every dollar meant the difference between prideful self-sufficiency and sharecropping. But working as a servant in a white man's house posed a special kind of peril for young black women. A well-known example of this is described in the most detailed narrative ever written by an enslaved African American woman, *Incidents in the Life of a Slave Girl*, in which an escaped slave woman attests to the special sexual cruelty of her master, who was a physician. The writer, Harriet Jacobs, had two children outside marriage before she outwitted slavery and the American South. I guess Celestia Hundley's story will never be completely known.

My investigations had taken up the day. While I was having certified copies of the records reproduced, I debated whether I should retrieve my grandparents' 1930 marriage record. I decided against it. I wanted to remain in communion with the people born in the era of enslavement, people I never laid eyes on, people whose names have never been uttered to me by another human being.

I certainly felt like I knew my grandparents quite well growing up, though of course that's not really true. It's nearly impossible for me to think of my grandmother in the cabins and creeks of Pittsylvania, in the state she is named for, instead of in the geography where I knew her, the decidedly urban east side of Cleveland, Ohio. My own son Nathaniel, when he talks on the telephone with his mother's parents, a couple who were born and raised in small towns in the southern Haitian countryside, and he hears their heavy Kreyol accents, I know that part of him thinks them otherworldly. Mainly, I think at three he hears their ancient age as much as he glows under the sheltering nimbus of their warm human affection. I certainly got that feeling on my birthday or at Christmas when my grandfather called from Blairs and my grandmother called from Cleveland. Grandpa Jackson talked country and was difficult to understand, especially compared to the clipped, precise English of my own father. But I knew, I took for granted in the same way I took my own health for granted, that he loved me and would call as long as he was able to.

And years later, when I reflect that he might have chosen a birthday card that he could not read, and signed a name on that card in an alphabet that was murky to him, or called me from a place that was not his home, I understand that I am only beginning to know the heavy trust of distant love.

7 · Land of the Civil War

A week before I embarked on my journey, I visited Chatham's web page. There the civic agents claim for Chatham the title a "true Southern town," by which they mean hospitable and friendly. But after I was there for a full day, I agreed it was genuinely Southern in one main aspect: the American Civil War continues to be fought. Some of the bloodiest battles in this long national conflict took place in nearby Danville: a massacre in 1883 and "Bloody Monday" in 1963. The name Bloody Monday kept alive a June civil rights march at Danville's City Hall, where police responded by tattooing the peaceful demonstrators with clubs and high-pressure water hoses, sending forty people to the hospital with severe injuries.[1] Martin Luther King Jr. said of that event, "Very seldom, if ever, have I heard of a police force being as brutal and vicious as the police force here in Danville, Virginia."[2]

The more remote county seat seems to reflect the eternal polarization. Black Americans left the Southside area in droves, not after the pain and violence of the Civil War, but after the pain and violence of World War I. But the ones who remained seem to have moved south to Danville. On my visit to Chatham in July of 2008, I saw mostly whites with suspicious looks on their faces, what the writer Chester Himes described as the "vinegar" expression. Writing a century ago about the attitudes common among white people in the county, Ellen Glasgow called it "the peculiar disfavor felt for the black man by the low-born white."[3]

Here's an example of what I mean. When we arrived in Chatham, I walked from the king's-ransom-charging bed-and-parfait to an old-time gas station for sodas. I was waiting in line behind an athletically dressed, earring-wearing African American man talking into a mobile phone. The man was of a slender build, about thirty, and the proverbial Hershey-bar color. I noticed him in particular, because we had a similar pattern of baldness—though the contrast between his hair and skin color did not accent the receding hairline to the degree that dark hair on light skin does my own.

I think it's rude to talk on the phone when interacting with human beings, but the contemporary world is so different from my presumptions. The talking man refused me any sign of recognition, which I considered another prickly sign of disrespect. He had his back to me and shielded the store counter from my use or view, though I was laden with packages. His ill-mannered behavior extended to the scanty white female clerk, who must have been his age, which is middle age here, and looked like she wished she were somewhere else. It was a hot day, and the man bought a can of beer, but it took forever for him and the cashier to conduct this transaction. They danced in a tempest of miscommunication, lengthy pauses, and ignoring each other, a miniature theater of maneuvers that simmered with tension. From the looks of things here in Chatham, I figured they probably conducted the same business just yesterday.

What I didn't reckon was that the white clerk would refuse to look me in the face too. She put my change down on the counter too, just as she had done with him, as if she expected me to be climbing into the back of the pickup truck. The customer after me, a white woman who I knew full well to be an alley barfly, was treated to customary pleasantries as she secured her ordinaries, cigarettes and beer. The clerk put the woman's change in her hand. I saw versions of this for two days straight, the meager, sober whites showing a specific preference for their own kind.

The afternoon experience in Chatham rekindled my own memories of the scruffy intimacies between black and white Americans. One July a quarter of a century ago, my dad had arranged a scholarship for me to take a twenty-one-day Outward Bound wilderness course at Hurricane Island, Maine. Outward Bound styles itself as a physical test like boot camp, combined with an inner spiritual journey. My father was on alert that entire summer, as I roamed the city on my bicycle, pressured both of my parents to be allowed to drive, and tried to arrange unchaperoned visits with my girlfriend, Renée. I am sure he wanted me to become able to withstand peer pressure. As director of the Druid Hill Avenue branch of the YMCA, my father also made the scholarships available to dozens of Baltimore teenagers, about half of whom were African Americans from West Baltimore. Fittingly, we made the eighteen-hour drive to Maine on a public school bus.

I was preparing my application to the US Military Academy at West

Point, and I had hoped the experience would resemble military wilderness training. But my course at the Hurricane Island Outward Bound School was really closer to a sailing expedition, compass, protractor, marine chart, and cold weather included. The defining moment took place when we removed the mast of the thirty-foot pulling boat, turned the vessel upside down in the water, righted it, and re-outfitted the boat. It was excruciating, but not in the manner I had anticipated.

On my boat, the *MacMillan Watch*, there were several of us from Baltimore, four African Americans out of twelve. Reggie and Philip and Sonya all lived up the street from my grandmother, a rough area in the northwest part of the city, not at all far from my own block. But while I had a Headmaster's scholarship to a suburban Jesuit prep school, they attended the neighborhood public school, where a boy had recently been shot dead after class. I had noticed Sonya early on, because she smoked cigarettes on the bus and made out with a guy from another part of town. She acted grown. And not much later in her life, she would have an intimate relationship with a man who later shot and killed a city police officer.

I had had exposure, considerable exposure by the time I got to high school, to middle-class white Americans. I knew, in a practiced way, what kind of food they ate, the clothes they deemed fashionable, the music they liked, the kind of daring they thought appropriate for teens, and something of what they held sacred. I admired them as a group and thought them quite different from the black people in my family, my church, and my neighborhood. My father and I had had some rows over my sense of belonging to white families. In retrospect, I guess he didn't want me to become an understudy, a mimic man.

But the familiarity with whites that I took for granted, whether I performed a role or not, was available to few of the other African American teenagers on the trip. The clothes that I packed for the expedition were inexpensive, but they closely resembled the deck shoes and fleece-and-nylon windbreakers of the white kids. Sonya's bags were crammed with form-fitting designer jeans and jelly-bean-colored sneakers; Reggie and Philip had brought baggy cotton sweat suits that remained wet for three weeks. In other words, the lives of the other black sailors on my boat had not moved out beyond lower Park Heights Avenue and Mondawmin Mall, working-class and sometimes-desperate black Baltimore. They did not know how to swim, and the things that they knew about survival did not seem to make a great difference on an open pulling boat in the chilly July waters of Penobscot Bay.

One of the indignities forced on all of us, black and white, was a morning bathing ritual called simply "dip." The boat's male and female Outward Bound instructors performed this mandatory cleansing nude and, more or less, without comment from us. (One night, Sonya snickered at the male crew chief's penis, and from then on I maneuvered so she would not observe me disrobed.) After a few days, the minor shock of collectively skinny-dipping in the water on those gray, overcast mornings became inconsequential, since the more gruesome and solitary cause of embarrassment happened when we moved our bowels from the "seat of ease"—the prow of the pulling boat. Most of the crew got used to the "dip"—except Sonya, Reggie, and Philip. Something about having to submit to public nudity and jump into the cold water, along with the possibility of inspection, touched on a deep issue of basic self-respect for three black teens, whose speech and clothes had already set them apart. After several bouts of insolence, hardheadedness, aversion to "dip," and increasing frustration all around, the instructors decided to withhold food from Sonya, Philip, and Reggie.

Now, no one was getting fat on the trip. Much of the actual work we had to do required taking a daily turn at the oars, which seemed fun at first; after five minutes and the eruption of blisters, it seemed like slavery. We were all ravenous at the end of every day. There were no regular meat rations in the locker, and bits of cured sausage were considered treats. In fact, meat was so rare that we would salvage these bits even when they fell into the putrid bilgewater that was always sloshing around the bottom of the boat. Despite their evident hunger, Philip and Reggie continued to refuse to "dip." They were small brown boys, sixteen and nineteen years old, with white knit caps covering their close-shaved heads, and they huddled together in silence, avoiding eye contact with the rest of the crew.

Sonya had seen something of life and figured she could manage the ordeal for the sake of breakfast. Long after everyone else was fully dressed and fed, she relented and agreed to jump into the water and make her way from the prow to the stern. She took her morning baptism in the nude, glaring at and freely cursing anyone who stole glances at her chocolate limbs and her parts outlined in eggplant. Of course, she was impossible to miss in the late morning. She alone was naked, her breasts slanted at odd angles as she awkwardly went overboard, trying to keep her hands on the gunwale to preserve her chemically straightened hair. To this day, I remain uncertain as to the greater test: steadfast resistance that makes you an outlaw, or drawn-out, public, humiliating submission.

Taken altogether, the four of us were like the compass points of African acculturation to colonial Virginia. I remembered that when I got home, from the exposure to the sun on the boat, my skin was as brown as it had ever been.

Another girl and I told the counselors at the evening meeting that we felt more uncomfortable with the techniques being used to impel cooperation than with the minor dissent of the anti-dippers. Besides, on several of the other boats, the black Baltimoreans completely rebelled and simply demanded to be sent home. But even though my neighborhood peers stuck it out through the entire course, the counselors decided to withhold completion certificates from Sonya, Philip, and Reggie. They were unclaimed, like people tossed overboard, and to Outward Bound School officialdom they would never exist. Something about that scene, about the wisps of Sonya's disheveled processed hair and her exposed, cold-water-nipped bosom, something about her shaming herself for food, remained with me.

I supposed that the shipboard-kin memories resurfaced in Chatham because that teenage trial was such a classic moment of ambiguity for me, one in which I was unsure about which side claimed my best allegiance. Should I have condemned my peers and taken the side of the privileged white majority? Did my willingness to overcome embarrassment and the chilly water measure my courage, or did it measure my submissiveness, my willingness to please no matter the cost? Phillis Wheatley wrote that it was God's "mercy" that had brought her from Senegambia to Boston, enabling her to secure Christian salvation and rescuing her from pagan idolatry. On the other hand, Pittsylvanian Paschal Price had defied enslavement—its protocols of chastisement as a well as its religion. Was one path truer, or even easier? I didn't feel like there was much justice anywhere. I consoled my haunted mind and eased my ancient confusion by window-shopping at the antique store on the sunny but deserted Main Street, and then headed back to the clerk's office, to the deed registers.

The clerks were surprised to see me return, and I smiled and headed back to the desks. The indexes for wills and deeds were grouped by decade, and I had to scout through four or five volumes to locate the years that were important: Deed Book 71 for 1877, Deed Book 84 for 1886, Will Book 4 for 1890–1904. The dust stirred as I unlimbered the registers from their racks and slung them over to the desks. I began looking up the names I had retrieved from the US census records, careful not to tear the pages with their labored cursive script.

I knew that to hit a home run—to find information about my enslaved ancestors prior to 1865—I would need to find a slave owner who had left a will and detailed his holdings, or to luck up on an inventory that mentioned the enslaved by name prior to the dismantling of the estate. Such legal inventories taken before the distribution of property amounted to the key occasion in the life of the enslaved when their names would have entered public documents, when their names would have been put down in books guarded by a county clerk.

And here is the nasty paradox about African American genealogical research: people whose earthly lives were about to become miserable because they had been sold can sometimes be recovered by their descendants; those who knew a modicum of family security tend to be obliterated by history. If you find a name, you are almost certainly reading about a casualty, even if that person kept functioning biologically well enough to produce your own family.

I knew that my grandfather's grandfather Granville Hundley either was born a slave or, more disastrously, was sold into his condition in Pittsylvania by the 1840s. Since learning his name in 2006, I had considered more and more these people who had spent nearly all their productive years in chains. Hundley would have been a teenager, perhaps a rowdy, perhaps a brooder, when Nat Turner's rebellion in Southampton took place, changing the terms of bondage in the United States. He would have been a man well into his middle years in 1859, when John Brown tried to take the arsenal at Harpers Ferry and initiate open race war. In Danville, a year after Brown's foiled revolution, the city executed a black man named Jordan, owned by B. W. Ogburn, for killing another enslaved man named Bob. In October of the same year, 1860, a sixty-seven-year-old planter was given eighteen years for "the murder of one of his female slaves, by whipping her so brutally as to cause her death."[4] In the country, a short distance up the rail line, did white people and black people talk freely of the court's heavy sentences to one another? Were those exceptions worked up to justify the humanity of the slave regime?

What kind of adjustment did a man like Granville Hundley make to the world of the Southside Virginia piedmont after the Union victory at Appomattox? Was my great-great-grandfather in the crowd in 1870 and 1871 when the black men Kit Hubbard and John Jackson, convicted of murdering the white shop owner Joe E. Anderson, were hung from a scaffold in a field one mile from Chatham? He faced a jumble of problems in the 1860s and 1870s quite different from the ones he had known in his early life. And yet, he persevered with a household of small children in those postwar years of 1865 and 1866, years of lean crops, disease, and the issuance of coercive labor contracts that the Freedmen's Bureau half-heartedly kept track of. But especially as I scrabble after Hundley's years in the area of Ringgold-Laurel Grove, I mull over the kinds of personalities he encountered from day to day—the people he ran into at the mill, or traded with, or borrowed tools from, or shared a footbridge across the creek with.

The setting and many of the particulars for the drama of Granville Hundley's life and the neighborhood that was his main boundary were captured in the 1870 survey of Pittsylvania County by US census taker J. W. Cole. Cole took a curious route to record roughly twenty-six thousand county residents living in the "subdivision north of the Dan River." He started his journey in Laurel Grove on June 1, 1870, toward the eastern edge of Pittsylvania, and then he apparently traveled west, then doubled back east, then jotted north and a bit further east, in a large loop but with smaller loops inside it. The first person enumerated was an African American named John Lindsey. Fifty-three pages later, on June 23, Cole enumerated Granville Hundley, the head of the 434th household living in the 431st dwelling in same Laurel Grove postal area as John Lindsey.[5] By that time, he had also been to Whitmell and Pleasant Gap, which was on the other side of the White Oak Mountain and the Virginia Midland Railway that ran north to south and connected Danville to Competition. Covering the four-hundred-plus families took Cole three weeks. That was one of his smaller loops. Nearing the completion of his circuit during the last seven days of August, Cole got to John Hundley, a white citizen living in the 5,834th building he'd visited. But the black and white Hundleys, in all probability, shared a common property line.

This terrain of my grandfather's grandfather, where footpaths were used by residents as frequently as roads and where people relied on specific varieties of poplar and oak trees to define property lines in legal documents, was a place dominated by white male heads of household. Many of these men had recent memories of the Civil War and not great prospects for financial success in agriculture. The multiple conscription acts passed by the Confederate government eventually drafted all able-bodied white men from the ages of seventeen to fifty; virtually everyone from Hundley's corner of Pittsylvania County had participated in what they called "The War between the States" and which to me is the Civil War. I wonder what Granville Hundley called it. Perhaps he just had a word for the end of it, Jubilee.

Hundley's neighbor Elisha Keen appears to have been a sergeant in I Company of the Fifty-Seventh Virginia Infantry, the "Pittsylvania Life

Guards," where he was joined by Granville Hundley's other neighbors, James Bullington and John Slaughter. But more of these farmers and artisans, including William Ferrell, who shared fences with Granville Hundley, his brother James Ferrell, William Jennings, Leonard Cole, Wilson Meyers, Champ Evans, and Joel Bennett, had served under Captain Daniel Townes in A Company of the Thirty-Eighth Virginia Infantry. At Gettysburg during the famous charge of General William Pickett's division in the direction of Cemetery Ridge, the "Pittsylvania Regiment," or the Thirty-Eighth Virginia Infantry, sustained a casualty rate of 40 percent. Of the seven companies comprising that regiment, no company had a higher casualty rate, particularly in terms of men shot dead on that afternoon, than A Company. They must have seen the fighting at its thickest. Joel Bennett was shot in the hand at Gettysburg, and another neighbor's boy, John Gunnel's twenty-year-old son, Joseph, was killed. T. R. Yeaman, who served in the Ringgold Battery—a Confederate artillery unit, whose uniforms bore red piping—lost his brother William there too.

The entwined lives of the former Confederate soldiers and the ex-slaves along these paths and unimproved roads simply must have been a miracle of understanding between 1870 and 1900, an age when black and white lived in the integrated style that, likely as not, the United States will never see again. Beverly Hall, who had served in E Company of the Thirty-Eighth Virginia Infantry CSA and charged the Federal batteries as a part of Pickett's division at Gettysburg, supported a family of seven by working at John Hubbard's gristmill. Beside him were three households of black Robinsons: eighteen-year-old William Robinson, his wife, Mary, and infant daughter; middle-aged Clement and Jane; and seventy-year-old Milly, her son, Wilson Taylor, and his son, Charles. Sixty-year-old James McNichols's household included a twenty-five-year-old son and a twenty-one-year-old black servant named William Hall. The households of Catherine Jones, Henry Clemens, William Mills, go back and forth, white and black, until the census enumerator got to the coach maker William Ferrell, who had a black wheelwright living on his premises, forty-year-old Goodrich Coles.[6] To understand the manner in which Hundley exercised freedom, I was drawn toward the county's part in the Civil War, a topic that continued to weigh heavily on the minds of the people who overtly shaped my ancestor's liberty, day in and day out.

The Confederate Army was in retreat after Gettysburg, and in a sense, General Robert E. Lee's failure to support Pickett's breakthrough cost the entire success of the rebellion. The historic defeat in Pennsylvania must have continued to weigh heavily on the minds and shape the outlook of these white men in between the neighborhoods of Spring Garden and Kentuck. It must have inflected the talk of the farmers as they clotted together off Old Richmond Road or on the public road to discuss the rain and the drought, to prize tobacco, to repair equipment, and of course, to engage in one of their favorite pastimes, sampling the corn whisky that they made themselves. It must have come up as they dealt with one proud black farmer in their midst, my great-great-grandfather.

The Thirty-Eighth Infantry's A Company had been organized in 1860 by Dan Townes in Kentuck, four miles from where Hundley was living in 1870. Townes collected the men during the buildup toward the presidential election, when the Southern militias became more vigilant and serious. Every neighborhood in the county had a militia, and three days' annual service was mandatory for men under the age of forty-five, though this typically amounted to nothing more than drinking practice at an old field. But the militias did double as a reserve for the slave patrol, the infamous "patterroller" in the eyes of the black enslaved and the black free. It's difficult to imagine that there was not an almost palpable animosity between black Pittsylvanians and the patrols, men who were paid twenty-five cents per eight-hour shift, and whom the enslaved referred to as "bugs." Kentucky slaves called them "the worst fellows that can be found," who stole money and would "act just as they please" with wives and daughters.[7] When it was known that the paterrollers were planning to break up an event, the enslaved would inform one another that there were "bugs in the wheat." Perhaps Hundley, perhaps the boyish Ned Jackson, viewed the secessionist armed forces as a huge slave patrol.

Captain Daniel Townes's Company, as A Company was known, went into service on May 30, 1861, traveling by railroad to the Battle of Bull Run. The men arrived too late to be involved in that scrap, but attended the rest of the conflict promptly. During the war, most of Pittsylvania's Confederate soldiers died at Chimborazo Hospital in Richmond of typhoid, diarrhea, bronchitis, or rubella. But life and death in the Thirty-Eighth Infantry didn't follow the accepted pattern. The regiment managed to get bloodied at Seven Pines and Malvern Hill in 1862, at Second Manassas and Fredericksburg, at Chester Station and Drewry's Bluff and Cold Harbor. During the difficult and deadly Battle of Malvern Hill, eleven men in the regiment were killed and seventy-two wounded. In May of 1863 at Drewry's Bluff, twenty-three rebels died in the field and seventy-seven were wounded. In both examples, the casualties depleted a regiment around four hundred strong.

"Patterollers" inspecting passes. From *Harper's Magazine*, 1860. Private collection.

None of what happened before or after compared to the blood spilled on July 3, 1863, at Gettysburg in Pennsylvania. Captain Townes's Company alone suffered eleven men killed and nineteen wounded. When the assault began at three o'clock that afternoon, the Thirty-Eighth Regiment and the Fifty-Seventh Regiment were side by side on the extreme left of Pickett's division. West Point graduate Lew Armistead led the brigade into battle by double-timing it out on foot with his men, waving a black slouch hat on his sword. Armistead's brigade marched in lines two men deep eighty yards in back of Dick Garnett's five regiments up front. The Pittsylvanians were actually the support brigade, but vanguard and rear guard made no difference on that afternoon.

The men of the Thirty-Eighth and the Fifty-Seventh crossed Emittsburg Road, made it up to the Codori Barn, reached a copse, and then finally pierced the Union line at what became known as "the Angle," a pocket close by a well-defended stone wall, where the Confederates took artillery fire the entire time and musket volley at the end. Rawley Martin, a lieutenant colonel from Chatham who led the Fifty-Third Virginia and marched on the immediate right of the "Pittsylvania Life Guards," later wrote that the individual Pittsylvania soldier saw the attack as "the most stupendous work of his life."[8] But when he was recovering from the battle in a hospital, he wrote that he no longer cared to discuss Gettysburg at all, which many of the men came to think of in the immediate aftermath as a sheer waste of life. But on that afternoon, Pickett's inspector general, Walter Harrison, was playfully literary in his description of mingling the Gettysburg water with Chambersburg whisky, and satirizing what the conflict would increasingly be seen to represent. He remarked after drinking a concoction in Peach Orchard just before beginning the storied climb to immortality, "Perhaps if the whiskey been of a *darker color*, we might have got up a miscegenation."[9]

Apparently, the Pittsylvanians reached as close as the Confederates got to victory that day. For a brief while they captured Union Battery A, a four-gun unit of three-inch ordnance rifles led by Lieutenant Alonzo Cushing, who died while firing deadly grapeshot into their ranks. But Armistead's short breach received no support. The Thirty-Eighth and the Fifty-Seventh fought against the Irish Sixty-Ninth Pennsylvania and the Seventy-Second Pennsylvania. The Virginia boys were plying a new trade—invading home turf—and the Union troops steadied themselves by yelling "Fredericksburg," the name of the battle where the Federal soldiers had undergone their own catastrophe a year earlier in Virginia. Armistead's advance with the Thirty-Eighth was the high-water mark of Pickett's Charge, and the Irish Union soldiers fought them back with rifle butts. The deadly embrace between combatant armies was so tight they had no room to fire.

The common man did not sacrifice himself alone. Brigade commander Armistead himself was mortally wounded, as was the Thirty-Eighth's regimental commander, Colonel Edmonds, as was A Company's commander, Captain Townes. Pickett's Charge characterized the valor and implausible chivalry of Southern men. The attack was compared to the Charge of the Light Brigade, and became a powerful source of romanticism for the South during the war and after. To the whites in the neighborhood of Spring Garden and Ringgold, the disaster at Gettysburg must have served as an emblem or a badge of their commitment to the "forlorn hope"— whose vanquishing must have looked a lot like black freedom.

The immense bloodletting leading to the Jubilee, the day slavery ended, could only have been to the enslaved some form of divine retribution. Nat Turner had claimed that his bloody rebellion against slaveholding whites was signaled by a dream in which he saw the heavens on fire and blood dripping from the cornstalks in the field. During the Battle of Antietam in 1862, more men apparently died at a faster rate than ever before in the annals of human warfare, and they were mown down like stalks in a cornfield. In the eyes of an enslaved African—maybe even someone like sixty-three-year-old Ringgold freedman Cuffee Macko, the man known to have held on to something of his African, probably Congo past and who had achieved freedom by 1860—Pickett's Charge of ten thousand groaning rebels, swinging across one open-field mile and gaining fortified higher ground; in an attack that General Robert E. Lee ordered to win the battle in which he definitively lost the war; where the Union artillery mangled the close ranks of the rebels, and then from behind a stone ridge riflemen raked the Southerners with gunfire; where a host of marching men were butchered into an orchard of gore: this too must have seemed like a divinely ordained retribution in kind for the depravity that was hereditary slavery.

After the obliteration of Pickett's division, Captain Townes was replaced by Richard Joyce, a twenty-six-year-old store clerk from Ringgold who worked for W. H. C. Reynolds, a successful merchant. Joyce lived in close proximity to the area's free blacks: the blacksmith John Foreman, the bricklayer Atlas Gie, Sokey Henderick, and the landowning William Anderson. Joyce himself owned a nineteen-year-old black man, whom he valued at close to nineteen hundred dollars. This young man very well may have traveled with the young captain of A Company during the war until Joyce was captured at Bermuda Hundred, the old inland Virginia slave ship port, in 1864.

I can only guess at the number of black Pittsylvania men who eyewitnessed Pickett's Charge while holding a horse's reins or carrying supplies. Certainly a tolerable number of African Americans marched with the gray. Seventy black men attempted, unsuccessfully, to join the Confederate ranks at Lynchburg when secession was announced.[10] In June of 1861, "a body of 150 armed picked negroes," mustered in with the First South Carolina Infantry, attacked Union troops near Vienna, Virginia.[11] Jeff Shields served as the bodyguard and valet of Stonewall Jackson; William Mack Lee cooked for Robert E. Lee and attended him throughout the war. Not many served the Confederacy like Holt Collier, a black sharpshooter from a Texas Cavalry regiment who went to war with his owner, Howell Hinds; but there are multiple accounts of black soldiers on duty as pickets, cannoneers, and sharpshooters, and even, at the Battle of Seven Pines, two black regiments fighting for the Confederacy.[12] Their motives were diverse. One black gunner for Confederate artillery at Bull Run recalled his hope "that the Yankees would whip" the Confederates. The man claimed he would have run over to the other side, "but our officers would have shot us."[13]

Escapees driving a wagon into Federal lines. From Edwin Forbes, "Life Studies of the Great Army" (1876). Confederate Miscellany, Emory University.

Free and enslaved blacks of Pittsylvania County came to the aid of the Confederacy too, especially as noncombatants. On October 3, 1862, the Virginia General Assembly passed an Act for the Public Defense, which required a percentage of enslaved men between the ages of sixteen and forty-five to serve the Confederacy, with the percentage to be at the governor's discretion. County clerks and justices of the peace were to be the direct agents procuring the men, and after the act was passed, the Confederate Engineering Bureau requested 4,500 black Virginians.[14] Pittsylvania was required to furnish 580 men, more than any other county, and it wasn't until March of 1863 that it got close to the requisite number.[15]

The national Confederate government and the State of Virginia passed the first of five acts conscripting free blacks to serve as labor battalions, which escalated to the last-ditch attempt of arming the slaves near the end of the war. The 1864 bill for the Conscription of Free Negroes fully covered indispensable black participation.

Sec. 1. The Congress of the Confederate States do enact that all male free negroes resident in the Confederate States between the ages of 18 and 50 years shall be held liable to perform such duties with the army or in conjunction with the military defenses of our country in the way of work upon fortifications or in the government works for the preparation of materials of War or in Military Hospitals as the Secretary of War may from time to time prescribe and while engaged in the performance of such duties shall receive rations and clothing and compensation at the rate of Eleven dollars a month under such rules & regulations as the said Secretary may establish—*Provided* that the Secretary of War with the approval of the President may exempt from the operation of this Act such free negroes as the interests of the country may require should be exempted or such as he may think proper to exempt on the grounds of justice, equity or necessity.[16]

Section 2 of the act then went on to requisition "male negro slaves," and Section 3 gave the secretary of war the power to "impress the services of as many male slaves as may be required from time to time to discharge the duties indicated in the first section." At the end, in March of 1865, the Confederate War Department requisitioned another 104 black men from Pittsylvania, and for the first time, the full quota was sent.[17] The planters in Danville might have liked sending the men off as labor better than the other looming alternative. Simultaneously, the front page of the *Danville Appeal* carried the headline "CONSCRIPTION OF NEGROES." At last the slaves themselves were to be impressed into the fight. "If this bill is to be adopted at all," the editorial admitted, "it ought to be done at once, so as to allow some little time for the arming, equipping, and drilling of negroes for service."[18] After the war, the Confederacy was prepared to grant black freedom to stave off defeat. Of course, by then the Confederate military situation was hopelessly desperate.

That I know of, I have no free ancestors from Pittsylvania who would have been conscripted; actual records of the enslaved sent to the battlefields are more difficult to glean. (On April 3, 1865, as the Confederate government at Richmond was collapsing, the records were burned, so the number of enslaved and free blacks who had ever labored hard for the Confederacy can only be inferentially known.) Since the Confederates ultimately ran a hospital in Danville, kept Union prisoners in tobacco warehouses, and used the city as its quartermaster's depot, there would have been plenty for blacks to do at home in Pittsylvania or the incorporated city of Danville.

Slaveholders received compensation for their men who built army

GUERRE D'AMÉRIQUE. — Arrière-garde du général Sherman, parti de Méridan pour se rendre à Selma.

Black "contrabands" carrying Federal wounded after battle, Meridian, Mississippi, February 1864. "Guerre d'Amerique," from *Le Monde Illustré*. Confederate Miscellany, Emory University.

roads, encampments, trenches, and breastworks. Black men worked skilled jobs as carpenters, blacksmiths, boatmen, iron foundry workers, colliers at the niter and mining works, and then as orderlies at the massive Chimborazo military hospital outside Richmond, a complex of more than one hundred buildings, which they built. They served as wood-cutters, sawyers, provisioners, foragers, cooks, hostlers, and teamsters. Ulysses S. Grant wrote in his memoirs that the four million enslaved in the aggregate were more worthwhile to the Confederacy than twelve million Northerners of the same age and sex.[19]

Grant believed in the value of enslaved labor because of the expectation of consistent daily production. If you chopped wood as an enslaved man, the expected output was a cord and a half per day. A cord is eight feet long, four feet high, and four feet deep. If your logs were slightly smaller in circumference than a paint can, say, eight inches in diameter and four feet long, you would need eighteen pieces for your bottom row, and you'd need at least six rows for a cord. And you would split a log of that size into quarters. The last time I picked up an axe and went against a rotted log that wanted to come apart, I am sure it took thirty licks. I was putting everything I had into those licks too: the beads of sweat were flying, and I blistered my hands.

My own bias is to doubt that the slaves' experience ditching and trucking for the Confederacy offered moments of the "stupendous work" that Lieutenant Colonel Rawley Martin believed had been experienced by white farmhands during Pickett's Charge. But despite the scarcity of information on the use of black labor during the Civil War, a picture of competition among skilled laborers increasingly emerges. Enslaved black men seem to have used the opportunity to develop more fully into skilled craftsmen during the war, which much of the freed population living in Virginia had already indulged in.

At the Clarksville Ordnance works, mainly devoted to a harness shop, the captain-in-charge, John Kane, wrote angrily to his superiors in Richmond, who sought to lower the pay for skilled black workers.

> You do not fully understand the class of free Negroes we have here when you say seventy to seventy five dollars … the Negroes to whom I refer are almost altogether carpenters, blacksmiths, or blacksmith helpers and selected as the best of that class of mechanics to be found in the neighborhood, some in fact superior workmen to many white men.
>
> We have one boy, although a slave, and whom we are now paying $182 per month who as a general workman is the best blacksmith in the shop; on piece work at home this boy excels in industry any of the workmen.[20]

One enslaved man named John working in the sawmill at Fluvanna County was employed annually for $1,500.[21] He must have been doing remarkably keen work, fast, and been good at supervising the others. The great Southern ironworks and foundry at Tredegar bought skilled slaves throughout the war; in 1864, for a man named Morris, it paid the very high price of $4,600.[22] In Lynchburg, a free black teamster named James Robinson gained a letter of recommendation from the president of the Old Dominion Iron and Nail Works. Robinson's advocate hoped to remove him from the conscription list because of the freedman's proven excellence as a trucker of iron material, with his collection of four wagons. Granville Hundley and his postwar neighborhood that included so many black artisans as well as his young neighbors like Nat Hutchings must have contributed in one way or another.

During the war, freedmen actually may have had it tougher than the enslaved. When it came time to send their own men, the slaveholders

Negro teamsters and Federal supply train. From Edwin Forbes, "Life Studies of the Great Army" (1876). Confederate Miscellany, Emory University.

were gravely reluctant to enlist as laborers their "full hands" or "No. 1 men" far from home or to expose them to frontier conditions. On the eve of a formidable military engagement, a Campbell County planter appealed to his son: "I write to tell you not to let Sam go into the fight with you. Keep him in the rear, for that nigger is worth a thousand dollars."[23] On the frontier, they preferred to have poor or disabled whites at work in the mines. In contrast, some Richmond-area blacks claimed they preferred mining coal, which under wartime conditions must have been treacherous, even compared with the labor conditions an enslaved man was accustomed to. But it is likely that blacks such as Booker T. Washington's stepfather, who later relocated his family to a West Virginia coal-mining town and put everybody to work, got their introduction to coal mining on account of Civil War exigencies.

The transformation from the agricultural to the industrial was under way. As one historian wrote, "Not only did [the Negro] constitute the major part of the required labor in the Valley blast furnaces, but he worked side by side with the white skilled mechanic as puddler, heater, and roller."[24] Increasingly large numbers of Virginia's enslaved male workers must have become conscious of the market value of their labor power.

Probably the biggest project in Pittsylvania during the war was the maintenance of the railroad line to Richmond and the construction of a new line extending to Greensboro, North Carolina. By 1862 eight hundred men were clearing a path eighty feet wide through forests and also tearing up the York River line for much-needed iron. The railroad operated a sawmill and used enslaved men to manufacture its crossties and bridge timber. In 1864 more than seven hundred enslaved blacks performed as firemen, brakemen, cleaners, coach maids, and machine-shop employees.[25] In a capacity similar to their antebellum jobs, black labor kept Virginia's railroad lines, bridges, and locomotives repaired and maintained throughout the war.

The war gave men a chance to display courage and skill and see something of the state. Boatmen who patrolled the James and Rappahannock Rivers in trousers and bandanas proudly displayed their formidable physiques. T. C. De Leon admired such men in a description in his 1890 book *Four Years in the Rebel Capitals*.

> A splendidly developed race are those Africans of the river boats, with shiny, black skins, through which the corded and tense muscles seem to be bursting, even in repose. Their only dress, as a general thing, is a pair of loose pantaloons, to which the more elegant add a fancy colored bandanna knotted about the head, with its wing-like ends flying in the wind; but shirts are a rarity in working hours and their absence shows a breadth of shoulder and depth of chest remarkable, when contrasted with the length and lank power in the nether limbs.[26]

The modern-day fetish of watching black young men racing, leaping, knocking one another on their backs, and eluding capture in football and other sports is profoundly anchored in the American joy derived from watching enslaved men and women "play out their strength" and dramatically transform feral lands into yards of Georgic precision.

Walt Whitman depicted this too in his 1855 masterwork *Leaves of Grass*.

> The negro holds firmly the reins of his four horses—the block swags underneath on its tied-over chain;
> The negro that drives the dray of the stone-yard—steady and tall he stands, pois'd on one leg on the string-piece;
> His blue shirt exposes his ample neck and breast, and loosens over his hip-band;

His glance is calm and commanding—he tosses the slouch of his hat away
   from his forehead;
The sun falls on his crispy hair and moustache—falls on the black of his
   polish'd and perfect limbs.

I behold the picturesque giant, and love him—and I do not stop there;
I go with the team also.[27]

I like Whitman's spirit, singing his body electric song to himself. He certainly was an enjoyer of masculine spectacle. His poem about comforting
the runaway slave also convinces me that at the end of the stanza he does
not liken his loving admiration of the "picturesque giant" to his fondness
for the dray horses pulling the wagon. Not to take anything away from
the white farmer and his Puritanism, his work ethic, and his whisky, but
the motivated and skilled "gangs" of blacks who performed heavy labor
in rhythm, with that African sense of time and splendor, introduced a
new quality of the sublime to these shores.

The boatmen performing their tasks with athletic grace were not merely
sports or hired hands. William Brackens, a free Negro, was in charge of
the Tredegar ironworks' small fleet of boatmen and bateaux. Up and
down the considerable network of waterways he sent a fleet of water-
men, navigating tricky rivers and creeks with watercraft loaded down
with pig iron. When he was impressed into service and taken to dig fortifications outside Richmond, his absence threw the ironworks managers
into a flurry of letter writing. "No one else understands the small tribu-
tary streams by which the metal is brought down," protested Tredegar's
owner, West Point graduate Joseph Reid Anderson, to the Confederate
secretary of the navy.[28] Brackens was returned to his boats.

The black free and enslaved men along Virginia's Roanoke, Staunton,
and Dan Rivers would have poled the boats as well, and one of their important cargoes was gunpowder, a key determinant of the fighting capacity of a nineteenth-century army. Gunpowder manufacture required
three essential ingredients: sulfur, charcoal, and niter, and southwestern Virginia was also home to the most intensive niter production of the
Confederacy. Pure niter abounded in limestone caves, and enslaved men
participated in both mining operations and in the eighteen-month-long
production of artificial niter in beds of decayed animal carcasses. In April
of 1864, the Confederate Army sent Lieutenant McCue to Pittsylvania to
conscript freedmen for the war industry. Half the men he enlisted that
spring went into the Confederate Engineering Bureau and the other portion to the Medical Department. Conscripted labor attached to the En-

gineering Bureau worked on railroads like the vital Danville–Richmond line or the Lynchburg–Tennessee line and on the Niter and Mining Bureau mining projects, along with the munitions work in Danville.

Captain E. S. Hutter commanded the arsenal at Danville, and he had twenty-one enslaved men at his discretion.[29] At the ordnance center at Danville, the same effort went on that consumed the other major centers for Confederate arms production. By November 1862, for example, the Richmond arsenal was turning out sixty thousand rounds of small-arms ammunition per day.[30] Ordnance work was dangerous: at the Richmond works, deadly accidents occurred when primed artillery shells exploded while being packed and loaded. At Petersburg they smelted lead into pellets to make bullet cartridges. The black teamsters trucked it all, including the heavy ten-inch cannon called "columbiads" that weighed ten tons and required thirty mules to move. After the Battles of Bull Run and Seven Days, hundreds of Negroes were hired to retrieve weapons from the battlefield and prepare them for future use. At the Danville armory, Candidus Bilhartz got a contract to manufacture breach-loading carbine rifles, and Mary Shelton's enslaved blacksmith worked there. I imagine Granville Hundley heard the munitions depot at Danville explode on April 10, 1865, just after Jeff Davis, president of the Confederacy, fled the city.

More common than munitions production and as important as transportation were the fortifications that black men built to protect Virginia from Union attack. A single pick man could keep two men busy with shovels, and an expert ditcher could shovel 8 or 10 cubic yards of earth in a day, baling earth 12 feet horizontally or half that distance vertically.[31] To put this kind of work in perspective, a cubic yard of earth, a square 3 feet long, 3 feet wide, and 3 feet deep, weighs 2,700 pounds—500 pounds more than a ton.

The black ditchers and carters built redoubts and sloped battlements considerably more sophisticated than simple trenches. Dennis Hart Mahan's classic 1848 *Treatise on Field Fortifications* provided the basic schemata that the Confederate engineers followed. The laborers excavated a trench and sloped both sides during the process. They formed the excavated soil into parapets on top of the trench. The parapets, earthen walls, protected the Confederate soldiers from fire and allowed them an unobstructed visual sweep of the battlefield; onrushing troops had no reprieve from the line of sight of the riflemen above them. Enslaved men reinforced the parapets with branches and wattle, and in the six months after the war was declared, Virginia's coasts, its northern boundary, and

Fredericksburg hospital burial detail, ca. 1864. In this photograph near the Union hospital at Fredericksburg, Virginia, a black burial detail goes about its grim work. Of the four men, though, only one, dressed in a clean white shirt, holds his gaze with the camera. In the distance, a white Union soldier in folded shirtsleeves seems to glare at the one black man who does not turn toward the camera at all, and whose head seems to be a blur of motion. Photographs of the day were stills that required subjects to hold their pose for several seconds, demanding a good deal of cooperation between photographer and photographed. In this case, that cooperation was incomplete. Photograph: Library of Congress.

its waterways were studded with defense fortifications. As even the 1939 film *Gone with the Wind* showed, white Southerners, like the film's heroine, Scarlett O'Hara, were quite pleased to be surrounded by black men digging earthworks to protect them from Yankee cannons. In March of 1864, the *Danville Appeal* reassured its readers that Danville would have her defenses built. "The negroes impressed and sent from Pittsylvania county to Richmond to work on fortifications for sixty days, will be released from the fortifications at the expiration of thirty days and sent to Danville to work on fortifications."[32] The defenses at Danville were constructed so formidably that the sloped ground protecting the bridge to the city can be seen today.

The occasion of the black laborers building the fortifications for Danville was one of the most curious elements of all the service that I find at occurring at the end of the war. The white people might have feared that Danville would be another Vicksburg, and that Union engineers, apparently an unimaginative lot of men, would attempt what they had done at Petersburg and at the Mississippi River town: to wit, tunnel far into the earth and plant demolitions to enable a breach of the city's defenses. Yet the work on the fortifications would have brought groups of black Americans in close contact with one another. When the black breast-work ditchers worked at Danville, they must have encountered captured black Federal troops, many of whom had been taken prisoner around Petersburg and were probably from Virginia. Throughout the Civil War, regular exchanges of convalescents were carried out between the two armies.

> Tuesday evening, a number of Yankee prisoners, apparently about two hundred, were sent from this place to Richmond, for the purpose of being exchanged. They were convalescents, as it is known the Federal government refuses to exchange any but the sick.
>
> In obedience to orders from the A and I General, all the slaves who were confined at this Post as prisoners of war have been sent to Camp Lee, from which place it is designed to return them to their owners. There remain here yet a few free negroes, captured in the battles below Petersburg, and a considerable number of regular blue bellies.[33]

In spite of the massacre of black soldiers in battles at Fort Pillow, Milliken's Bend, Poison Springs, Plymouth, and the Crater, the Confederate Congress's 1863 law designating black soldiers "slaves in arms," and the field commanders' general inclination never to take black prisoners, the policy of "no quarter" was not uniformly applied.[34] Still, it seems that if the black soldiers who went to Camp Lee, where fifty-three years later my own grandfather drilled and outfitted for World War I, were returned to their owners, they would have faced a considerable amount of chastisement, if not execution, for running away and joining the Federal army. They were enslaved men who had taken up arms against whites, and the penalty was death. I wonder what my ancestor Granville Hundley would have thought, and the boy Edward, seeing those men on the road to Camp Lee, or glimpsing those not-so-regular African American "blue bellies" left in Danville in April 1865. On Pittsylvania roads, black Virginians forced south in coffles shared a path with captured black and white Union troops who had been paroled from Danville and were headed north to the thicket of battle at Petersburg. Together they fell like a mighty cross on the land.

8 · The Will

On May 22, 1877, my great-grandmother Celestia's sixty-two-year-old father paid two hundred dollars for the privilege of becoming a landowner. It had been twelve years since Granville Hundley was "shot free," as the saying went—emancipated from slavery by the Union victory of arms. That price bought him fifty acres, more or less, by Sandy Creek, where he had lived at least thirty years, maybe longer. How he had amassed the money or gathered the determination to do it, I never learned from those meager courthouse registers, but I took great pleasure from his triumph. His having borne enslavement for half a century and then scraped by for a dozen free years convinced me that for him, owning the land must have overlapped with the dream of his own physical freedom.

Recorded on the county deed register as one "Granvel Hundley," he bought the following tract from the man he had known well, John Hundley:

> A parcel of land lying in the County of Pittsylvania and adjoining the lands of Dr. Edward Williams, William E. Ferrell, John Hundley + others, beginning at Smith Old Path where Dr. Edward's line crosses the same. Thence the Old Path to cross paths that lead to Hubbard's Mill. Thence straight line to a large poplar in William E. Ferrell line at an elbow, thence Ferrell line to John Hubbard to Dr. Edward Williams line to the Old Smith path at the beginning supposed to contained fifty acres more or less.[1]

Granville Hundley must have had a gambler's instincts to have felt confident enough to buy his ground by Smith's Old Path after he had gone beyond his sixtieth year of life. By 1877 he had outlived a great number of his peers, black or white. Part of his experience must have been doggedly lonely. Since many of the black men I have known passed away in their fifties, and people live longer today than they had in the nine-

Hundley
from
Hundley

This deed made and entered into this the 22'd day of May 1877 — between John Hundley of the first part and Granvel Hundley of the second part, all of the county of Pittsylvania and State of Virginia Witnesseth that the said John Hundley for and in consideration of the sum of five hundred dollars, the receipt of which is hereby acknowledged by the said John Hundley, have sold unto the said Granvel Hundley his heirs and assigns forever, a certain tract or parcel of land lying in the county of Pittsylvania and adjoining the lands of D[r] Edward Williams, Williams & others, beginning at Smith & others, beginning at Smith fence John Hubbard & others, beginning at Smith fence where D[r] Edward Williams line crosses old path where D[r] Edward Williams line crosses the same, thence the old path to cross path that leads to Hubbards mill, thence straight line to a large poplar in William E. Ferrell line at an elbow, thence Ferrell line to John Hubbard line to thence Hubbards line D[r] Edward Williams line over the creek, thence Williams line to the old smith path at the beginning supposed to contained fifty acres more or less, and the said John Hundley do hereby and by these presents warrant a good and legal title to the above described lands with all

Granvel Hundley, 1877 deed. Clerk's Office, Pittsylvania County, Virginia.

teenth century, I imagine that Hundley's longevity and ownership of land made him a unique figure in the neighborhood.

There was another difference that he had little chance to shape. Somehow, perhaps even during slavery, Hundley got what black folks called "half a white man's chance": he became one of a select few who learned something about dealing with white men, conducting business transactions, and saving money. He must have been skilled so that, in spite of his advanced years, he could imagine himself capable of identifying profitable land and then making that land yield. He did not place a higher value on goods that might be enjoyed at once over those that were durable, and both kinds might have drawn untoward attention to him. He obeyed the ready homily of Freedmen's Bureau Commissioner Colonel Brown, who advised, "Better for you to remain than looking for something better."

The size of the parcel itself was really just a working farm for one active man. The rough area is something like a square quarter of a mile. One hand could comfortably plow one of those 440-yard lengths with an ox in two days. To conserve so well that he could buy property, Granville Hundley must have been stubborn, a person set in his ways, the kind of man who said no a lot more than he said yes. It's quite difficult to figure out where his resources would have come from. Samuel Wilson, for example, paid black workers like Nat Hairston and Gil and Elbert Wilson seventy-two dollars for making his tobacco crop in the years 1866 and 1867.[2] The highest annual wages he paid went to prime and, one assumes, young workers like Elias and Clifton Hairston and James Wilson: one hundred dollars. Other workers, men, women, and children, received a range of smaller amounts, as little as twenty dollars for a season. I suspect it would have been difficult to keep even a small family in "groceries"— bacon and cornmeal—for twelve months at any of those wages, and it is unclear what kind of rent those workers had to pay.[3] After slavery, same as today, lengthy illness or infirmity spelled catastrophe.

Becoming a farmer that year was a complicated move for a black man. An 1876 editorial examining racial lines in the upcoming election reflected local sentiment concerning the freedmen.

The biggest political card yet. The carpet-baggers of Mississippi and Louisiana are telling the negroes that [Rutherford B.] Hayes is a black man— one of their own race and color—who will not only give every negro "his forty acres and a mule," but put the bottom rail on top, and keep it "thar."

It is said that it takes like wildfire with the negroes, and any attempt of the Democrats to deny the truth of the statement, is hooted down by them as one of "dem d——d Democratic lies." What a country—what suffrage—what a party![4]

Louisiana and Mississippi sent blacks to the US Senate, so those states were especially held up to scorn. Political realities in Virginia were similarly multiracial, if not as spectacularly successful for black individuals. In 1880 the famously interracial and anti-Bourbon Readjuster Party sent William Mahone to the Senate from Virginia and then placed William Cameron in the governor's mansion the next year. Granville Hundley could have joined the Readjuster Party, which came into being the year before he bought his property, and had the tangible impact of putting blacks on the Danville City Council. But on the ground, "forty acres and a mule" was being understood by many whites as a metaphor for putting the bottom rail on the top, a metaphor for something deeply undesirable.

◆ ◆ ◆

My sense of the precise location of Hundley's fifty-acre parcel, hemmed in by the Smith Old Path, Hubbard's Mill, Dr. Edward Williams's property, a large poplar tree, and ex-infantryman William Ferrell's land was well beyond murky; I was sifting sludge. The road names had changed, new roads had been added to the old places, and I had found no nineteenth-century detail maps of the county. The semiofficial nature of the place-names only added confusion to the surveyor's legally precise records of the plots.

In 1880 the US census enumerator, a man named J. B. Callaway, described his route through the Pittsylvania district quite near my ancestors. He traveled

> [until] the Telegraph road crossed the Tunstall District line, thence along the Telegraph road to Mountain Road near Joe Hendley's thence down the Mountain Road to Ringgold Road at Malmaison thence up Ringgold Road to the Danville and off the Mountain Road near Griffith Evans' thence down said Mountain Road to Birch Creek, thence down Birch Creek to Halifax Co. line.[5]

My relatives lived in the adjacent district and were enumerated in that census by a man named Wheatley, who only noted that he was covering the line of households west of a road "from Danville via Chatham to the old Campbelite church." The adjoining path followed by Callaway more closely touched on my family's neighborhood roads and landmarks.

The modern-day Ringgold-Church Road connects to Malmaison Road within an area that includes in its rough circumference the edges of Birch Creek. Mountain Road is about a mile and a quarter north and parallel to Birch Creek, and Mountain Road smacks into the throat of Old Richmond Road. The modern-day Keeling neighborhood is shaped like a black-eyed-pea pointing northeast and between Birch and Sandy Creeks. The shape includes Malmaison Road and a few small paths such as Richardson and Kesee Lane. Keeling Drive, a highway lined by small farms, is in the center.

In Granville Hundley's time, Keeling Drive must have been a farmer's simple, unimproved road that connected two large thoroughfares: the stage road between Danville and the Pittsylvania County Courthouse (today's Route 29) and Old Richmond Road headed to the state capitol. Back in the day, roads were named for their destination; by the time of World War I, IQ-crazed America gave numbers to all its roads. Edward Williams put his impressive house on his land in an area that had been first owned in 1766 and 1767 by James Terry, Benjamin Terry, and John King. Hundley's place seems to have been a northwestern boundary for census taker J. B. Callaway. No man named Joe Hendley lived in the county, but John Hundley did. His farm lay somewhere between Edward Williams's Road to the east and Telegraph Road carrying news between Chatham and Danville on the west, surely off the gravel-embedded macadams that swing into wooded bottoms and abut or cross Sandy Creek.

Irishman James McNichols was the white farmer whose property was closest to Granville Hundley's, and according to a 1926 postal map, he lived at the junction of Keeling Drive and modern-day Chestnut Level Road. I feel vaguely certain that today's Route 29, Sandy Creek, Malmaison Road, and Keeling Drive were the general borders of my great-great-grandfather Granville Hundley's land. I'd have to say the mystery of the old farm and the old dwelling was one hidden in plain sight: every time I had been to Blairs in the last five years, I'd blundered across these same roads. All that I was missing for absolute certainty was a tangible landmark.

Hundley's fifty acres were not merely a testament to his individual prowess; it meant something concrete to the others around him. A combination of family and friends constituted a little village on his acres by Sandy Creek. In 1880 between Granville Hundley and the next land-

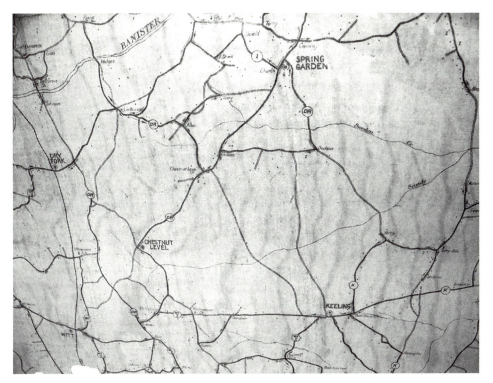

1926 Pittsylvania County postal route map. Library of Virginia, Richmond.

owner, William Ferrell, were some five African American households, including my great–grandparents'. (That year was tough; it saw Hundley unable to work for eight months, perhaps due to sickness, perhaps due to accident.) Hundley and his wife, Charity, had living in their house Paul Miller, a fourteen-year-old boy who worked the farm. Closest to them was the next-oldest person, Lucretia Jones, age fifty and living by herself. Hundley's daughter, Adelaide, her husband, Jordan Carter, and their three daughters were next. Then my own great-grandparents, Edward and Celestia, and young Charlie. Then Sarah and Isaac Carter and their six children. Edward and the thirty-eight-year-old Carter were farm laborers, while Jordan Carter and Granville Hundley were listed in the US census as farmers. One black man in the area, a twenty-two-year-old named Hugh Garland, could read.

Hundley owned the land, so I wondered what particular quality Jordan Carter might have had to elevate his occupational status. I guessed that the two Carters were brothers, though a wealthy county planter named Jesse Carter had owned scores of people in 1860, perhaps causing the name to be quite common. Paul Miller, Jordan Carter, Isaac Carter, and Edward Jackson must have worked the Hundley forty acres, as did their sons when they became old enough. At the time in Pittsylvania, a few women, like Sukey Smith and Ella Jones, continued to work the fields in the same capacity as when they were enslaved, but the gravitation to Victorian-era gender norm patterns was under way.

All the people on Hundley's land inhabited some version of the weather-beaten wooden houses that straggle along the shaded overgrowth or bake in the middle of fields lined with red-clay furrows that I had visited in the summer of 2008. The oldest structures in the area today are the tobacco barns made of squared timber, *V*-notched at the corners and daubed with clay at the seams. Now they all have roofs that are finished in tin, but they would have had wooden shingles a century and a half ago, and the cabins occupied by people would have been constructed along a similar plan. Some of the dwellings, however, resembled modern houses in that they had porches and overhanging roofs, windows, and the appearance of two or three rooms. The interiors were faced with coarse boards that were nailed up, milled lumber perhaps; but the exterior covering seems well within the ability of a person familiar with sawyering and the ability to set himself to a blistering task for long hours. The biggest difference between the two dwelling types, I suppose, is that the cabins typically had dirt floors, whereas the lumber houses would have been built on a wooden deck and may have had stone piers for a foundation. No structure that had wooden posts sunk into the ground could have endured the sun and the rain to exist today, but you can almost imagine people arguing the merits of one type of dwelling over the other. My preference would have gone to whichever was better insulated in winter, which was likely the log cabin dug into the earth.

What sort of attitudes loomed outside the small Hundley camp? I assume the whites Hundley worked with or for, the men who had known him when he was chattel, perhaps even liked or admired him by the time his bought his land, and told him the farm was a good bargain and that he was vigorous enough to make the land pay. John Hubbard, who owned and operated a mill on his land, was a fifty-year-old farmer in 1877; William Ferrell was thirty-five; and Edward Williams was forty-two. Perhaps they showed Hundley respect on account of his years and drive.

His closest neighbor was Ferrell, the veteran of the Thirty-Eighth Infantry and a wagon maker whose land was valued at about $300. He too had bought his modest thirty-acre lot—"from Hubbard's mill gate to the Ringgold Road to Harry Shelton's old line"—from John Hundley, in

Tobacco barn at Chestnut Level near Keeling, Virginia, 2011, detail. Photograph: Lawrence Jackson.

April 1876 for \$130 in gold.[6] The most considerable property was that of Dr. Edward Williams, the neighborhood squire whose father was from England.[7] He also had the most impressive house around, an 1856-built, two-story frame dwelling with three brick chimneys, valued at better than \$500 and sitting on 475 acres with several outbuildings.[8] Williams's land was valuated at \$2,000, and he was the rare person in sufficiently flush domestic circumstances to have a servant, thirty-year-old Martha

Adams, who boarded with her children. The county's gentry and tobacco merchants like Robert Wilson owned buildings worth about $4,000 total. Williams wasn't in that class, but in the years to come he would have a street named for him by the headwaters of Sandy Creek, between the districts of Beavers and Keeling. In 1869 he kept two fine horses valued together at $150 as well as a decent carriage and personal property that totaled about $370, including four cows, two fat hogs, and a $20 pocket watch.[9] He was the most well-to-do man whom my ancestor Granville Hundley regularly saw.

On the east side of Williams's house were seven African American families of farmworkers with no more than $200 among them. Undoubtedly, some of these people had been owned by Williams five years earlier and continued to work his land. Williams owned enough people in 1860—$9,000 worth of them—to employ a professional overseer named Washington Posey. Just west of Williams was a miner born in New York who had purchased a large parcel of land, about the same size as the one Williams himself owned. The Irishman McNichols, who had married a Virginia woman and taken to farming, headed the next household. There was also a nearby dry-goods merchant. For Pittsylvania, this mix of different people was nearly cosmopolitan.

Possibly the neighborhood's oldest resident when Granville Hundley became a property owner was John Hundley, whose birth year was recorded in the 1880 census as 1784. The ancient man had only dwindling wealth toward the end of the century. In 1870 his land had been valued at $1,000, and he had $600 worth of personal estate, much of which must have been cash money, since his home was a common wooden building and since a man his age had little need for a riding horse and little ability to provide proper care for cows and pigs.

A decade later, when he died, Hundley was still prospecting and making land deals. On the last day of August in 1883, his estate was dissolved by his neighbors Levi Hall, tavern owner Walter Beavers, and sixty-three-year old Berry Hughes. The executor, James Lanier, filed "An Account of Sales of the Personal Property of John Hundley Died." Hundley's household and his solvent bonds were valued at $1,747.97.[10] He had lived a remarkably long life, perhaps ninety-nine years. The US census of 1880 gave, for the first time, his occupation as carpenter. If my great-great-grandfather had been owned by this white man, that's the kind of work he would have done too, and it might be a possible clue to the source of his modest savings in the years after slavery.

The appraising of John Hundley's household would have required literate men skilled in accounting to conduct the job. Inside his living quarters, his single most-expensive possession was a $5 bureau. But on his property, his brewing apparatus—his "still, worm & cap," by which he distilled fruit or corn or some other grain to make potable alcohol—was worth $3 more than the bureau. Hundley had a rifle and two shotguns that couldn't fetch as much as $3. But his revolver, evidently of a recent vintage, commanded the price of $4.50. Smith & Wesson was advertising its single- and double-action .32-, .38-, and .44-caliber models at the time.

Near the end of his life, Hundley had lent out large sums to his relatives, probably to his nephews or their children, and his neighbors. There was a bond from J. B. Hundley for $300, and in January of 1882 he had credited $833.33 (a perfect third of $2,500) to his neighbor and the will's executor, James Lanier. At some point in the late 1870s, Hundley had sold Lanier a parcel of land: "197 acres, from Fall Creek to Danville and Pittsylvania Court House Road, bonded by Walter Beavers on South and East and James A. Lanier on North&West to James Lanier for $2500."[11] To the end of his life, Hundley, the son of a rather well-to-do man and from a fairly prominent family, continued to do what he had been doing since at least the 1840s: he was a land speculator who supported himself by conducting real estate deals around the Sandy Creek and Birch Creek areas.

I believe that white John and mulatto Granville Hundley had a bond. I suppose not very long before he died, John Hundley registered his will, in which he split his estate into sixths, giving equal shares to Charles, Thomas, Caleb, and William Hundley and Mary and Elizabeth Fuller. That was exactly the way Granville Hundley wrote his will four years later in 1887, parceling out his goods in sixths. Out of John Hundley's final inventory, when Lanier executed the will and sold off the estate on August 31, 1883, Granville Hundley purchased a single "lot of tools" for 60 cents.[12] Neighbors Ferrell and McNichols bought cheaper lots of tools, and James Lanier bought one worth 75 cents. But Granville Hundley was the only colored man to purchase anything from Hundley's estate, which, considering the neighborhood, makes the affair seem more like a wake than a flea market. To me, the circumstance is one of solemnity. I presume that Granville Hundley knew those household effects rather well.

My great-great-grandfather being the only colored man to obtain anything from Hundley's estate cemented for me, in the absence of anything like a bill of sale at the Pittsylvania County Courthouse, that John Hundley had once owned him. Granville Hundley bought the land eleven years after emancipation, and he knew the household effects well enough to desire and secure a pouch's worth of tools. Based on this teacup's worth of evidence—the fact that he saved money in the aftermath of slavery, bought land from his former slave master, and then participated in the final dissolution of that same person's estate—I think that my ancestor could have interacted with the whites around him on a basis of equity and dignity. The odds that he would continue being able to do that, however, had begun to stack against him.

In November of the year that John Hundley's estate was dissolved, a white man named George Lea fired a concealed pistol at a black man named George Adams in the middle of Danville's Main Street. Attracted by the sound of gunfire, white men attending a lecture by George Cabell, the Democratic congressman from Danville, emerged from the opera house and began shooting into a black crowd, killing five, and violently assaulting blacks at every opportunity.[13] The Democrat mob violence continued for several days, and the interracial Readjuster Party was driven from office by the next year. The guarded optimism that Southside black freeholders must have felt after the Great Jubilee of emancipation formally had begun to sour.

At three o'clock on October 19, 1886, Granville Hundley filed with the county clerk a homestead exemption that granted tax relief based on his property's registered value. In a way, that day, nine years after he had bought his own farm, must have been a kind of general referendum on emancipation. Charles Bilhartz, born in Bavaria and the son of Candidus Bilhartz, a coach maker and gun manufacturer during the Civil War, was the notary public who signed the deed and entered it for my ancestor.

It was an ironic moment for a man who had spent fifty years in bondage in a state where it had been illegal for him to be taught to read. Hundley, whose genetic material I carry but cannot trace because he was on my grandfather's maternal line, was in all likelihood at least a fourth-generation American, whose African and English forebears probably came to this country a generation before the Revolutionary War. My great-great-grandfather had his exemption notarized for him by a man for whom English was a second language. The classic pattern of immigrant whites' status quickly moving past that of the formerly enslaved—even people such as Jews, southern Italians (particularly Sicilians), non-Castilian Spaniards, Arabs, and Irish, who never before would have been considered "white"—was established. National public sentiment shifted on the topic of how freedmen should be treated to the point that even a Northern paper like the *New York Times* could write, "We are now, we hope, past that general humbuggery of social and mental equality that followed the war and was preached North and South."[14]

On his homestead exemption, Granville Hundley claimed property in three categories: land, crops, and material. His tract was

in Pittsylvania County, Virginia on waters of Sandy Creek containing 40 acres more or less&valued at $3.00 per acre.		$120.00
crop of corn 10 barrels valued at $2.50 per Bbl		$25.00
1 curing of Tobacco	" "	$7.00
1 carry all+harness	" "	$5.00

The total of his farm and effects came to $157, and in those years Hundley also had pulling his two-wheel carryall a $30 horse, a sharp improvement over the $10 animal he had owned when he bought his land. Hundley also had four head of cattle (probably cows), three hogs, and $3 worth of firearms.[15]

Forty to fifty acres a dominion did not make, and the land he had bought seemed to have already dipped in value. Creek bottomland was sought after for farming, but it needed to be cleared and buildings put up for it to rise in value, the energetic work of youth. Land, even the freedman's hallowed morsel, turned out to be a weak investment after the war, especially for a man already in his sixties whose most vigorous years were well behind him.

Hundley would not have planted all of his acreage at any one time, if that were even possible. He had a couple of acres for corn and maybe a small parcel, prime land, which he had mauled and fertilized for tobacco. Every year a sizable percentage needed to lie fallow, and the fast-growing weeds and shrubs and saplings quickly overtook whatever was left unattended. Every growing season, land would have to be reclaimed, and manured and limed. It was a cycle of hard, unending, regular work. And I was uncertain if Hundley's cupboard of ten 200-pound-barrels of corn and a seven-dollar curing of tobacco—less than 100 pounds total, depending on the grade—made it worth his efforts.

Besides, the year of his exemption, tobacco was a perilous investment. In June of 1886, Pittsylvania farmers were taking nine cents per pound for their crop, which was up half a penny from April, but quite a bit distant from the tidy mark in January 1885 of thirteen cents.[16] On October 1, 1886, a surprise frost ruined crops in the field. By December of that year, Pittsylvania County's great human economic engine, William Sutherlin, admitted that "the extreme low price of tobacco and the dullness of the trade with manufacturers and dealers, is causing great anxiety among farmers in this section of Virginia and North Carolina."[17] Granville Hundley had got half a white man's chance, but then he had all a white man's trouble.

Perhaps he had miscalculated when to cut the stalks, grown too much of the crop, or was unable to produce a fine and sought-after grade of Bright Leaf, or maybe the weather had conspired against him. Even if he had as much as one hundred pounds, that would have been only enough to prize into a small barrel. Growing a crop that size seems merely a gesture to me, a way of limping along with the tenor of the place and the old time. It also strikes me as evidence of a grail for him that I hadn't perceived, a dream beyond emancipation and even landownership itself: the dream of belonging to the planter class.

I'm not even certain how much tobacco my ancestor personally cultivated during his life in bondage, though I doubt he would have waited until he was seventy-one to tempt fate with a new and complex crop. Maybe Granville had worked during slavery in some sort of trade, like carpentry, and he knew how to build tobacco barns or hogsheads better than cultivating the weed. Which is not to rule out that the small crop might also have provided his only cash money, to pay his taxes and the like, or maybe to allow him to receive credit from a local merchant. But 1886 was a devastating year. By its end, moderate-grade Virginia tobacco averaged three cents a pound.[18]

Facing financial ruin toward the end of his life after having survived slavery and then actually having joined the tiny percentage of freeholders must have stung. The conservative wisdom of landownership and self-reliant sustenance farming that a man like Hundley must have stood for would not have served his children particularly well. That year probably crushed the dreams of many a black laborer aspiring to own a tobacco farm. The traditional wisdom that Hundley could offer would have been doomed.

The modest white men who had fought for the Confederacy, who with their children would be delirious over the war in Cuba and the Philippines, in the main were deeply opposed to three things, none of which had much to do with the social-equality chimera that propelled the *Plessy* Supreme Court decision of 1896. They resisted the education of freedmen, they tried their best to prevent freedmen from using the ballot, and they bitterly resented the economic independence of freedmen that came about through self-supporting farms.

Paradoxically, while freed blacks, before and after slavery, were disparaged as a class, whites enjoyed intimate affection with individual blacks. On occasion the public attitudes seemed even deliberately generous. In that hard year of 1886, the *Danville Register & Bee* reprinted an article reporting the decapitation of a black man. Locomotive mishaps of all kinds killed Virginians frequently, and the derailment of the mail train "Old 97" in 1903 that slew nine became the source of folk ballads; but black men in particular were known to be found lying headless across the rails. "Last Tuesday morning, the body of a negro man named Patrick Moon was found on the railroad track, near Barksdale depot," began the short news brief, reprinted from the Halifax paper.

> He had been run over by some train not known. Moon lived at Meadville and had been to Danville to sell his tobacco. Some think he was murdered and placed upon the track. It was "only a poor coloured man," and yet the hearts of his wife and children must feel the grief that those of the bluest blood would experience. The *Record* extends its sympathies to them in this hour of their withering woe.[19]

The Barksdale depot was the stop after Sutherlin and the first stop in Halifax on the Danville–Richmond line. Perhaps knowing about these printed words publicly extending sympathy and using a vocabulary apart from the day-to-day would have consoled Patrick Moon's family. I guess that if I could not read, and if people I admired or at least acknowledged as very powerful could read, and they read this to me, I would be uplifted and feeling better. Being invoked in the web of a socially esteemed skill, a connection to the impressive technology of the written word, must have mattered for something. And obviously the editors of both the *Halifax Record* and the *Danville Bee* were invested in the appearance of a certain kind of liberal notion of tolerance and charity. Perhaps this attitude was also evident in some of Granville Hundley's dealings with his white neighbors.

But the mildly liberal solicitousness of this newspaper article was outdone by spiraling outrage expressed in Southern papers after the Civil War. In the same December 1886 newspaper, but on the front page, was an account of a lynching in South Carolina, "A Negro Hung and Riddled with Bullets," "for attempting to commit an outrageous assault upon a respectable young white girl."[20] I suspect that the "several hundred negroes" who tried to protect the condemned, Caesar Robinson, doubted the legitimacy of the rape charge, but after a gun battle they were driven off, or at least that was what the *Danville Register & Bee* claimed. Another newspaper in that city favored the return of the whipping post for penitentiary-bound "rogues," five times as likely to be black as white.[21] Lacerating force would shape the freedman's future.

A few weeks before this spate of accounts, on the eve of the November election, Danville police killed a black Democrat named James Hargrove.

The *Danville Register* seemed objective when it reprinted a Republican version of the story: "The condition of affairs here is an outrage upon civilization: just prior to every election a few colored men are murdered here to intimidate them from voting their honest sentiments."[22] But the Democrat-inclined *Register* determined that Hargrove had not been martyred on the altar of white supremacy. The black man was "killed by an officer in defense of his own life." In addition to asserting that Hargrove's death was a justifiable homicide, the paper took a swipe at black Southsiders. Since the black man was "a democrat...it is said on good authority that the colored people refused to give him a Christian burial for that reason." Toward the end of his days, my grandfather's grandfather Granville Hundley knew this increasingly tense climate; but it was nearly the total horizon of life for my father's grandfather Edward Jackson.

The year of the homestead exemption and the tobacco-crop disaster convinced Hundley of something: the end of his time was near. Ten years after officially joining the landowning class, on January 25, 1887, he made his will, saying that he possessed "forty acres, more or less...situated... on Sandy Creek and adjoining lands of Dr. E. Williams, William Ferrell and others."[23] He probably made the will because his health had begun to fail. He kept at the land, however, until he died around 1893. His life might be said to have boiled down to ten vital years of landowning freedom between 1877 and 1887.

Even though the entire act of filing a will at the Pittsylvania County Courthouse in Chatham in the 1880s must have been rare—or even prestigious—for an African American, it might also have been the act of a haunted man, fearful that his heirs would never possess the fruit of his long struggle. In Virginia after slavery had ended, the relations between blacks and whites took one turn after another. When Granville Hundley himself left this earth and his holdings were apportioned to his six children, his property became humble sustenance land that might have been difficult for them to profit from enough to even pay their annual property tax.

On the twenty-first of March, 1893, the will was proved by the oath of Ned Adams and entered under the authority of attorney James Lanier, the same man who had handled John Hundley's affairs. Granville Hundley, born around the time that our national anthem was written in Baltimore's harbor, was deceased. Two men had witnessed his will: thirty-four-year-old Ned Adams, who lived a couple of fields away, as well as Rasmus Mayhan. These were Granville Hundley's black male comrades, and they observed something in the county that was rare then and rare today: a colored man passing on an inheritance to his children. The white executor Lanier owned Sandy Creek property along with Dr. Williams, Levi Hall, and John Hundley. I never found any muster roll showing these men to have been in the Confederate armed forces, but these white landowners had known Granville Hundley in slavery, and they had known him in freedom. These men constituted a parallel peer group for him, after a fashion, and for a while Hundley must have represented to them an acceptable version of reputable black freedom.

In the first clause of my great-great-grandfather's will, he gave all his land to his twenty-six-year-old son John, who lived at the time with his older sister, Harriet Robinson. Harriet was twenty years older than John, and apparently the order determined John to be the executor of sorts, which probably made sense because he was the only person who had the legal last name of Hundley. It may have also been significant that African American John Hundley had never been enslaved to any man. In any event, the will instructed John to parcel out the land to himself and the rest of his siblings: one-sixth each to Granville's oldest son, Nat Henry Hutchings, daughter Fanny Fulch, daughter Harriet Robinson (called "Robertson" in the will), daughter Adelaide Carter, and daughter Celestia Jackson, my great-grandmother.

I had known from the US census of 1870 that Hutchings was a neighbor; now I know that he was also kin. Although their houses were within calling distance, I never would have imagined the paternal-filial relation until I read Granville Hundley's will. Hutchings and wife Permelia had several daughters, Martha, Mary, and Fanny, and two sons, Granville and newborn Robert—a group of names that binds tighter the family connection for me. In terms of my father's grandparents, I figure his grandfather Edward Jackson had a hand in naming the oldest children: William, Edward, Lily, and John. Then in 1895 and 1900, Celestia named the ones my parents took me to visit before the end of the 1960s: my grandfather and my twin great-aunts. My great-grandmother named her last children after her older brother, Nathaniel, and his two children, her nieces Mary and Martha. I never knew that my grandfather and father had a middle name, Henry, until I looked at the census of 1920 when either Edward or Celestia listed "Nat Henry" as their twenty-four-year-old son. My father was a junior, so his name would have to have been the same.

By naming my own son Nathaniel, I have participated in a family tradition that had an antebellum history that I knew nothing about, that I guess my own father knew nothing about.

Nathaniel Hutchings's oldest son, Granville, born a couple of months

I do hereby constitute and appoint Thomas W Lanier exe cutor of this my last will and testament. In witness whereof I have hereunto set my — and affixed my seal this 25th day of January 1887

Granville Hundley {seal}

Teste
Beverly Mayhan
Ned his × Adams
mark

Granville Hundley, 1887 will. Clerk's Office, Pittsylvania County, Virginia.

after the Civil War had begun, had his own large family by the end of the
century. The son respected the same naming traditions that connected
him to his grandfather. Granville Hutchings had a daughter named Ellie,
a daughter named Cornelia (for his mother), a daughter named Elsie,
and a daughter named Morning (recorded by the census taker, Charles
Lovelace, as "Moaning") like his grandfather's wife, and his aunt Celestia's mother. Perhaps even my grandfather's younger sister Martha named
my modern-day cousin, whose name sounds like "Carnel" to me, after
this woman Cornelia. (It became harder to track when the surnames of
Granville Hundley's and Nathaniel Hutchings's children were turned
into "Hunley" and "Hutchins" and "Hunly" and "Huchins.") All in all,
I think the persistent naming of children for an older relative is a good
thing. It is, after all, the resumption of the African way.

The reason Granville Hundley's son Nathaniel chose to carry the last
name Hutchings had something to do with the complex tangle of race
and slavery, a tangle I was unable to untie. Nathaniel Hutchings had lost
about twenty-five years of his life to slavery, and probably in Pittsylvania. Perhaps he was a child from an early slave marriage that Granville
Hundley had consummated before he met my great-great-grandmother,
a woman called Morning on county court marriage records and Charity on the census. Perhaps this woman Morning was a wife after slavery who insisted that the teenager keep the name of another household?
Of course, Morning and Charity might not be the same person. What if
my great-grandmother Celestia gave her real mother's name, Morning,
on her 1878 marriage certificate, but lived with a woman called Charity in
the immediate aftermath of slavery?

Another possibility was that Nathaniel deliberately chose not to take
the name Hundley. Consider black Civil War hero Robert Small's testimony concerning the problem of surnames among the ex-slave population: "Very few take their father's names—they choose them for
themselves."[24] This was a declaration of a practice, not an explanation of
it, so the rationale behind the choosing of different names earlier continued to puzzle me. But I found a clear explanation in the remarks of a black
character in a postbellum novel set about twenty miles south of Pittsylvania. Nimbus Ware rejects his owner's name, saying, "I ain't a-gwine ter
brand my chillen wid no sech slave-mark! Nebber!... I ain't gwine ter
war his name ner giv it ter my chillen ter mind 'em dat der daddy wuz
jes anudder man's critter at one time."[25] It was certainly possible that for
their own reasons, sons like Nathaniel Henry Hutchings and Edward
Jackson might have deeply resented the white men who owned their

fathers, even if the fathers had made peace with the same people. Perhaps an element of lingering bitterness was the key to Edward Jackson's name-change mystery as well.

The county register held a single record of marriage for Nat Hutchings, to eighteen-year-old Mary Jane Coleman, which took place on September 22, 1885. It was at least his second marriage, and he identified himself on the register as a widower. Hutchings verified that his father's name was Granville Hundley, but for his mother's name he left a blank. How could his mother have been unknown? I asked myself. And then I answered: What if she had been white?

The 1870 US census taker J. W. Cole classified both Hundley and Hutchings as mulattoes in appearance. Would Hundley, Granville and Nathaniel both, have sought to keep such an 1841 scandal from the county record, or might they have been disinclined to share that kind of information with one of the county's particular clerks? Could Granville Hundley's having fathered a child with a white woman in his late twenties have anything to do with the fact that he only seems to show up as an enslaved man with John Hundley on an 1845 tax list? Was Hutchings protecting his father in 1885 by refusing to reveal his real mother? There really were many possibilities, and my fancy seemed to alight on the most sensational one.

Only rough guesses shed light on the household relation of the father and son before the war. In 1860 the physician John M. Hutchings owned a twenty-one-year-old male whom he described as mulatto in appearance, along with fifteen other people who lived in three houses and worked perhaps as much as seven hundred acres.[26] Hutchings also owned several young girls (Celestia could have been among them) and a thirty-nine-year-old woman who could have been Morning, and the physician-farmer probably employed an overseer named Willis Patterson. Hutchings lived in Pleasant Gap, pretty close to the middle of the White Oak Mountain range—which seemed, at least when I thought of the family as having lived either in Danville or near the depot at Ringgold, prohibitively far.

But slave marriage and family life took place at a distance, I reminded myself. I had been getting so close to these people, my ancestors, that I had started to imagine their lives under conditions similar to my own. But a husband and wife and their natural children sharing the same cabin day in and day out was irregular, partly because most owners had smallish crews of the enslaved: a handful of working-age adults and twice as many children. On top of that, black men and women disliked the day-

In the Gap of the Peaks of Otter, Virginia.

Gap Otter, Virginia. Note roadway and fencing. From Edward King, *The Great South* (1875).

to-day indignity of observing their spouses at the utter mercy of another human being. Perhaps Granville Hundley didn't think so much of picking his way along darkened paths after work for a tough eight or nine miles between Sandy Creek and the Pleasant Gap neighborhood over a twenty-five year span. Maybe he strengthened his constitution by handling the distance, a "right smart step," and seeing his family near the White Oak Mountain during slavery time when they seemed not to have lived together. Maybe Granville himself had been owned by Hutchings at the time of Nathaniel's birth and then, after joining John Hundley's household in 1845, he became best known to his new Sandy Creek neighborhood by that name?

My grandfather probably knew this uncle, whose first and middle names he shared. In 1900 Nathaniel Hutchings was still living with wife Mary, his junior in age by thirty years. They had many children in the household: eighteen-year-old George; fifteen-year-old Laura; ten-year-old Ella; eight-year-old Benjamin; six-year-old Phoebe; three-year-old Aleas; and one-year-old Nat H. My grandfather Nathaniel Henry Jackson and his first cousin Nathaniel Henry Hutchings might have grown up together and been playmates.

A year after Granville Hundley died, a sea change throughout Virginia brought about the voting method the nation would adopt in 1896 with the Supreme Court's *Plessy* decision. Even if he had done something extraordinary like join the radical party in the 1870s, my great-grandfather Edward, who never learned to read or write, would almost certainly have had his vote removed from the ballot box along with those of his black friends when Virginia state senator M. L. Walton successfully sponsored the secret ballot law in 1894. The law prohibited symbols or party names on the ballot, and required voters to cross out the names of all the candidates they rejected in the space of 150 seconds. Then Governor Phillip McKinney admitted that the new law effectively disenfranchised blacks: "Negroes often hesitated in getting a Democratic election judge to assist them in marking their ballots; others were timid or ashamed to acknowledge their ignorance; and many who attempted to vote could not correctly mark their ballots in the allotted time."[27] Black political participation in Virginia was essentially finished, and with it much of the aspirations of freedmen for a life better than what they had known in slavery.

By 1902 when Pittsylvania Democrat Claude Swanson became one of Virginia's senators to the US Congress, adjoining neighborhoods like Ringgold and Laurel Grove had 2 people voting Republican and 146 for Swanson. In Keeling, 59 voted for Swanson and 1 person for the Republicans, and in Kentuck 103 for Swanson and 1 for Davis, the Republican candidate.[28] In Virginia overall, an estimated 42 percent of people voting against the Democratic Party in 1893 dropped to 2 percent by 1900.[29] When blacks complained that their rights were being trampled, they were accused of "vile slander" or called "Colored Kickers," who frothed for race war by voicing unwarranted grievances.[30]

In the late 1880s, the Danville newspapers topped off the disenfranchisement and the reports regaling black violence and buffoonery with new advertisements featuring black caricatures for "Gold Dust Twins" soap and "Ethiopian Pile Ointment" salve. White people were bombarded with images that helped to erase their moral compass when it came to black Americans. The early advertisements complemented the headlines on the marquis at the Danville Academy of Music. In March of 1886, the duo James McIntyre and Thomas Heath along with thirty-five other vaudevillians arrived in town to perform their famous minstrel show, "McIntyre and Heath's Model Minstrels."[31] The two blackface entertainers performed skits as Alexander Hambeltonian, the clowning stable boy, and Henry Jones, the sharpie. Their popular drama "Ham Tree" involved their climbing a tree three hundred feet high to find the holy pork rump. McIntyre and Heath were still in their twenties when they entertained Danville with those enduring blackface routines. They would have careers

Advertisement, *Danville (VA) Register*, January 1885. Microfilm, Library of Virginia.

for half a century and would influence their field widely, from Ziegfeld Follies star Bert Williams to cinema icon Al Jolson.

Seven years after her father had died, Celestia and her husband, Edward Jackson, were still farming for a living, and I suppose by Sandy Creek. But in spite of Granville Hundley's having left her about eight acres, the Jacksons, married twenty-two years, no longer worked land that they owned.[32] In the years since Hundley's death, they had become renters—"metayers," W. E. B. Du Bois would have called them in his 1903 collection *The Souls of Black Folk*. Perhaps they had become Colored Kickers, and resented having to cultivate relationships with whites of the new breed, who drilled in the militia, the Danville Grays. Perhaps Edward had joined Danville's African American militia, the Douglass Guards, which doesn't seem to have lasted in public after 1884. It would be so easy to fit them into the narrative that includes the loss of voting rights, the Supreme Court decision, and the end of the Readjuster Party, but I'd bet their slipping downward was cozier than that, with an almost tactile sense of gloom and identifiable culprits close at hand.

The US census of 1920 marked my twenty-four-year-old grandfather Nathaniel Jackson, like his slave-born parents, as unable to read or write.

However, my great-aunts, five years younger than their brother, were considered literate. Perhaps Edward and Celestia abandoned Granville Hundley's dream of farm life to move a little closer to a school, so that at least some of their children would learn. Perhaps the scuttling of the yeoman vision was as simple as that: relinquish the land to move within walking distance of a school that would take your children.

When I worked on a master's degree in Ohio in 1991, I met two of my grandfather's nieces. My cousin Elizabeth, a statuesque woman who had moved from Danville to Cincinnati in the mid-twentieth century, showed me a black and white photograph of her mother, my grandfather's sister Sally; I could remember her from visits to Blairs during my childhood. In the picture, Aunt Sally, big-boned in the same way as her daughter Elizabeth, was standing in front of the chinked-in cabin that had been the family home; my cousin said to me, "We've come a long way." Then her son, a dealer in Afrocentric books who has children my age, told me something that his mother didn't say, but must have told him. He said that his great-grandmother—he did not say or seem to know her name, but mentioned her only as mother to Sally and Nat— had knocked a white man off his horse after he tried to molest or interfere with her children. I can't recall precisely which word my cousin's son used, but somehow the horseman had threatened the children, and Celestia had responded with her fists.

At the time I learned this, I had imagined that it must have been a mythical quarrel with a plantation-style "riding boss." But now I am sure it was not that. If my grandfather were a boy, even if only the age of my young son Mitchell, it might have had something to do with their losing their farm, a triangle of events including Granville Hundley's death in 1893, my grandfather Nathaniel Jackson's birth in 1895, and the US census of 1900 that shows the family back at square one. A generation later, the Jacksons were starting out with what they had the day after slavery ended.

9 · The Reckoning

Frederick Douglass's favorite line from Abraham Lincoln's 1865 inaugural address was "until all the wealth piled by the bond-man's two hundred and fifty years of unrequited toil shall be sunk, and until every drop of blood drawn with the lash, shall be paid by another drawn with the sword."[1] But overwhelmingly, the rest of the country preferred the "with malice toward none" part of the address. I suspect that included my great-great-grandfather Granville Hundley, and maybe even his cohort of men and women, who had spent so many years of their lives enslaved. Perhaps the very opportunity for some years of freedom was inspiration enough for him to turn his hand to farming in the 1870s. Granville Hundley, whatever complex choices he made, had built up enough savings under slavery so that he could have a stake in some land five years after bondage. He lived his whole life among black and white neighbors, seemingly maintaining good relationships with everyone, but he especially seems to have forged a tie, during bondage and beyond, with his owner, John Hundley.

By contrast, his son-in-law Edward Jackson probably never cast the strong relationships with whites that his wife Celestia's father did. He never amassed any capital, nor is it clear that his children were able to.

It would take the expansion of heavy industry and global military conflict to moderately improve the circumstances of my family. The migration of African Americans like my relatives to Washington, D.C., and the major cities of Ohio, Pennsylvania, and Maryland changed the demographics of Pittsylvania County entirely, from approximate racial parity among its 52,602 residents in 1880 to roughly 11 whites for every black among its 61,271 inhabitants by 1930. Black people simply fled the county. When my dad was born in Danville in 1932 in a warren of frame houses south of William Sutherlin's mansion, which by then was the public library that no one my father was related to could use, the logic of white supremacy in Pittsylvania was not merely an aesthetic logic — it was a logic of ineluctable human force. My grandparents took my dad to Roanoke, where my grandmother's family had moved. After they divorced, my grandfather, a railroad fireman, returned to his hometown.

So there's no little surprise that what I finally come to about my Virginia heritage and what got passed on to me is this: we survived slavery as a people by ever making ourselves into something that white people couldn't assimilate. We became nuggets of obdurateness, but without ever fixing who we were or, for that matter, putting too much faith in whom we were with. I guess this was so because we didn't always have the means to tell our young people what we knew, and we counted on the fact of their stumbling and imprecision to make them rely on and develop their imagination. But since the contours of the message became the key to unlocking the message itself, they had also invested their faith in a slow and maddening and torturous process. Undoubtedly this is grave ancestral wisdom, but to at least one of its recipients, it feels perplexing and incomplete.

American liberal scholarship doesn't try to quantify uncertainty among the enslaved or their descendants. The academics who write about slavery see strong family bonds among the enslaved, and they're not of a single mind that the enslavement was condemned by its survivors. In the remarkable research and writings of the respected scholarly elite, I nearly always come across a kind of waffling over the issue of slavery as well as the Civil War and its aftermath. The general line of reasoning holds that the oppressive legal and condign power was regularly creased and wrinkled and overcome by the wonders of human agency.

Here are the words of Melvin Ely, an academic whose diligence in the archives I admire: "White authorities and white neighbors, for all their moral failings and acts of callousness, left space in which free blacks could act as something other than slaves."[2] Well, did the whites *leave* a space, or did the blacks, free and enslaved alike, *take* the space? To me, this distinction makes all the difference and turns things around.

A prizewinning historian, Ely insists on making a meaningful distinction between Virginia laws and actual behavior in the Old South. "White ambivalence or lassitude often, and the decent impulses of white individuals sometimes, created openings within a system whose benighted racial credo seemed to rule out any sort of flexibility," he states in a recent work. This is an enlightened contemporary view that seeks new anchoring points for racial relations. Ely warns us away from "the easy conclusion that contempt for blacks is unvarying among whites." But this enlightened perspective always seems to reach the same plateau: "The real shame of the Old South was that white people recognized the humanity of blacks in dozens of ways every day, yet kept them in bondage or second-class citizenship despite that knowledge."[3] The final analysis has to be about white power and magnanimity.

Then I read a narrative account from Louis Hughes, a mulatto born in Virginia and sold in Richmond, who lived and worked in Memphis and labored at the Confederate saltworks near Mobile during the war. In June of 1865, well after the Civil War had ended, Hughes and his family were still being held in bondage on a Mississippi plantation by a cutthroat who had ridden with Nathan Bedford Forrest, the professional slave dealer, Confederate general responsible for massacres of black soldiers, and, after the war, the founder of the Ku Klux Klan. An intelligent, well-traveled man, Hughes realized he was free but still had to "escape" from the plantation, make his way to Memphis, and then pay Union cavalrymen to engage in a ruse to secure freedom for himself and his family.[4] Hughes's ex-owner, William McGhee, intended to either re-enslave him and his family or kill them all.

Even if Ely's depiction is more of a representative truth than Hughes's experience was, and even if every library in North America and Europe confirms that reality, I am not consoled. Just as soon as I am presented with evidence of possible decency of white settlers, I have to contend with a transcript of horror that's more gruesome than what I was capable of imagining.

When we black Americans who barely know the legal names of our own grandparents, we whose presence in this country dates back for ten or eleven generations—when we look back to the era of bondage, we do this from the perspective of the families that we know today. The now grandfatherly male cousins who have never, in all their lives, had regular employment. The people known by "street" names, who never grew into adult names. The sisters, aunts, and female cousins raising children in poverty, sometimes with genteel flair, sometimes not. We are seeing immigrants of every hue offer lip service to our historic plight, take advantage of the legislation that we pioneered for two centuries, and then pass us by. We are thinking about the mental illness that seems as much a coping style as a neurological disorder. We are thinking about a people who, as long as they can recall, have experienced a simmering anger that bubbled under the surface and that was sometimes dampened by doses of alcohol. We are thinking about black people using illegal and frowned-upon narcotic remedies for a hundred years for the same reason that tens of millions of Americans ever used Dexamyl, methamphetamines, and Prozac. We are thinking about neglected communities and decaying houses and public services that operate under multiple standards. We are thinking that in every new place we have ever traveled in the United States, we found a community with posh homes, quaint, comfortable businesses that catered to desires we had yet to form fully, and regular traditions we found enchanting and seductive—and yet, just on the other side of the tracks were the crumbling huts for us; and even when they wore fresh coats of lavender or lime or canary or fuchsia paint, it didn't shrink the blemish on the country that willed this.

Somehow there is no fitting in for us as a group with all our history. My ancestors in the nineteenth century married in droves. They were people from small communities who couldn't put down their father's name or their own birthday on an official document, or they walked to the altar with their outside children. They were semirural women related to me who had one occupation: "keeping house." And then to see them coming together in the 1870s and 1880s, and knowing how it would only fall apart in the next generation on their pilgrimage to the cities, is too much. As soon as they left the farm and the crop and went to work in towns for wages, the family fell apart, and it fell further apart when they moved to the Northern urban areas. Maybe it should have fallen apart, and I am not sure that it didn't remind them of another enslavement: women to their men, and men to their children.

◆   ◆   ◆

I suspect that what happened between the generations of Granville Hundley and Edward Jackson was a gross injustice compounded. I think that Hundley could look at freedom in and of itself as a great-enough thing to wipe out what Thomas Jefferson famously called the "ten thousand recollections by the blacks, of the injuries they have sustained."[5] I doubt if Edward Jackson was able to do that, if the fiat that ended outright bondage was enough for him. I think that he might have just as easily considered the past of slavery wrong and unjust, an attitude of bitterness that would have interfered with any strategic diplomacy with whites.

And here I find Thomas Jefferson's outrageous disingenuousness haunting us still. He was a unique man who must have had his share of sleepless nights. He well understood the ethical disaster brought on by the tobacco economy, but he could not raise his own ethical standards enough to escape the vulgar prejudice of his day. Yet, it would not have been impossible to do.

The black Boston poet Phillis Wheatley died in 1784, a year before Jefferson's views on the Negro became widely known. Wheatley was well respected at the intellectual hub of the colonies and loomed as an example of a genuine African *philosophe*. Voltaire reviewed her work, and she was very nearly presented at the Court of St. James to the king and queen of England.[6] She considered herself a "vent'rous *Afric* in her [Wheatley's own] great design." Her most famous poem entertaining issues of race and identity, "On Being Brought from Africa to America," shows Wheatley using the certified tools at hand—Christianity and the classics—to argue against racial prejudice and bigotry. The range of this black teenager's impressive talent and political effort reached its peak with her 1773 "To Maecenas," an allegorical poem that compares the situation of the talented African in America to the talented African in classical Rome. The difference was that Maecenas, the unprejudiced Roman patron of the arts, did not exist on the American scene.

The poem contains a kernel of historical controversy because of an intriguing footnote. In the past, Maecenas has aided Homer, Virgil, and eventually Terence, nearly a contemporary of Cicero's. Beside Terence's name, Wheatley places an asterisk directing the reader's attention to a note at the bottom of the page which reads, "He was an African by birth." The Carthaginian Terence for Wheatley is inspired by the fullness of Roman society, "all the choir," and he has "his soul replenished, and his bosom fired."[7] Roman society from top to bottom assists in cultivating and embracing Terence's precocious talent. Yet Wheatley ponders why this "one alone of Afric's sable race" receives nourishment from Rome, the imperial power that had enslaved him. She questions the absence of succor for a woman such as herself writing in colonial America.

Though she did not live to see it, Wheatley's question, and her evidence in the footnote, was roughly dismissed by Americans of power, starting with Jefferson. In *Notes on the State of Virginia*, the book that Southern extremists quoted from memory during the constitutional debates over the slavery question, Jefferson had condemned Wheatley in a passage following a discourse on the foul odors of black people and the assertion that African-descended men lusted after white women, because whites belonged to a higher species: "Religion indeed has produced a Phyllis Whately [*sic*]; but it could not produce a poet. The compositions published under her name are beneath the dignity of criticism. The heroes of the Dunciad are to her, as Hercules to the author of that poem."[8] Jefferson, who had obtained his classical education from the renowned liberal George Wythe, went on to turn Wheatley's very own self-footnoted argument in "To Maecenas" against her. "Epictetus, Terence, and Phaedrus, were slaves," he averred. "But they were of the race of whites. It is not their condition then, but nature, which has produced this distinction."[9] Jefferson combated Wheatley by redefining antiquity.

Of course, as Wheatley determinedly informs her reader, Terence — that is, Publius Terentius Afer, as his name appeared on all his works — was an African, born in Carthage and hardly "of the race of whites."[10] According to records from Jefferson's library, which he later sold to Congress, Jefferson owned two books by Roman poet Publius Terentius Afer. In the 1725 quarto *Terentius Bentleii*, the poet's name is written as "Publii Terentii Afri Comoediae." The first name is his rank, the second is his given name, the third is his place of origin or family name, and the last is his occupation. In the 1740 octavo *Delphini*, the name appears as "P. Terentii Carthaginensis Afri."[11] The cognomen Afer denoted the regional origin of the Roman poet, and was a common addition used to indicate foreigners. Terence, born about 195 BC, lived at the end of the era of the Second Punic War, a political event that must have brought thousands of Africans in contact with Roman Empire. He was described in Jefferson's copy of Suetonius's *Life of Terence* as *colore fusco*, which means "dark complected."[12]

Like other white Virginians who were educated in the 1760s, Jefferson read, in addition to Terence, Suetonius's *Vitae Caesarum*. Suetonius would have informed him of the complexion of Terence. Though *Vitae Caesarum* is not indexed in his library (*Opera omnia quae extant* is the Suetonius text listed in E. Millicent Sowerby's catalog), *Lives of the Caesars* is certainly where Jefferson obtained his knowledge of the treatment of slaves in Augustan Rome.[13] He drew an extended analogy between colonial Virginian slavery and what he knew of classical slavery in *Notes on the State of Virginia*.

The notes he made on Terence's plays and preserved in his literary commonplace book while a student at William and Mary are also extremely revealing. Some are taken from Terence's play *Andria*, and they range over the profitability of conformity and the onerous burden of truth-telling. Remarkably enough, Jefferson was attracted to the following passage:

> He fell in easily with the ways of all his acquaintances, gave himself up to his company, and joined heartily in their pursuits; never opposed anyone,

never put himself ahead of anybody. That keeps clear of jealousy and is the simplest way of getting a good name and making friends.

SOSIA: A wise start in life. Nowadays it's complaisance that makes friends and truthfulness is the mother of unpopularity.[14]

Jefferson's notebook entries during his student years afford an intriguing interpretation of his vociferous condemnation of Wheatley in 1784. His surprising and unsubstantiated declaration of a "white" Terence attaches well to a credo that embraces common prejudice for a comfortable, popular life.

Jefferson was always uncomfortable with the institution of slavery, but he also wanted, like most of us, to be well liked. In the "Original Draught of the Declaration of Independence," he excoriated King George for waging

> a cruel war against human nature itself, violating it's most sacred rights of life and liberty in the persons of a distant people who never offended him, captivating and carrying them into slavery in another hemisphere, or to incur miserable death in their transportation hither . . . the *Christian* king of Great Britain determined to keep open a market where MEN should be bought and sold.[15]

Jefferson was not a maverick or alone in his sentiments: the great majority of the half a million freedpeople in 1860 were descendants of people freed in the famous waves of manumission during the last quarter of the eighteenth century, before the introduction of the cotton gin, when chattel slavery seemed about to collapse under the weight of its contradictions. But at the Second Continental Congress in Philadelphia in the summer of 1776, Jefferson's strong antislavery sentiment was "the mother of unpopularity." His determination eight years later to dismiss Wheatley—a reader of Suetonius's *Vitae Caesarum* who had won her manumission partly on the excellence of her own Latin skill—along with his decision to whiten Terence, ironically mimics *Andria*'s lines about the benefits of conformity. When confronted with the mind and body of a black woman whom he could not possess, Jefferson rested his case on the common-law prejudice of the day.

If, like not more than a few prominent American statesmen, Jefferson willfully manipulated the evidence, what can we expect from the lesser men? The incontinent example he set has been dutifully followed by generations of American writers and thinkers: it's what led Ralph Ellison to label America a nation "ethically schizophrenic."[16] Here's an example of what Ellison meant. In Vermont I once saw the gentle Haitian novelist Edwidge Danticat being taken to task by a middle-aged white American who demanded to be told this: precisely what portion of her talent did she owe to her years of education in the United States? The Middlebury man was incapable of conceiving of the debts he owed to Ms. Danticat. He could not bring himself to acknowledge that Haiti's defeat of Napoleon enabled the Louisiana Purchase, enabling the cotton fortunes and another sixty years of slavery. He registered no inkling of the US Marine occupation of Haiti between 1915 and 1934, the massacres, the bayoneted children, the gutting of the national treasury, or our overthrow of Haiti's labor government in 1957 and the installation of the bloody Duvalier regime. Ms. Danticat's interrogator showed no awareness that on account of a simple feature like skin color, on a visit to the United States a few years later, Ms. Danticat's uncle would perish chained to the bed of a Florida hospital after being unjustly detained and denied medical care.

I have confronted the same kind of impasse on my journey to the lives of my ancestors. What is the link between the people I met and the people I never could meet, or really even hear stories about, and my own modern life that involves air travel three or four times a year, sometimes even to foreign lands, that lodges me on occasion in stories-high glass and steel towers, and on rare occasion casts my image across a digital screen? The rapid movement across space and time creates a mirage. The disembodied human voices and images electrically and digitally conveyed are illusions of meaning. I am more interested in looking for myself by way of my gathering these ancestors of mine; I want my travel to go in that direction. Besides, what is the value of knowing they are there if I do not reach back to them? In searching for them, I can change them for myself, and they can live again.

Yet I can't make my way to them fully. Black American I may be, but I find the ethical schizophrenia, the Jefferson plague, the "ambivalence or lassitude" afflicting me too. There is a note at the bottom of this onscreen page that I have been typing into my computer for many years. In bold it says, "Talk to people from the area. Look up your relatives as far as it goes." I have made it to blood kin exactly twice, in 2004 and very briefly in 2006, to living, breathing people descended from the same line as I am. But mostly I have spent my time in the library, the place where the landholders' records are kept. Why doesn't my research culminate in an affectionate family reunion? Liberal white writers seem much more authoritative and convincing in making these connections than I.

In early 2009 I attended a lecture by the journalist Douglas A. Blackmon, a white Mississippian based in Atlanta who had written a book about the greatest crime that occurred in the United States between 1870 and 1950: the Southern vagrancy laws and work-gang system of debt peonage. Blackmon served as the southern bureau chief of the *Wall Street Journal*. Toward the end of his lecture, hosted by a Unitarian church, my young sons were quite restless, and the white parishioners at the Unitarian Church began to take it upon themselves to hush my children so they could better understand Blackmon's peerless research. At this time Mr. Blackmon mentioned that in the course of his uncovering the precise manner in which Southern companies and politicians had re-enslaved tens of thousands of black men for almost another century after the Civil War—a condition I knew of only through legends worked into fictions like August Wilson's *Joe Turner's Come and Gone*, Ralph Ellison's character Brother Tarp in *Invisible Man*, and John Killens's *Youngblood*—he had befriended a descendant of one of these cruelly abused men whose lives ended prematurely. So now the successful white man from the *Wall Street Journal*, who even though he was under the weather looked wholesomely fed and lovingly cared for, was going to guide another descendant of African American peasants into the world of the published word.

I had worked twenty years to move toward the circles of influence and prestige connoted by the name *Wall Street Journal*. (The newspaper's regular black pundit is a man named Shelby Steele, who like my high school classmate hasn't given his whole heart to another African American since Booker T. Washington.) I would be embarrassed to admit to my black friends what I have undergone, the willed amputations to create a desirable professional career, or at least one I might have called desirable had I had the opportunity to pluck it from the ether twenty years ago. But I do not, despite my own having been culled, experience a kind of sensual quickening when I ease near cavities of power. I am internally warring, and suspicious of myself.

And Blackmon's determination to help this black man "tell his story" strikes me as absurd, not simply because it justifies the white man, but because the model is so patently slave-like: black labor is a resource to be exploited, or in this case a black man's family history of oppression, which will be put into words and guided into print. The project will be more humiliating to me if the man's "voice" is deliberately crafted and sustained, the way that William Lloyd Garrison and L. Maria Child hoped to guide Frederick Douglass and Harriet Jacobs.

And maybe I want that as well, a desire I have been unable to admit to myself, perhaps like the desire of the "natural" athlete: to experience the fulfillment of acceptance, a hearty embrace from the social community if only for accepting myself as a natural metaphor, a body, accepting my own history as a story or a voice. What does it mean for me to think of my life relative to being a black man in pursuit of white acceptance? Is this the value of Granville Hundley's life, and the difference between his and Edward Jackson's, Hundley thinking of himself in light of Edward Williams, James Lanier, Levi Hall, William Ferrell, and ancient John Hundley, and his son-in-law thumbing his nose at them, sucking his teeth or spitting on the ground, and picking his own name, being for himself in spite of the consequences, and one of the consequences being his obscurity to his immediate descendants, just sixty years after he walked the earth?

Admittedly too, Blackmon's gesture makes me feel guilt. I have to inspire myself to resume contact with my own relatives, whom my father lost touch with a quarter of a century before my grandfather died. My dad graduated from a black high school named for one of Roanoke's pioneering New Negroes, Lucy Addison. Then he went to college in Baltimore and worked for the housing authority after he got out of the army. He began a professional career in 1960 at a time when his dollar, his credit, and his degree went as far as they have ever gone. His bubble was burst by the spiraling inflation of 1973 caused by the oil crisis, the new wrinkle to our people's cycle of credit, speculation, and misfortune.

But it was my father's distance from the country, from his struggling kinfolks, that helped to ensure not just our respectability but the sense of another kind of future. We grew up with ties to the past, yes, but not obligations to it. A stone has a past, but only people serve out duties to their kind. We were a new breed. No blood kin angling toward us for the resources that we had, no one relying on us for a medical procedure, a new roof, a carburetor, bail money, expensive medicine, or a trip to seek another medical opinion. No sister or aunt fleeing an abusive maniac and having to lodge herself and her children with us for ten weeks or ten years. Today I find myself accomplished but reluctant to engage fully in the lives of the people to whom I am tendering an amazing connection, whose joint ancestors I share, whose story is as fully, obviously more fully theirs than it is mine. I have traveled one hundred and fifty years inside to learn how far outside I am.

White Americans' willingness to tell a story they are intrigued by but distant from, and black Americans' reluctance to bore into the same topic at depth, suggests that whites understand our history as a puzzle, and we blacks pick at it like a sore. I guess it is this difference that allows Blackmon to be the magnanimous philanthropist. And it is this too that keeps me ugly, small, covetous, stingy, niggardly.

10 · My Inheritance

I made a fell swoop through central Virginia in the late winter of 2009, from the Southside up through Charlottesville to Richmond, and then I doubled back to Danville. A cool misty rain prevailed through forests filled with gray leafless trees. The trip was filled with extraordinary surprises.

I spent a day in Charlottesville, where my sister had attended the state's flagship university. I recalled my family admiring The Lawn, where select undergraduates were housed in rows of early nineteenth-century brick motels with wood-burning fireplaces. In a week and a half, my sister would be calling the school Mr. Jefferson's University. By contrast, when it had been time for my father to attend college, he would have been wasting his time to have submitted an application to the best public university in the state of his birth. We breakfasted in a student café called The Treehouse, where we couldn't avoid noticing a pimply, hatchet-faced white undergraduate shoveling his eggs and bacon into his mouth, it seemed with both hands. My father looked with disgust on the boy eating breakfast. "He's going to run the country one day," he said, clearly and, I thought, loud enough to be overheard. "He should eat properly." As the iron-tapped heels of my father's penny loafers scraped the brick paths during that trip in 1981, his thoughts must have contained wry combinations of resentment, surprise, and regard—layered conjunctions of the present and the past.

I gave a drizzly Saturday to the university's Albert and Shirley Small Special Collections Library, beginning with the computerized index for Pittsylvania County holdings. The library, two underground floors completed in 2004, was designed in a manner guaranteed to be a marvel for old-time Virginians. Quaint but technologically modern, and finished in a blend of wood and brick that Jefferson would have understood as complementary to his overall design, it fulfilled some kind of longing for beauty within me too.

I considered the items that I might get at within an afternoon. The Hairston family papers were there, so I looked up the scraps of paper they used to make contracts with freedmen in the years after the Civil War, and thumbed through their account books which showed, among other things, how much they paid to have a physician ride up to a slave cabin and administer a potion. I photographed nineteenth-century Virginia county maps, putting them underneath a table to block the fluorescent light and jerry-rigging chairs to keep the glare off the Mylar protective coverings. I tracked down some of the records from the Bright Leaf tobacco manufacturing company, printed on corporate stationery emblazoned by the symbol of their wealth.

Small Special Collections closes at five o'clock on Saturdays. Each special collections library is unique, but they all demand a myriad of paper application forms that have to go to their librarians, who then bring out the requested materials—sometimes only one at a time, and sometimes only two or three times per day. The librarians at Small were trying to be helpful, though we had some misfires along the way, since I had to explain to the staff—from docent, to work-study student, to curator, to assistant director—the kinds of things I was looking for, my purpose, and my professional credentials, and all this with the clock running. Of all the requests I placed that afternoon, the one I knew least about was a simple series of records called Pittsylvania County Ledgers. I submitted a call slip for it only because it was supposed to contain some antebellum materials. It was the last box I opened, late in the afternoon, around the time that fatigue was setting in.

The ledgers were commonplace books, and I looked through them as carefully as I could. As usual, I was hunting for needles and pinheads. The last item in the box, left out of the enumeration in the computer catalog entry, was a worn calfskin account book about the size of a checkbook. On its front I could decipher a name inked in cursive handwriting: V Dickison. Vincent Dickenson was a son of the highly esteemed Pittsylvanian Rev. Griffith Dickenson, who also had a son named Griffith, who was one of John Hundley's trading partners. I had dredged up a personal account book of an estate sale.

In his will of 1843, Rev. Dickenson attested that he was "of tolerable health and disposing mind." "In disposing of my negroes," he continued, "I desire every feeling of humanity to be regarded in parting Husband + wife, Parent + child."[1] A Revolutionary War veteran, Dickenson lived in eastern Pittsylvania and departed his earthly life at the age of eighty-six on October 16, 1843. Part of the chiseled inscription on his soapstone

BANNER WAREHOUSE

FOR THE SALE OF

LEAF TOBACCO,

LEA, NOELL & CO., Proprietors.

JNO. G. LEA.
CHAS. D. NOELL. }   Danville, Va., *June 3* 1885

Sales of Tobacco Made for *Ben Corbin*

No.			
	1 8 6 0 $		
	3 0 0	10	3 0 0 0
	1 6 6 5	70	6 3 2 6 0

ATTENTION!
Examine all calculations, and should errors occur, come at once and have correction made.

Warehouse Charges,   6 5 2 6 0

Auction Fees,

Commissions 2½ per ct. *3 r d*   7 2 8

NET PROCEEDS, $ 6 4 5 0 2

Bright Leaf Tobacco stationery. Albert and Shirley Small Special Collections Library, University of Virginia.

Cover of Vincent Dickinson's 1860 ledger. Albert and Shirley Small Special Collections Library, University of Virginia.

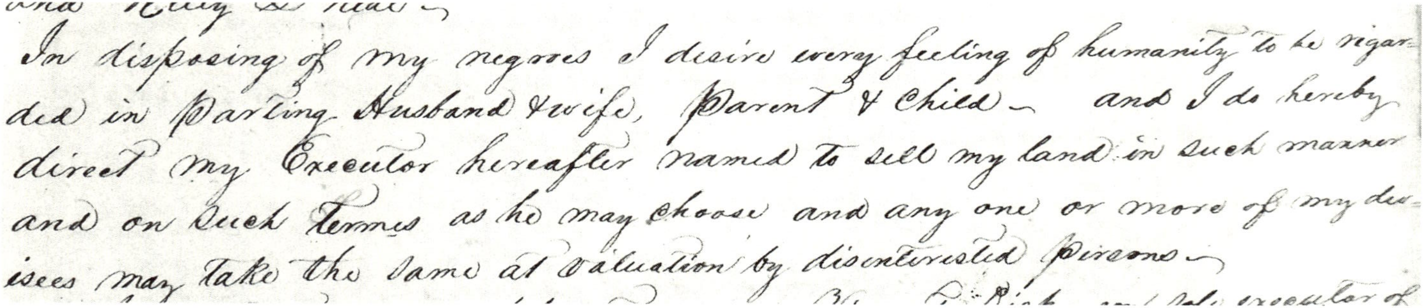
In disposing of my negroes I desire every feeling of humanity to be regar-
ded in Parting Husband & wife, Parent & Child— and I do hereby
direct my Executor hereafter named to sell my land in such manner
and on such Terms as he may choose and any one or more of my dev-
isees may take the same at valuation by disinterested persons—

Griffith Dickenson, 1843 will. Pittsylvania County, Virginia. Clerk's Office, Pittsylvania County, Virginia.

Griffith Dickenson home, Pittsylvania County, Virginia. Photograph: Library of Virginia, Richmond.

graveyard memorial proclaims that that he had "died trusting in a crucified Savior."[2]

The pious reverend had lived well in a two-story, six-room house built about 1800, seven miles southeast of a Pittsylvania town today called Gretna, ten miles north of Chatham. Constructed with hand-hewn beams, two large chimneys on either side, and two sets of stairs, one in front and one in the back for servants, one assumes, it was a basic farmhouse made elegant by the gables, windows, and piazza extending from the front and one side of the home. By the mid-1850s, the eldest son, Vincent Dickenson, came into possession of a good portion of his father's estate.

Vincent Dickenson was a literate man who wrote in a nice, tidy script. He was seventy-four in 1860, and was keeping four Negro houses on his place. His oldest slave was a sixty-year-old black man, and he also owned four women in their twenties and eleven children under the age of ten.[3] Among the children were two boys who Dickenson said were four years old at the time—roughly the age of my great-grandfather Edward.

In that year, time or bad luck or profligate habit caught up with Vincent Dickenson. He had borrowed money from Joseph Terry, at least ten thousand dollars over time, and the bill came due. In April he prepared to liquidate his estate, beginning with his 888-acre home parcel on the Stinking River and another that size by Brushy Mountain. Then, on June 12, 1860, neighbors from Pittsylvania poured onto the Dickenson farm and bought his carryalls and iron tools, the plows, scythes, and cradles, and they proceeded to purchase his sixteen enslaved people. Dickenson had probably set up a table on his large porch to conduct the business while his property crowded the yard.

The script of the ledger that I held was perfectly legible, as were the abbreviations Vincent Dickenson used. On page five, at the bottom, I saw clearly the intimate hand noting that on June 14, 1860, he was "receiving 1690.00 Geo W Hall for purch of Sandy."[4] An enslaved man named Sandy who had belonged to the Dickenson estate had been sold to Pittsylvania's professional "Negro Trader," George Hall.

I am not able to put into words how I was affected by reading this line. I could mainly consider what the event must have meant to my ancestor Edward Jackson, who on the day before he got married told the county clerk that Sandy Dickerson was his father.

I found a transcendent value contained in this leather-bound ledger with its translucent onionskin pages. The ledger itself took on the heft of a slave's chains, lashed like a whip, burned like a hot brand, and a great deal more. It was an actual physical object held in the hand and written on by the man who had sold Sandy Dickerson; the same man who had held an ancestor of mine in bondage owned it. It was a document that in a sense directed me, shaped my own life, because of its withering power over one of my forebears. And of course it was a document I would like personally to destroy—not because I wished for another past, but because I thought it cruel that even documents of the injustice should be so lovingly preserved. And with all the precautions that the illustrious university had taken in constructing this climate-controlled bunker, where security cameras and portraits and busts of Washington and Jefferson, Emerson, Longfellow, and William Cullen Bryant oversaw my perch, I doubt they had factored in the possibility of a slave's descendant's tears erasing the ledger of slavery. Or his phlegm, for that matter.

I was reminded of a sentence from a famous book: "If you go there— you who never was there—if you go there and stand in the place where it was, it will happen again; it will be there for you, waiting for you."[5] And it is one thing to read about it, and another when it happens to you.

And I am not sure if I want to be standing in the Dickenson yard,

1860

June 13. Amt bro forw'd   2442.09
"   "   D Oliver   "   1 00
"   "   A W Thompson   "   17 50
"   "   S J Minstain   "   7 57
"   "   N N Witcher   "   2 00
"   "   Nath Hobson for
         negro Dick   }   1265 00
"   "   W Coles Jr   "   8 00
"   "   same pur money
         of Bell   }   1280 00
"   "   John Gilbert   "   5 75
"   "   Ro Wilson pur
         money of Leroy
         Little Henry &   }
         Young Reuben   4521 00
"   "   W Coles Jr for Horse "   96 00
"   14   Gro W Hall for hire
         of Sandy   }   1690 00
"   "   Jas Carter hunter "   42 25
"   "   L Scruggs   "   3 00
"   "   "   over $ 11381.16

Sandy Dickerson sale page from Vincent Dickinson's 1860 ledger. Albert and Shirley
Small Special Collections Library, University of Virginia.

seven miles southeast of Gretna, on June 14, 1860, while the factors make their decisions from the porch, where the son of the preacher placates the people he owns with the ever-ready Bible verse that pious masters dished up to quiet the enslaved: Chronicles 2:17, "Ye shall not need to fight . . . stand ye still, and see the salvation of the Lord."[6]

So I stood up and walked out of the room and tried to regain my composure, thinking how any kind of sentimentality, anger, or weepy sadness was the worst response. I wished I could find one of the library's black custodians to talk to, who could relate to what had happened. It was one of those times when you need your people.

When I piece the ledger together with some background from the county courthouse and the US census, I am able to produce a story that makes sense to me.

For $1,690 his earthly master sold Sandy, a forty-year-old blacksmith, to George Hall in 1860. Thomas Martin purchased Sandy's wife, Jennie, and her children, Patsy and Lankford, for $2,050.[7] Sandy may have been sold out of the county immediately, though he seems to have made it back to Pittsylvania by 1870; but he and Jenny and Patsy and Lankford were not living together that year. Perhaps Jennie had died; perhaps she joined "$50,000 Worth of Negroes" destined for the Southern market. It was a part of the sad irony of what was called the "chattel principle," setting a price and exchanging a piece of currency.[8] Sandy had become so good at what he did, he had made so much of himself under enslavement, that even in the eyes of masters predisposed to keeping families together, he *and* his family were too expensive to purchase in a single lot. Husband and wife were separated from each other, and from their children, most likely forever.

I will never know if the person who grew to be the man Edward Jackson was in that yard by the gabled frame house that day. There is a decent probability that he was, and it might conceivably have been the last time he saw his mother. Moreover, this could explain Edward's first career in domestic service, if he had been groomed early on to wait the Dickensons' parlor table. There were even oblique clues explaining his arrival on the farm of Levi Hall by 1870, perhaps fifteen miles due south of the Dickenson place. Griffith Dickenson had married a woman named Susanna Shelton, and my ancestor Edward Jackson may have somehow belonged to her as a dower slave, which might have prevented his sale and consequent mention in the wills of any Dickensons. Levi Hall's in-laws were Nancy and Henry Shelton, who had bought Sandy Creek land early in the nineteenth century, and probably Susanna Shelton was

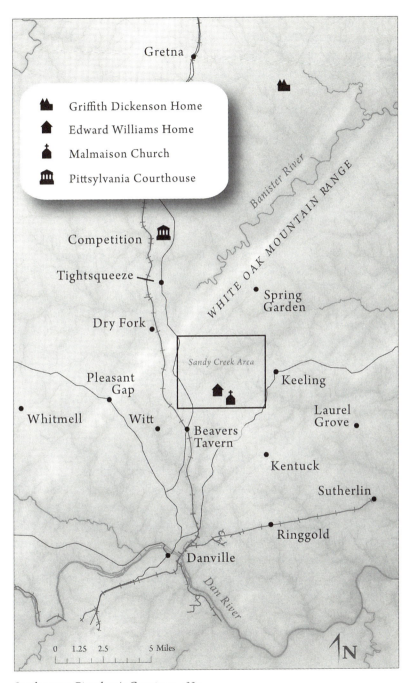

Southeastern Pittsylvania County, ca. 1880.

related to them. If my reconstruction of the events was even slightly accurate, how did the two parents and the children brave that fateful day? Did they recite to each other, "God moves in mysterious ways. His wonders to perform"? Although I wanted to find a piece of tangible proof connecting Edward to Sandy and Jennie, was I better off without such a burden, such a cavern that I had to then fill with remorse? If a little boy named Edward had fallen into the hands of Sandy Creek slave owners after that June day on Dickenson's farm in 1860, was acute trauma behind his choice of another name? Was selecting a new name his way of countering the death of his mother or the end of his childhood?

Perhaps his picking the Jackson surname was as simple as this. In the 1840s John Hubbard, the proprietor of the Sandy Creek mill, married a woman named Ann Eliza Jackson. In his 1846 will, Ann's father, William Jackson, left his daughter and his son-in-law several tracts of land north of Birch Creek. Jackson was an affluent planter and miller, and he controlled a firm by the name of Kirby, Jackson and Anderson; he also operated a mill on Birch Creek called Jackson and Anderson Mill.[9] The acres planted by the tobacco farmer Levi Hall lay in what Hall called Fall Level, probably not quite a mile south of Sandy Creek, and probably somewhere between Fall Creek to the west and Birch Creek to the east, on the other side of the road from Edward Williams. The Jackson mill couldn't have been far from Levi Hall's place, and perhaps Edward knew Reuben, Billy, Phillis, Jane, Alice, or Dick, who had been owned by Jackson in 1846; perhaps he knew that they said Jackson was a decent man. Maybe the black people living between the two creeks knew Ann Hubbard to possess excellent human qualities, but her husband did not have the same kind reputation, so Edward connected her estimable qualities to her Jackson origins. Perhaps he would have taken any local name other than Dickenson. The triumph was that I was finally able to take my great-grandfather Edward Jackson at his word: I believe Sandy and Jennie Dickerson were his parents.

I think it doubtful that slave-swapping Vincent Dickenson could have imagined that one of Sandy's descendants would one afternoon retrieve the account and reinterpret the meaning of the ledger. The clouds from that day might release a drop of life if I can leap forward too.

◆ ◆ ◆

Two somber days later, after a trip to the libraries and old-time rookeries of Richmond, I retraced my route back to Danville by way of Route

29. Along the way, I stopped at the antique markets a few miles south of Charlottesville, where I found a copy of the famous (to me) poster "The Colored Man Is No Slacker," which I had seen advertised in museum catalogs. I bought the poster and would have paid whatever I had to for it to render homage to my grandfather Nathaniel Jackson, who had served in France during World War I. My mother and sister considered his military record a step in the direction of an aristocratic character, while it seemed to me that he had been conscripted unfairly. Newsreels and photographs from that time showing the Negro troops who weren't medal winners, when the men were aboard ship or dancing, tend to emphasize the comic or grotesque, as did the Army and the War Department themselves. General Ballou of the Ninety-Second Division issued the infamous Order No. 40 that had blacks arrested for talking to white Frenchwomen, and Pershing's command followed it up even more infamously on August 7, 1918, by sending to the French High Command a memo, "Secret Information Concerning Black American Troops." The "Secret" was that black Americans were really animals disguised as men.

Yet the images glowing from the wartime-era poster I purchased were the opposite of degradation. The poster emphasizes patriotism, discipline, middle-class homeownership, propriety, and sexual restraint. In it a good-looking somber man embraces a slim-waisted, soft-haired woman in a blue dress with a lace collar. They bid each other adieu from a white-columned porch with red and yellow roses in planters, and the soldier touches her hand one last time before he turns to march off with his unit in their Sam Browns and khaki.

By the time I swung through Chatham it was almost dusk, and I had spent almost my entire trip in libraries. I had hoped to walk the grounds of Keeling to get a feel for what the place could have been like when my ancestors lived there. So I pulled off the highway at Spring Garden Road, hoping for something to attach itself to me viscerally. The road dipped and bent, and soon enough I got to a crossroads at Chestnut Level Road. There stood a weather-beaten store with a faded red sign that once said Grocery. I scouted inside the place, thinking I might discover something of value from the nineteenth century. But the grocery preserved another era. Sometime between 1965 and 1975, it had become a television warehouse of sorts. The local kids have had a time of it kicking in the cathode ray tubes around the shop, and in the center of the building the roof had collapsed. Here and there I could see late-1960s motorcycle helmets such as were worn on *The Partridge Family* and *The Mod Squad* television shows, headgear without all the astronaut-style padding of today.

"Colored Man Is No Slacker." US Army recruitment poster, World War I.

I was bemused, I suppose, looking for a poster or another item to coin-
cide with the early twentieth-century exterior. Instead, the shop appears
to have been in its heyday when I was making childhood visits to nearby
Blairs. At that time, I don't think my father would have wanted to know
what was out here, which must be quite close to where his father had

Tobacco barn at Chestnut Level near Keeling, Virginia, 2011. Photograph: Lawrence Jackson.

been born. I took a digital picture of the exterior for posterity, to signify a past I was unable to recapture.

I meandered along Chestnut Level Road, headed south, and came upon Hunter's Lane, which I took. There were very attractive rolling fields etched with furrows and dotted with nineteenth-century tobacco barns made of squared logs notched with *V*s at each corner. There were also distinctly shabby trailer homes that gave you the sense of either the imitation of life or a hive of human punishment. It was after five o'clock on Friday night, and I knew what would happen after the drinking began. Tim McGraw's song "Down on the Farm" had been playing on the ubiquitous country music radio stations that characterize the essential nature of the American native in the same way that Rush Limbaugh does.

Curiously, I was not being haunted by the song I remembered so clearly from the era of my family's Danville trips: Joan Baez singing "The Night They Drove Old Dixie Down." With her sultry folk style, Baez squeezed my five-year-old emotions with the only line I could ever distinguish from the final stanza, "He was just eighteen, proud and brave / But a Yankee laid him in his grave." Although it didn't take all that long for me to pick sides in the Civil War, it wasn't until writing this book that I even knew that Danville was the locale of the lyric, that Stoneman's cavalry were my people's liberators, not rogue bandits. Between that song and "Billy Don't Be a Hero," the soundtrack of my early childhood seemed haunted by Civil War death. But McGraw's "Down on the Farm" eschews politics. It is a nostalgic pastoral for the open-field bonfires, the drinking contests, the rough courtship and jousting that goes on, and declares, "Ain't no closing time, ain't no cover charge, / Just country boys and girls getting down on the farm."

Of course today, like in the earlier time, only hardworking members of the middle class own farms; farming is not quite a working man's occupation. The "getting down" now is going to include crack and crystal meth. I began to see the evidence even more after I turned off in the direction of Keeling at Edward Williams Road. At the bottom of the hill I saw what looked like a very old store or tobacco barn. I had observed the top of the building from satellite pictures of the area on Google Maps. Up close I could see spray-painted marijuana leaves and gang-sign regalia that the young white kids get from MTV and rap videos. While I padded around the turf outside the building in search of leaves and stones and espied the running creek, the neighborhood kids raced automobiles along the bumpy gravel road. But even though the boys raised a spray of granite chips as they took their two-door American economy cars and shiny flatbed trucks up and down the path, the wan girls in the passenger seats waved as they went by. There is a world of humanity in a wave.

Inside the old barn, which perhaps seemed like a store because its roof had such a largea overhang, I found a dead pit bull shrouded in pillowcases. The carcass was beginning to smell. I thought of then imprisoned quarterback Michael Vick, and the old Virginia traditions of animal combat. Outside again, I investigated the creek, stepping over the broken Bud Light and Icehouse beer bottles, American beers made from corn. The creek itself was four or five feet wide and flowed quite readily. The banks might have been no higher than four feet, but it was easy to see how after a good rain the road would be impassable. The likelihood of a flooded road gave a specific salience to the contemporary saying you hear from black Americans: "I'll be there, God willing and if the creek don't rise."

After checking the tree leaves—maple, oak, elm, and sweet gum, just like in front of my own house in Georgia—I drove to the top of the hill. I observed what seemed to be a new house with a very large and impressive barn. Unchained dogs barked at me as I drove past. After I had cleared the house I noticed a compact graveyard. I had been ragging myself the entire trip about driving too far in the wrong direction before turning

Tobacco barn by Sandy Creek, 2011. Photograph: Lawrence Jackson.

around, so I backed up my station wagon, a Volkswagen, and drove up to the tombstones. The dogs edged closer to the car, though they barked no more aggressively than before. I noticed then that the hounds were protective but not vicious breeds, an old English Labrador mix and some kind of husky or other. Since it was the country I prepared myself for the possibility of someone running over to the car with a rifle, but after half a minute I didn't see or hear anything other than mild baying and yelping.

I drove to the other side of the house, where I saw an assortment of later-model cars and trucks. I considered my chances with the quickly reconnoitering hounds and got out of the car. A woman wearing thick-frame glasses cut at oblique angles called to me from the yard. Although she was white, she immediately brought to mind my mother's next-door neighbor from Prince Edward County who vaguely resembled Billie Holiday, in the way that a number of women on my old block in Baltimore did. Maybe this white woman had some Native American in her face.

She was articulate, unembarrassed, and straightforward, unworried by her encounter with a strange man from Georgia. She told me, straightaway, that this was Dr. Edward Williams's house, erected in 1856, and that

Edward Williams's 1856 house, 2011. Photograph: Lawrence Jackson.

he was buried in the graveyard. Indeed. After several years, I had found precisely what I was after: one of the concrete boundaries of Granville Hundley's 1877 land tract. I confirmed her words at the graveyard, and then she directed me to her husband, the owner of the house. Frederick Chandler invited me into his parlor, and his wife joked that I had been welcomed to his "inner sanctuary."

Over the fireplace were racked eighteenth- and nineteenth-century muzzle-loading muskets and rifles. The two muskets would have operated by a piece of flint striking steel and igniting a pan of black powder, hence the saying "keep your powder dry"—otherwise, your rifle won't be able to fire. One of the rifles was an exquisite, early nineteenth-century Kentucky long rifle, such as Andrew Jackson and Davy Crockett would have handled. The last was an 1853 Enfield. Frederick Chandler collects the rifles of the frontier and the rifles of the Confederacy, and already I knew a great deal about this man. The 1861 rifle manufactured by the armory in Springfield, Massachusetts, would never hang on this wall.

The Chandlers revealed that Edward Williams called this very house Malmaison, and that the road took its name from the house. I had thought the road was called that name because it was home to a brothel. Rather, Edward Williams had imagined himself as Napoleon and his wife as Josephine, so they had named their house for Napoleon's quarters. I learned that Dr. Edward Williams expired in 1906 in the living room of his home after inserting a turkey quill as a catheter. Chandler verified that a mill, such as would have belonged to John Hubbard, once stood at the bottom of the hill where I had taken pictures of the creek, Sandy Creek. He also thought that up the road, on one side or the other of the creek, was a farm that had belonged to Levi Hall. John Hundley, who lived by himself and was one hundred when he died more than a century ago, he had not heard about.

I tried to share my sense of joy. Mrs. Chandler extended her own sense of warm hospitality and gave me a quick tour of the home, which they had just painted, inside and out, and restored to its nineteenth-century specifications. And she had outfitted both the original living room and one upstairs bedroom with antique dolls and children's furniture; in the upstairs room there was also a becoming linen wedding dress that, after my research and a greater appreciation for the culture of the nineteenth century it instilled, I found alluring.

The Chandlers were cheerful and gregarious. But our divergent pasts spoke loudly in Dr. Williams's old home. In the hallway they kept a bust of General Lee, who had freed his slaves, I should add, and in the corner of the kitchen they had four black ceramic figures, "smiling darkies." It was precisely the kind of thing that might reflect ownership of a wrenching past or an ironic sense of humor if the figures were in a black person's house, but it says the opposite in a white person's house. It was a sure sign that the Chandlers had no genuine black friends. To me, the essence of all this is whether or not you believe that Africans had been savages in need of some element of European enlightenment to become human beings like anyone who can read this. That's the great divide, plain and simple. Since the time I became responsible for my own education, I have tried never to waver on this single point, and it keeps me busy. I believe that the historical record of contact between Africa and Europe excludes Africa, and most completely when it pretends to be inclusive. And yet, I was the African descendant, more kin to Henri Christophe than to Napoleon, in their revived Malmaison, a guest, a recipient of their time, their knowledge, their hospitality. The Chandlers invited me to have coffee.

I thought about June 5, 1917, when my grandfather registered for the draft. The registration took place near Beaver's Tavern. At the tenth question on the form, after asking whether or not he was single or married, my grandfather was asked about his race. The inducting officer, J. C. Blair, wrote simply "African."[10] Since even Blair could get to the heart of the

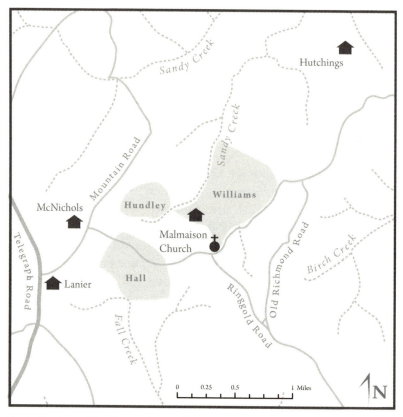

Sandy Creek area, Pittsylvania County, Virginia, ca. 1880: Granville Hundley farm, 40–50 acres; Edward Williams farm, 475 acres; Levi Hall farm, 197 acres; Nannie and Granville Hutchings home; James McNichols home; James Lanier home.

matter, my course was clear. With the image of Dickenson's calfskin ledger crowding my mind, I politely declined the Chandlers' libation ritual.

I drove away thinking the encounter extraordinary and remarkable, at the very least on account of the questions that it put to rest. Perhaps it is a sign of the age of Obama, or perhaps I am like the seamstress and writer Elizabeth Keckley, who visited her former owners after the war and bragged of how well she had been treated. I wondered what the memory of the contact would be like for the Chandlers.

◆　◆　◆

At Mary's Cafeteria just north of the Dan River, I stopped for a little supper. It was the only home-style place I had seen in Danville, which surprised me. The city of Lynchburg, where I had an outstanding dinner and breakfast, offered a feast of culinary excitement compared with the slate of deep-fried frozen food that seemed to be the only thing available within an hour either way of Danville. Mary's fare near closing time tasted like canned food to my mouth. I got green beans, corn, lima beans, and a dish called macaroni and cheese that was so bland I had to pickle it in salt. I noticed the African Americans around me, who naturally enough ran the known world's range of skin colors and hues, picking their way through dinner, and I recognized that I was possibly, perhaps probably, distantly related to them all.

A man sat in front of me with his shoulders upright. He wore a black leather baseball cap, which to us signifies the generation of the singer Frankie Beverly—who, together with the group Maze, is the African American version of Jimmy Buffett—and a leather jacket. He was light colored, and the Afro spilling from beneath his cap was turning gray. Seated at the table, he appeared to be a man of some stature, and I wondered if he could be some version of Granville Hundley or his son Nathaniel Henry Hutchings. I had seen a photograph of men working in a tobacco warehouse in Lynchburg, and based on what my father and grandfather looked like, I had already formed the perfect mental image of Edward Jackson, who, I had decided, was something of a dandy.

A young man just over five and a half feet tall with the shoulders of a linebacker and the commanding head of a stage actor was clearing the trays. His forearms were an ornate tapestry of tattoos. He struck up a conversation with me, asking if I was Muslim on the basis of the style of beard I was wearing, which in Philadelphia and coastal New Jersey is called a "Sunni." He told me he was from Newark, one of the only places I have ever been that reminded me of the impossible circumstances of my hometown. He then divulged that he had been institutionalized. The euphemisms that we use for this—"caught up" and "in the system"—have an obvious conspiratorial quality.

Kareem impressed me as being completely earnest and a formidable adversary if aroused. He also struck me as the embodiment of the African American who is beloved by individual white Americans who know him personally in a relation of at least minor deference, and yet is simultaneously kept at bay if that relation of deference is ever narrowed. He told me he was a Galloway on his mother's side, a name I had come across several times during my analysis of the US census records. Some of his people were free before the Civil War and lived near Sandy Creek.

I didn't miss the irony that his forays into the underground economy of our day had backfired and reduced him now to a kind of neoslavery. His attitude that mixed forbearance with resignation in the face of the odds was more similar to our ancestors' approach to slavery and its aftermath than he could possibly know, than I could possibly know, or than I could tell Kareem if I did. We exchanged a few war stories, gripped each other twice, and then, feeling some responsibility for him as a younger man, I encouraged him to prepare for the future with a guarded ambitiousness. Our ancestors had survived enslavement just a few miles from each other, and for generations; it was our duty at least to carry on.

NOTES

CHAPTER TWO

1. Julian R. Meade, *I Live in Virginia* (New York: Longmans, Green, 1935), 3, 50.

2. Thomas Nelson Page, *Social Life in Old Virginia before the War* (New York: Scribner, 1897), 28.

3. www.census.gov/genealogy/www/data/2000surnames. Washington was 86 percent black; Jefferson was 75 percent.

4. Ralph Ellison, "Hidden Name and Complex Fate," in *Shadow and Act* (1964; New York: Vintage, 1995), 148.

5. These others were in wide use as names for slaves: Phillis or Fillis for Fili, which meant "lost" or "abandoned" in Manding and Bambara; and from the Akan language: Jemmy for Kwame, a Saturday-born male; Cuffee for Kufi, a Friday-born male; and Juba for a Monday-born female. Allan Kulikoff, *Tobacco & Slaves: The Development of Southern Cultures in the Chesapeake* (Chapel Hill: University of North Carolina Press, 1986), 325; thanks to Kwesi Degraft Hanson.

6. Ellison, "Hidden Name and Complex Fate," 149.

7. "Martin Jackson," in *Voices from Slavery*, ed. Norman Yetman (Mineola, NY: Dover, 2000), 174.

8. US Bureau of the Census, *Measuring America: The Decennial Censuses from 1790–2000* (Washington, DC: Government Printing Office, April 2002), 14.

9. Patricia Samford, *Subfloor Pits and the Archaeology of Slavery in Colonial Virginia* (Tuscaloosa: University of Alabama Press, 2007), 131.

10. Levi Hall, "Homestead Exemption," Pittsylvania County, Virginia, Deed Book, vol. 70, p. 11. Pittsylvania County Courthouse, Chatham, VA.

11. "Levi Hall," Claiborne and Jeter Day Book, 1855, p. 50. Rare Books, Manuscripts and Special Collections Library, Duke University.

12. "Levi Hall," Pittsylvania County Marriage Register, vol. 1, 1767–1862, p. 125; "Levi Hall," Pittsylvania County Land Book, 1870, p. 15. Pittsylvania County Courthouse, Chatham, VA.

13. Lorena S. Walsh, *From Calabar to Carter's Grove: The History of a Virginia Slave Community* (Charlottesville: University Press of Virginia, 1997), 161. In the sixteenth and seventeenth centuries, a frank was a hog pen, and the verb *frank* meant "to fatten."

14. Lynda J. Morgan, *Emancipation in the Tobacco Belt, 1850–1870* (Athens: University of Georgia Press, 1992), 176.

15. The descriptions of Pittsylvania's historic plantation homes are drawn from the

National Historic Register applications for historic sites made from Pittsylvania County, Virginia. These are archived at the Virginia Department of Historic Resources: http://www.dhr.virginia.gov/registers/Counties/register_Pittsylvania .htm. Windsor 071–0035; Mountain View 071–0025; Woodlawn 071–0037.

16. Page, *Social Life in Old Virginia*, 22.

CHAPTER THREE

1. Ellen Glasgow, *The Deliverance: A Romance of the Tobacco Fields* (New York: Doubleday and Page, 1904), 6.

2. L. Beatrice Hairston, *A Brief History of Danville, Virginia—1728–1954* (Richmond: Dietz, 1955), 2.

3. Frederick Siegel, *The Roots of Southern Distinctiveness: Tobacco and Society in Danville, Virginia 1780–1865* (Chapel Hill: University of North Carolina Press, 1987), 16.

4. Siegel, *Roots*, 88.

5. Thomas Jefferson, "Subjects of Commerce," from *Notes on the State of Virginia* (1787), in *The Portable Thomas Jefferson*, ed. Merrill Peterson (New York: Penguin, 1975), 218–19.

6. Hairston, *Brief History*, 7.

7. Nannie Tilley, quoted in Siegel, *Roots*, 95.

8. Lorena S. Walsh, *From Calabar to Carter's Grove: The History of a Virginia Slave Community* (Charlottesville: University Press of Virginia, 1997), 63–64.

9. Henrietta Perry, quoted in Siegel, *Roots*, 98.

10. Samuel C. Shelton, "The Culture and Management of Tobacco," *Southern Planter and Farmer* (February 1867): 12.

11. Advertisement, "Fire Insurance," *Danville (VA) Register*, no date. Also in *Danville Republican*, March 31, 1854.

12. Albion Tourgeé, *Bricks without Straw* (1880; Durham: Duke University Press, 2009), 262.

13. 1860 US Census, Pittsylvania County, Virginia, Pittsylvania County Courthouse, Chatham, VA; Joseph Kennedy, *Eighth Census—Volume III: Agriculture in the United States for 1860, State of Virginia* (Washington, DC: Government Printing Office, 1872), 159. Pittsylvania exported 7,053,962 pounds of tobacco.

14. Francis Walker, *Ninth Census—Volume III: The Statistics of the Wealth and Industry of the United States* (Washington, DC: Government Printing Office, 1872), n.p. Many thanks to Drew Swanson and Erica Brucho for help with these figures.

15. Frederick Law Olmsted, *The Cotton Kingdom: A Traveler's Observations on Cotton and Slavery in the American Slave States, Based upon Three Former Volumes of Journeys and Investigations by the Same Author*, ed. Arthur M. Schlesinger Sr. (1861; New York: Modern Library, 1984), 70.

16. Steven Deyle, "The Irony of Liberty: Origins of the Domestic Slave Trade," *Journal of the Early Republic* (Spring 1992): 50; Phillip D. Morgan and Michael L. Nichols, "Slaves in Piedmont Virginia, 1720–1790," *William and Mary Quarterly* (April 1989): 236.

17. Thomas Jefferson, quoted in Deyle, "The Irony of Liberty," 51.

18. Joseph Holmes, First Supplemental Series, Georgia Narratives, V04s 11 June 1937, Mobile, Alabama, p. 3. Slave Narratives, Federal Writers' Project; Manuscript Division, Library of Congress.

19. Allan Kulikoff, "The Origins of Afro-American Society in Tidewater Maryland and Virginia, 1700 to 1790," *William and Mary Quarterly* (April 1978): 236-37.

20. James Weldon Johnson, *The Autobiography of an Ex-Colored Man* (1912); reprinted in *Three Negro Classics* (New York: Avon, 1965), 423.

21. Olauduh Equiano, *The Interesting Narrative of the Life of Olauduh Equiano; or, Gustavus Vassa, the African, Written by Himself* (1789); reprinted in *The Classic Slave Narratives*, ed. Henry Louis Gates Jr. (New York: Signet Classics), 109.

22. Deyle, "The Irony of Liberty," 44.

23. Elige Davison, quoted in *From Sundown to Sunup: The Making of the Black Community*, vol. 1 of *The American Slave: A Composite Autobiography*, ed. George Rawick (Westport, CT: Greenwood Press, 1972), 88.

24. W. E. B. Du Bois, *Black Reconstruction* (1935; New York: Free Press, 1998), 44.

25. Thomas Jefferson, "Laws," from *Notes on the State of Virginia* (1787), in Peterson, *The Portable Thomas Jefferson*, 187.

26. Richard G. Lowe and Randolph B. Campbell, "The Slave-Breeding Hypothesis: A Demographic Comment on the 'Buying' and 'Selling' States," *Journal of Southern History* (August 1976): 405.

27. William McLoughlin, "Red Indians, Black Slavery and White Racism: America's Slaveholding Indians," *American Quarterly* 26, no. 4 (October 1974): 375-83; R. Haliburton Jr., *Red over Black: Black Slavery among the Cherokee Indians* (Westport, CT: Greenwood Press, 1977), 191; Theda Perdue, *Slavery and the Evolution of Cherokee Society, 1540-1866* (Knoxville: University of Tennessee Press, 1979), 70-72.

28. "Public Sale of a Large Number of Valuable Slaves," *Danville (VA) Register*, October 26, 1849.

29. "30 or 40 Likely Negroes For Sale," *Danville (VA) Register*, July 7, 1860.

30. Lorenzo Ivy, quoted in *Weevils in the Wheat: Interviews with Virginia Ex-Slaves*, ed. Charles L. Perdue Jr. et al. (Charlottesville: University Press of Virginia, 1976), 151.

31. Henry Box Brown, *Narrative of the Life of Henry Box Brown* (1851; New York: Oxford University Press, 2002), 60.

32. James A. Mitchell, Account Book 1834-35; Rare Books, Manuscripts and Special Collections Library, Duke University.

33. Henry Bibb, *Narrative of the Life and Adventures of Henry Bibb, An American Slave* (1850; Madison: University of Wisconsin Press, 2001), 91.

34. Henry Wiencek, *The Hairstons: An American Family in Black and White* (New York: St. Martin's Press, 1999), 70.

35. Anthony E. Kaye, *Joining Places: Slave Neighborhoods in the Old South* (Chapel Hill: University of North Carolina Press, 2007), 28-29.

36. Siegel, *Roots*, 108.

37. "William T. Sutherlin," 1860 US Census, Schedule 1, Pittsylvania, Virginia, p. 130.

38. "William T. Sutherlin," 1860 US Census, Schedule 2 (Slave Inhabitants), Pittsylvania, Virginia, p. 52.

39. Siegel, *Roots*, 131.

40. Myrta Avary, *Dixie after the War* (Boston: Houghton Mifflin, 1937), 48.

41. Wiencek, *The Hairstons*, 76–77.

42. "Samuel Hairston," 1860 US Census, Schedule 1, Pittsylvania, Virginia, p. 56; "Ruth Hairston," 1860 US Census, Schedule 1, Pittsylvania, Virginia, p. 57; "Samuel Hairston," 1860 US Census, Schedule 2 (Slave Inhabitants), Pittsylvania, Virginia, p. 52.

43. "The Richest Man in Virginia," *DeBow's Review* (January 1855): 53.

44. Peter Kolchin, *American Slavery, 1619–1877* (New York: Hill and Wang, 2003), 101, 256 table 5.

45. Siegel, *Roots*, 88–89, 82.

46. These figures are drawn from the 1860 Schedule 2, the slave schedule, for Pittsylvania County, Virginia. My thanks to Yoshi Furuiki and George Gordon-Smith for helping me to identify the planters. Drew Addison graciously helped to correct the figures.

47. Siegel, *Roots*, 76

48. Barbara Heath, "Space and Place within Plantation Quarters in Virginia, 1700–1825," in *Cabin, Quarter, Plantation: Architecture and Landscapes of North American Slavery* (New Haven, CT: Yale University Press, 2010), 158, 164.

49. Herman Melton, *"Thirty Nine Lashes Well Laid On": Crime and Punishment in Southside Virginia, 1750–1950* (Herman Melton, 2001), 104.

50. John C. Willis, "From the Dictates of Pride to the Paths of Righteousness: Slave Honor and Christianity in Antebellum Virginia," in *The Edge of the South: Life in Nineteenth Century Virginia*, ed. Edward Ayers and John Willis (Charlottesville: University Press of Virginia, 1991), 38.

51. "Robert Wilson," 1860 US Census, Schedule 1, Pittsylvania, Virginia, p. 79; "Robert Wilson," 1860 US Census, Schedule 2 (Slave Inhabitants), Pittsylvania, Virginia, pp. 66–67.

52. "Mrs. Bird Walton," in *Weevils in the Wheat*, 299.

53. Ishrael Massie, in ibid., xlii.

54. Olmsted, *The Cotton Kingdom*, 74.

55. Solomon Northup, *Twelve Years a Slave: Narrative of Solomon Northup, a Citizen of New York Kidnapped in Washington City in 1841 and Rescued in 1853 from a Cotton Plantation near the Red River in Louisiana* (1854; Mineola, NY: Dover, 1970), 224.

56. *1788–1790*, vol. 30 of *The Writings of George Washington 1745–1799*, ed. John Fitzpatrick (Washington, DC: Government Printing Office, 1931–44), 175.

57. Lynda J. Morgan, *Emancipation in the Tobacco Belt, 1850–1870* (Athens: University of Georgia Press, 1992), 52.

58. Melton, *"Thirty-Nine Lashes Well Laid On,"* 69–79.

59. "The Scaffold in Virginia," *New York Herald*, December 11, 1870, 4.

60. Fannie Berry interview, in *Virginia Slave Narratives: A Folk History of Slavery in Virginia from Interviews with Former Slaves* (Bedford, MA: Applewood, 2006), 2.

61. Fannie Berry, in *Weevils in the Wheat*, 48.

62. Tim Thornton, First Supplemental Series, Georgia Narratives, Vo4s, p. 611. Slave Narratives, Federal Writers' Project; Manuscript Division, Library of Congress.

63. John Carrington, letter to J. M. Sutherlin, September 27, 1858; Thomas Sutherlin Papers, Rare Books, Manuscripts and Special Collections Library, Duke University.

64. "Mrs. Bird Walton," in *Weevils in the Wheat*, 298.

65. "George Price and John R. Price," 1860 US Census, Schedule 1, Pittsylvania, Virginia, Danville, p. 52; 1860 US Census, Schedule 1, Pittsylvania, Virginia, Ruth Hairston, p. 57; 1860 US Census, Schedule 2 (Slave Inhabitants), Pittsylvania, Virginia, George Price and John R. Price, p. 64.

66. John Booker, letter to Charity Blair, December 22, 1863; Booker Papers, University of Virginia Library.

67. John T. Trowbridge, *The Desolate South, 1865–1866*, ed. Gordon Carrol (Boston: Little, Brown, 1956), 90.

68. Herman Melton, *Southside Virginia* (Charleston, SC: History Press, 2006), 57–60.

69. Herman Melton, *Pittsylvania's Nineteenth Century Grist Mills* (Herman Melton, 1991), 210.

CHAPTER FOUR

1. "General Orders" and "Highly Important General Orders from Maj. Gen. Wright to the Citizens of Danville," *Sixth Corps*, May 8, 1865.

2. James Smith, "Virginia During Reconstruction" (PhD diss., University of Virginia, 1960), 390.

3. Edmund Ruffin, *The Diary of Edmund Ruffin*, vol. 3, *A Dream Shattered June, 1863–June, 1865*, ed. William Scarborough (Baton Rouge: Louisiana State University Press, 1989), April 27, 1865, p. 867.

4. "To Servants," *Danville (VA) Daily News Era*, June 1, 1865.

5. Quoted in Lawrence M. Clark, "A Brief History of the Education of African Americans in Danville, Virginia: From Dan's Hill to Langston High School," online at www.vcdh.virginia.edu/cslk/danville/media/pdfs/brief_history.pdf.

6. Quoted in Richard John Dennett, *The South As It Is* (New York: Viking, 1965), 95.

7. Quoted in Henry Wiencek, *The Hairstons: An American Family in Black and White* (New York: St. Martin's Griffin, 1999), 197.

8. Jeffrey Kerr-Ritchie, *Freedpeople in the Tobacco South* (Chapel Hill: University of North Carolina Press, 1999), 87.

9. Quoted in Richard John Dennett, *The South As It Is* (1865; New York: Viking, 1965), 95.

10. Ibid., 78.

11. Bird Ferrell, letter to P. W. Ferrell, November 23, 1865; folder 1858–1894, William T. Sutherlin Papers, Rare Books, Manuscripts and Special Collections Library, Duke University.

12. Bird Ferrell, letter to P. W. Ferrell, September 14, 1868.

13. William Duncan to Asa Holland, cited in Smith, "Virginia during Reconstruction," 392.

14. William Duncan, letter to wife, cited in ibid., 409.

15. "William Duncan," 1860 US Census, Schedule 1, Pittsylvania, Virginia, p. 280.

16. Betty Saunders, quoted in Smith, "Virginia during Reconstruction," 392.

17. Kerr-Ritchie, *Freedpeople*, 104.

18. Ibid.

19. Observer, "Let the Plow Be King and Cuffee His Prime Minister," *Southern Planter and Farmer* (August 1867): 1, 7.

20. Kerr-Ritchie, *Freedpeople*, 108.

21. "Mr. Editor," *Danville (VA) Register*, January 3, 1868.

22. Maud Carter Clement, *The History of Pittsylvania County* (1929; Lynchburg, VA: Lipscomb, 1988), 254.

23. "An Ordinance to Allow Cost," *Danville (VA) Register*, June 25, 1867.

24. "Confederate Monument," Report pages 2–3, Location no. 202, Historic Sites, Pittsylvania County Map, Library of Virginia, Richmond.

25. Clement, *The History of Pittsylvania County*, 254.

26. Howard K. Beale, "On Rewriting Reconstruction History," *American Historical Review* 45, no. 4 (July 1940): 808; See W. E. B. Du Bois, "The Propaganda of History," in *Black Reconstruction* (1935, New York: Free Press, 1992), 711–29.

27. Du Bois, "The Propaganda of History," 719. Du Bois quotes from William A. Dunning's *Reconstruction, Political and Economic, 1865–1877* (New York: Harper, 1907).

28. Clement, *The History of Pittsylvania County*, 255.

29. Ibid., 256.

30. Ibid.

31. Myrta Avary, *Dixie after the War* (New York: Doubleday, Page, 1906), 181.

32. Ibid., 203.

33. James McDonald, *Life in Old Virginia* (Norfolk, VA: Old Virginia Publishing, 1907), 172.

34. "Colored Procession," *Danville (VA) Register*, January 3, 1868.

35. "A Relic," *Danville (VA) Register*, October 5, 1870.

36. "John Keen," 1870 US Census, Schedule 1, Pittsylvania, Virginia, p. 51.

37. "Records Relating to Murders and Outrages," Records of the Assistant Commissioner for the State of Virginia, Bureau of Refugees, Freedmen, and Abandoned Lands, 1865–1869. National Archives, Washington, DC, microfilm no. 1048, roll 59, p. 3, case 49 and case 60; p. 4, case 79 and case 84.

38. Smith, "Virginia during Reconstruction," 416–17. From the Samuel Hairston Papers, Alderman Library, University of Virginia.

39. "Records Relating to Murders and Outrages."

40. "Colonel Brown's Address to the Freedmen of Virginia," "Appendix One," in Kerr-Ritchie, *Freedpeople*, 251–52.

41. Ibid., 251.

42. "Ann Benedict," 1870 US Census, Schedule 1, Pittsylvania, Virginia, Chatham, p. 764; R. W. Manly Report, Bureau of Refugees, Freedmen, and Abandoned Lands, August 1870, National Archives, Washington, DC, microfilm no. 1048, roll 47.

43. "Report of School Buildings Owned by BRFAL," Bureau of Refugees, Freedmen, and Abandoned Lands, May 1869. National Archives, Washington, DC, microfilm no. 1048, roll 47.

44. L. Beatrice Hairston, *A Brief History of Danville, Virginia—1728–1954* (Richmond, VA: Dietz, 1955), 61.

45. R. L. Manly, Education Consolidated Report, Bureau of Refugees, Freedmen, and Abandoned Lands, June 1866. National Archives, Washington, DC, microfilm no. 1048, roll 47.

46. R. L. Manly, Education Consolidated Report, Bureau of Refugees, Freedmen, and Abandoned Lands, February 1868. National Archives, Washington, DC, microfilm no. 1048, roll 47.

47. Joe Anderson, "Historical Sketches of Shockoe Baptist Church of Pittsylvania County," 1903. Albert and Shirley Small Special Collections Library, University of Virginia.

48. R. L. Manly, Education Consolidated Report, Bureau of Refugees, Freedmen, and Abandoned Lands, February 1868. National Archives, Washington, DC, microfilm no. 1048, roll 47.

49. Du Bois, "The Propaganda of History," 716.

50. Booker T. Washington, *Up From Slavery*, in *Three Negro Classics* (New York: Avon, 1965), 59.

51. US Department of Agriculture, Bureau of Soils, Map of Pittsylvania County, Virginia, 1918. Library of Virginia, Richmond.

52. Ellen Glasgow, *The Deliverance: A Romance of the Tobacco Fields* (New York: Doubleday and Page, 1904), 7.

53. "William Carper," 1910 US Census, Pittsylvania County, Virginia, Chatham Magisterial District 95.

54. Jane Guild, *Black Laws of Virginia* (1936; New York: Negro Universities Press, 1969), 181.

55. "Ned Jackson," 1910 US Census, Pittsylvania County, Virginia, Chatham Magisterial District 94.

CHAPTER FIVE

1. Lorena S. Walsh, *From Calabar to Carter's Grove: The History of a Virginia Slave Community* (Charlottesville: University Press of Virginia, 1997), 170.

2. David Blight, ed., *A Slave No More* (New York: Harcourt, 2007).

3. Frederick Douglass, *The Narrative of the Life of Frederick Douglass* (1845), in *Classic Slave Narratives*, ed. Henry Louis Gates Jr. (New York: Signet Classics, 2002), 372.

4. Jane Guild, *Black Laws of Virginia* (1936; New York: Negro Universities Press, 1969), 176.

5. Jeffrey Kerr-Ritchie, *Freedpeople in the Tobacco South* (Chapel Hill: University of North Carolina Press, 1999), 94.

6. Brenda Stevenson, *Life in Black and White: Family and Community in the Slave South* (New York: Oxford University Press, 1996), 207–12. Stevenson uses the example of George Washington, a comparatively humane master who enslaved 319 people on several farms in 1799, to highlight the fact that more than 70 percent of the "married" couples lived alone. See also John Blassingame, *The Slave Community: Plantation Life in the Antebellum South* (New York: Oxford University Press, 1979), 162–63.

7. Lorenzo Ivy, quoted in *Weevils in the Wheat: Interviews with Virginia Ex-Slaves*, ed. Charles L. Perdue Jr. et al. (Charlottesville: University Press of Virginia, 1976), 151.

8. Frederick Law Olmsted, *The Cotton Kingdom: A Traveler's Observations on Cotton and Slavery in the American Slave States, Based upon Three Former Volumes of Journeys and Investigations by the Same Author*, ed. Arthur M. Schlesinger Sr. (1861; New York: Modern Library, 1984), 71.

9. "Descendants of Ambrose Hundley," and "Ambrose Hundley," folder "Hundley, Divers, Parker, Doss," Virginia Genealogy Room, Danville Public Library, Danville, VA.

10. Marian Dodson Chiarito, *Old Survey Book I 1746–1782 Pittsylvania County Virginia* (Nashville: Clarkston Press, 1988), 363.

11. Caleb Hundley Inventory, Accounts Current, vol. 13, Pittsylvania County, 1840–1843, p. 217. Pittsylvania County Courthouse, Chatham, VA.

12. Caleb Hundley, Personal Property Tax, Pittsylvania, Virginia, 1834. Pittsylvania County Courthouse, Chatham, VA.

13. Caleb Hundley, Deed Book. vol. 22, Pittsylvania County, June 20, 1831, pp. 235–36. Pittsylvania County Courthouse, Chatham, VA.

14. Caleb Hundley, Deed Book, vol. 44, Pittsylvania County, November 14, 1840, p. 222; John Hundley, Deed Book, vol. 49, Pittsylvania County, January 31, 1845, n.p. Pittsylvania County Courthouse, Chatham, VA.

15. John Hundley, Deed Book, vol. 32, Pittsylvania County, June 20, 1831, n.p. Pittsylvania County Courthouse, Chatham, VA.

16. John Hundley, Personal Property Tax, Pittsylvania, Virginia, 1845, 1848. Pittsylvania County Courthouse, Chatham, VA.

17. Phillip D. Morgan and Michael L. Nichols, "Slaves in Piedmont Virginia, 1720–1790," *William and Mary Quarterly* (April 1989): 233.

18. "Mary Shelton," 1860 US Census, Schedule 1, Pittsylvania, Virginia, Southern District, Ringgold.

19. Henry Wiencek, *The Hairstons: An American Family in Black and White* (New York: St. Martin's Press, 1999), 186.

20. Susan Westbury, "The Slaves of Colonial Virginia: Where They Came From," *William and Mary Quarterly* (April 1985), 235–36, tables 2 and 3.

21. Morgan and Nichols, "Slaves in Piedmont Virginia," 247.

22. Douglass Chambers, *Murder at Montpelier: Igbo Africans in Virginia* (Jackson: University of Mississippi, Press, 2005), 18, 62, 160.

23. Ibid., table 5.6, p. 82.

24. "Cuffee Walton," 1870 US Census, Schedule 1, Pittsylvania, Virginia, Southern District, Ringgold, p. 15; "Doctor Day," 1870 US Census, Schedule 1, Pittsylvania, Virginia, Southern District, Ringgold, p. 51.

25. Walsh, *From Calabar to Carter's Grove*, 81.

26. John Thornton, "Central African Names and African-American Naming Patterns," *William and Mary Quarterly* 50, no. 4 (October 1993): 735.

27. Maude Carter Clement, *The History of Pittsylvania County* (1929; Baltimore: Regional, 1976), 252.

28. "Nannie Echols," "1 60 F B," 1860 US Census, Schedule 2, Slave Schedule, Pittsylvania, Virginia, Southern District, p. 30.

29. Lorenzo Ivy, quoted in Perdue, *Weevils in the Wheat*, 151, 153.

30. Advertisement, "$100 REWARD," *Danville (VA) Appeal*, March 7, 1863.

31. Advertisement, "$200 REWARD," *Danville (VA) Appeal*, September 2, 1864.

32. Sidney Mintz and Richard Price, *The Birth of African American Culture* (Boston: Beacon, 1992), 43–44.

33. 1860 US Census, Pittsylvania, Virginia, Southern District, pp. 173–247.

34. "Sokey Henderick," 1860 US Census, Schedule 1, Pittsylvania, Virginia, Southern District, Ringgold, p. 191.

35. "Jesse Booker," 1860 US Census, Schedule 1, Pittsylvania County, Virginia, Southern District, Whitmell, p. 6; Luther Porter Jackson, "The Virginia Free Negro Farmer and Property Owner, 1830–1860," *Journal of Negro History* (October 1939): 433.

36. Alva H. Griffith, transcriber and compiler, *Pittsylvania County, Virginia: Register of Free Negroes and Related Documentation* (Westminster, MD: Heritage Books, 2007), 10, 235.

37. Heads of household "John Foreman," Willis Gie," and "Sukey Henderick," 1860 US Census, Schedule 1, Pittsylvania County, Virginia, Southern District, Ringgold, pp. 190–91.

38. Jackson, "The Virginia Free Negro Farmer," 390.

39. Ibid., 391.

40. Guild, *Black Laws of Virginia*, 72.

41. "Will of John Ward, Sr. Pittsylvania County," in Griffith, *Pittsylvania County, Virginia*, 270.

42. Ibid., 268.

43. County Clerk Tunstall, in ibid., 59.

44. "Found Dead," *Danville (VA) Republican*, March 31, 1854.

45. James Terry, land survey, March 25, 1766, in Chiarito, *Old Survey Book I*, 145.

CHAPTER SIX

1. "George Waller," 1860 US Census, Schedule 1, Henry County, Virginia, p. 127; "George Waller," 1860 US Census, Schedule 2 (Slave Inhabitants), Henry County, Virginia, p. 40.

2. "David Breedlove," 1860 US Census, North District of Pittsylvania County, Virginia, p. 29.

3. "Edward Jackson and Celestia Hundley, Marriage License, Virginia, Pittsylvania County," Register of Marriages Pittsylvania County, vol. 1, 1861–1900, p. 97, #41. Pittsylvania County Courthouse, Chatham, VA.

4. "Geo. L. Noell," 1880 US Census, "Inhabitants in Danville in the County of Pittsylvania, State of Virginia," p. 1.

5. "A Cruel Parient," *Danville (VA) Register*, January 3, 1868.

6. Jason Whitehead, letter to Langhorne Scruggs, February 19, 1857; Langhorne Scruggs Papers, folder 1855–1859, Rare Books, Manuscripts and Special Collections Library, Duke University.

7. Edward Jackson, Death Register Index, Virginia Bureau of Vital Statistics, Reel 6 1944 A-K, Library of Virginia, Richmond.

8. Jay B. Hubbell, "A Persimmon Beer Dance in Ante-Bellum Virginia," *Southern Literary Messenger* 5, no. 5 (November–December 1943): 463. Hubbell reprints an 1838 article by William B. Smith that appeared in the *Farmer's Register*.

9. I am making these guesses based on the US census of 1870 and the 1918 Pittsylvania Postal Delivery Map in the Library of Virginia map room. The map includes individual buildings and some household names, which I assume belonged to literate households regularly receiving mail.

10. On the US census of 1870 and Edward Jackson's marriage certificate, the blacksmith Sandy Dickerson always has his name spelled with an *r* between the *e* and the *s*. The additional county records for the family of Griffith Dickenson are typically spelled with an *n* between the *e* and the *s*, and occasionally the name is given as Dickinson. The alteration of spelling between blacks and whites in Pittsylvania who shared the same family names and sometimes the same family histories was common.

11. Hundley and Burnett, January 18, 1841, Pittsylvania County Deeds Book, vol. 44, pp. 326–27; Hundley and Prewitt, May 16, 1842, Pittsylvania County Deeds Book, vol. 46, pp. 70–71; Hundley and Prewett, January 18, 1845, Pittsylvania County Deeds Book, vol. 49, pp. 142–43; Hundley and Evans, September 15, 1845, Pittsylvania County Deeds Book, vol. 49, pp. 363–64. Pittsylvania County Courthouse, Chatham, VA.

CHAPTER SEVEN

1. James Forman, "Machine Guns in Danville," in *The Making of Black Revolutionaries* (Seattle: University of Washington Press, 1997), 326–29.

2. Martin Luther King Jr., July 11, 1963, Danville, Virginia; archived in William Thomas, "Television News and the Civil Rights Struggle: The Views in Virginia and Mississippi," *Southern Spaces* (November 3, 2004): 25; online at http://www.southern spaces.org/contents/2004/thomas/4a.htm.

3. Ellen Glasgow, *The Deliverance: A Romance of the Tobacco Fields* (New York: Doubleday and Page, 1904), 9.

4. Quoted in Edward Pollock, *Illustrated Sketch Book of Danville, Virginia, Its Manufactures and Commerce* (Danville, VA: E. R. Waddill and Bros., 1885), 40.

5. "Granville Hundley," 1870 US Census, Pittsylvania County, Virginia, subdivision north of the Dan River, p. 54.

6. 1880 US Census, "Inhabitants in Dan River District in the County of Pittsylvania, State of Virginia," pp. 9–10.

7. John Blassingame, *Slave Testimony: Two Centuries of Letters, Speeches, Interviews and Autobiographies* (Baton Rouge: Louisiana State University Press, 1977), 157.

8. Rawley Martin, "Rawley Martin's Account," in *Pickett's Charge: Eyewitness Accounts of the Battle of Gettysburg*, ed. Richard Rollins (Mechanicsburg, PA: Stackpole Books, 2005), 80.

9. Quoted in Walter Harrison, *Pickett's Men: A Fragment of War History* (New York: Van Nostrand, 1870), 78.

10. Benjamin Quarles, *The Negro in the Civil War* (1953; New York: Da Capo, 1989), 36–37.

11. Ervin L. Jordan Jr., *Black Confederates and Afro-Yankees* (Charlottesville: University Press of Virginia, 1995), 217.

12. Donald Cartmell, *The Civil War Up Close* (Franklin Lakes, NJ: New Page Books, 2004), 176; Jordan, *Black Confederates*, 218.

13. Jordan, *Black Confederates*, 225.

14. Ibid., Appendix A: Racial Population of Virginia's 148 Counties, 1860, 315.

15. James H. Brewer, *The Confederate Negro: Virginia's Craftsmen and Military Laborers, 1861–1865* (Durham, NC: Duke University Press, 1969), 142–44: Table 6.2, "Requisition for 4,500 Slaves by Cunties, October 1862"; table 6.3, "Requisition for 4,500 Slaves by Counties, November 1862"; and table 6.4, "Requisition for 2,832 Slaves by Counties, March 11, 1863."

16. "Conscription of Free Negroes: A Bill," passed February 17, 1864, in *In View of the Great Want of Labor: A Legislative History of African American Conscription in the Confederacy*, by E. Renee Ingram (Westminster, MD: Willowbend Books, 1999), 14.

17. Jordan, *Black Confederates*, 66.

18. "Conscription of Negroes," *Danville (VA) Appeal*, March 4, 1865, p. 1.

19. Brewer, *The Confederate Negro*, 6.

20. Ibid., 44.

21. Ibid., 21.

22. Ibid., 64.

23. Quoted in Jordan, *Black Confederates*, 218.

24. Brewer, *The Confederate Negro*, 52.

25. Ibid., 86.

26. T. C. De Leon, *Four Years in the Rebel Capitals* (1890), quoted in ibid., 19.

27. Walt Whitman, "Song of Myself," in *Leaves of Grass* (1885; New York: W. W. Norton, 1973), 39–40.

28. Joseph Reid Anderson, letter to Confederate secretary of the Navy, quoted in Brewer, *The Confederate Negro*, 71.

29. Ibid., 41.

30. Ibid., 38.

31. Ibid., 132.

32. "The Negroes Impressed," *Danville (VA) Appeal*, March 3, 1864.

33. "Leaving," *Danville (VA) Register*, September 2, 1864.

34. Quarles, *The Negro in the Civil War*, 205–7; James Hollandsworth Jr., "The Execution of White Officers from Black Units by Confederate Forces during the Civil War," *Louisiana History* 35, no. 4 (Autumn 1994): 484–85; Herbert Aptheker, "Negro Casualties in the Civil War," *Journal of Negro History* 32, no. 1 (January 1947): 41–46; Chandra Manning, *What This Cruel War Was Over: Soldiers, Slavery, and the Civil War* (New York: Knopf, 2007), 175–77.

CHAPTER EIGHT

1. "Hundley from Hundley," deed of land transfer, John Hundley to Granville Hundley, May 22, 1877, Deed Book, vol. 71, Pittsylvania County, 1877, p. 72. Pittsylvania County Courthouse, Chatham, VA.

2. Samuel Wilson Receipts; Samuel Wilson Papers, box 2, folder "Wages Paid," Albert and Shirley Small Special Collections Library, University of Virginia.

3. Lynda J. Morgan, *Emancipation in Virginia's Tobacco Belt, 1850–1870* (Athens: University of Georgia Press, 1992), 201. In 1865 in Richmond, black mechanics at the tobacco factories reported that "starvation is Cirten" on account of the high rents combined with wages they were being paid, which amounted to less than what they had earned as enslaved laborers.

4. "The Biggest Political Card," *Danville (VA) Bee*, August 29, 1876.

5. J. B. Callaway, 1880 US Census, Enumeration District 169, Danville Magisterial District, Pittsylvania County, Virginia. The census takers recorded the parameters of their districts in descriptions at the beginning of the districts, found on the website Ancestry.com.

6. "John Hundley," Deed Book, vol. 69, Pittsylvania County, Virginia, p. 98. Pittsylvania County Courthouse, Chatham, VA.

7. Edward Williams, 1880 US Census, Pittsylvania County, Virginia, Dan River Magisterial District 168, p. 8. Williams's plot was the only one of this group ever surveyed and registered at the county clerk's office.

8. "Edward Williams," 1870 Land Book, Pittsylvania County, Virginia, p. 33. Pittsylvania County Courthouse, Chatham, VA.

9. "Edward Williams" entry, "Persons, Property and Other Subjects of Taxation," *Auditor of Public Accounts Personal Property Tax*, Pittsylvania County, Virginia, 1869. Reel 693, Library of Virginia, Richmond.

10. "John Hundley," August 31, 1883; Accounts Current, book 45, March 1883–January 1884, Pittsylvania County, Virginia, p. 395. Pittsylvania County Courthouse, Chatham, VA.

11. "Hundley and Lanier," Deed Book, vol. 73, Pittsylvania County, Virginia, p. 7. Pittsylvania County Courthouse, Chatham, VA.

12. "John Hundley," August 31, 1883; Accounts Current, book 45, March 1883–January 1884, Pittsylvania County, Virginia, p. 386. Pittsylvania County Courthouse, Chatham, VA.

13. Jane Dailey, *Before Jim Crow: The Politics of Race in Postemancipation Virginia* (Chapel Hill: University of North Carolina Press, 2000), 119–25.

14. "The Great South," review of *The South: Its Industrial, Financial and Political Condition*, by A. K. McClure, *New York Times*, August 28, 1886, p. 3.

15. Granville Hundley, "Homestead Exemption," October 19, 1886, Deed Book, vol. 89, 1886, Pittsylvania County, Virginia, p. 481, Pittsylvania County Clerk's Office, Chatham, VA; "Granville Hundley" entry, "Persons, Property and Other Subjects of Taxation," *Auditor of Public Accounts Personal Property Tax*, Pittsylvania County, Virginia, 1880, reel 1119, Library of Virginia, Richmond.

16. "The Tobacco Trade," *New York Times*, June 4, 1886, p. 1; "The Tobacco Trade," *New York Times*, February 3, 1886, p. 1.

17. William T. Sutherlin, "Something about Tobacco," *Danville (VA) Register*, December 15, 1886.

18. "Tobacco Prices Higher," *New York Times*, July 29, 1887, p. 8.

19. "Fatal Accident," *Danville (VA) Bee*, December 8, 1876.

20. "A Negro Hung and Riddled with Bullets," *Danville (VA) Register & Bee*, December 8, 1886.

21. "Crowding the Penitentiary," *Danville (VA) Times*, March 15, 1886.

22. "A Republican's Dirty Work," *Danville (VA) Register*, November 10, 1886.

23. Granville Hundley, "Last Will and Testament," January 25, 1887; Will Book, vol. 4, 1890–1907, Pittsylvania County, Virginia, pp. 93–94. Pittsylvania County Courthouse, Chatham, VA.

24. Robert Small, quoted in John Blassingame, *Slave Testimony: Two Centuries of Letters, Speeches, Interviews and Autobiographies* (Baton Rouge: Louisiana State University Press, 1977), 374.

25. Albion Tourgeé, *Bricks without Straw* (1880; Durham, NC: Duke University Press, 2009), 119.

26. "John M. Hutchings," 1860 US Census, Schedule 1, Free Inhabitants in the Southern District of Pittsylvania County, Virginia, p. 88, and Schedule 2, Slave Inhabitants in the Southern District of Pittsylvania County, Virginia, p. 97.

27. Gov. Phillip McKinney, quoted in Dailey, *Before Jim Crow*, 160–61.

28. "Vote of Pittsylvania," *Twice-a-Week Register and Farrago*, November 7, 1902.

29. Dailey, *Before Jim Crow*, 161.

30. "A Vile Slander" and "Colored Kickers," *Danville (VA) Times*, June 27, 1889.

31. "Minstrels," *Danville (VA) Register*, March 8, 1886.

32. "Ned Jackson," 1900 US Census, Pittsylvania County, Virginia, Dan River Magisterial District, sheet 8.

CHAPTER NINE

1. Abraham Lincoln, quoted in Christopher Breiseth, "Lincoln and Frederick Douglass: Another Debate," *Journal of the Illinois State Historical Society* (February 1975): 22.

2. Melvin Patrick Ely, *Israel on the Appomattox* (New York: Knopf, 2007), 439.

3. Ibid., 344.

4. Stephen Ash, *A Year in the South: Four Lives in 1865* (New York: Palgrave, 2002), 127–42; Louis Hughes, *Thirty Years a Slave: From Bondage to Freedom* (Milwaukee, 1897).

5. Thomas Jefferson, *Notes on the State of Virginia*, in *The Portable Thomas Jefferson*, ed. Merrill D. Peterson (New York: Penguin, 1975), 186.

6. Frances Smith Foster, *Written by Herself: Literary Production by African American Women 1746–1892* (Bloomington: University of Indiana Press, 1993), 38, 43.

7. Phillis Wheatley, "To Maecenas," in *Memoirs and Poems of Phillis Wheatley* (Boston, 1838), 45.

8. Jefferson, *Notes on the State of Virginia*, 189.

9. Ibid., 191.

10. The debates over Suetonius's employment of the word *fuscus* to describe Terence seem no closer to ending; see Walter Forehand, *The Life of Terence* (Boston: G. K. Hall, 1985), 5–6. In these matters, the diligent and conservative classical scholar Frank Snowden stakes his reputation that Terence was black skinned: *Blacks in Antiquity* (Cambridge, MA: Harvard University Press, 1970), 16, 188.

11. E. Millicent Sowerby, comp., *Catalogue of the Library of Thomas Jefferson* (Washington, DC: Library of Congress, 1952–59), 4:549. The two Terence entries are respectively #4576 and #4577.

12. Forehand, *The Life of Terence*, 5–6.

13. Peterson, *The Portable Thomas Jefferson*, 190.

14. Douglas Wilson, *Jefferson's Literary Commonplace Book* (Princeton, NJ: Princeton University Press, 1988), 145.

15. Thomas Jefferson, "Original Rough Draught of the Declaration of Independence," June 1776, LOC p. 3; online at http://www.loc.gov/exhibits/treasures/images/decp3.jpg.

16. Ralph Ellison, "Beating That Boy," in *Shadow and Act* (1964; New York: Random House, 1995), 99.

CHAPTER TEN

To protect privacy, I have changed the names of two persons in this chapter.

1. Griffith Dickerson, "Last Will and Testament," August 29, 1843, Will Book, vol. 1, Pittsylvania County, Virginia, pp. 470–73.

2. Lona Dalton, "Dickerson Graveyard: Survey Report," Library of Virginia, Richmond; online at http://lvaimage.lib.va.us/VHI/html/21/0091.htmlReport HomePage.p.2.

3. "Vincent Dickenson," 1860 US Census, Schedule 2—Slave Inhabitants, Pittsylvania County, Virginia, p. 157.

4. V. Dickinson, inventory; Box Mss. Folios 38-81 2m-ledgers, Albert and Shirley Small Special Collections Library, University of Virginia.

5. Toni Morrison, *Beloved* (1987; New York: Knopf, 2006), 47.

6. Martin Delany, *Blake: or, The Huts of America* (1859; Boston: Beacon, 1970), 38.

7. Vincent Dickenson, April 17, 1860, Deed Book, vol. 59, Pittsylvania County, Virginia, pp. 150–51. Pittsylvania County Courthouse, Chatham, VA.

8. Walter Johnson, *Soul by Soul: Life inside the Antebellum Slave Market* (Cambridge, MA: Harvard University Press, 1999), 19.

9. William Jackson, "Last Will and Testament," June 24, 1846, Will Book, vol. 2, Pittsylvania County, Virginia. Pittsylvania County Courthouse, Chatham, VA. I am indebted to Dan Ricketts for calling William Jackson's will to my attention.

10. Nat Jackson, draft registration card, June 5, 1917.

INDEX

Act for the Public Defense, 152

Adams, George, 172

Adams, Martha, 169–70

Adams, Ned, 176

Addison, Drew, 220n46

Africa, 9, 28–29, 55, 84, 103, 125, 213

African Americans, 13, 20, 24–26, 131, 193; African customs, survival of among, 105–6, 110; birth records of, 125; black infant mortality, as "smothered," 102; black labor, during Civil War, 154–55; black women, and labor force, 94; breeding of, and slavery, 54–55, 56–57; color code used for, 113; as Colored Kickers, 182–83; common surnames of, 114; Confederacy, black labor in, 159–60; in Confederate army, 8; conscription of, during Civil War, 152–53; cultural formation of, 108–9; disenfranchising of, 182; as domestic servants, 42; dwellings of, 34, 37; and education, 88–89, 90–93; enslavement, erasing of, attempts to, 54–55; genealogy of, 6, 28, 145; and hidey-holes, 34, 37; and labor system, 97; light skin, preference for among, 57; migration of, to North, 185, 188; mob violence against, 172; names of, 1, 28–29, 60, 61, 123, 128, 180, 187, 206; naming practices of, 104–5, 110–11; naming practices of, as African way, 179; naming practices of, and African ways, adaptation of, 30–32, 95; naming practices, defiant creativity of, 110–11; out-of-wedlock birth rates among, and slavery, 124–25; reinvention of, after slavery, 138; and slave names, 217n5; slavery, as not a topic of conversation among, 28; troops, during World War I, directive against, 207; unknown fathers of, 126; as U.S. citizens, 86; white acceptance, 194, 215; white Americans, exposure of to by, 142–44; white Americans, guilt-based defensiveness of toward, 122–23; "Zip Coon" caricatures of, 132. *See also* freedmen; slavery; slaves

Alabama, 57

Albert and Shirley Small Special Collections Library, 196–97

Alexandria (Virginia), 65

American Revolution, 48

Amos 'n' Andy (radio program), 132

Ancestry.com, 33

Anderson, Joseph E., 69

Anderson, Joe, 89, 91

Anderson, Joe E., 145

Anderson, Joseph Reid, 158

Anderson, Claude, 59, 67–68

Anderson, Samuel, 102

Anderson, William, 110–11, 151

Andria (Terence), 190–91

Angola, 105

Appomattox (Virginia), 105

Arkansas, 57

Armistead, Lew, 149–50

Armstrong, Samuel, 92

Army of Northern Virginia, 74

Astor, William B., 64

Atlantic slave trade, 103

Hutchings, Permelia, 177
Hutchings, Phoebe, 181
Hutter, E. S., 159
Hyde, Thomas, 74

Inge, H., 88
Igbo, 37; naming practices of, 104
Incidents in the Life of a Slave Girl
  (Jacobs), 139
integration, 3
interracial marriage, 3
Invisible Man (Ellison), 128, 193
Ivy, Lorenzo, 58–59, 97, 107

Jackson and Anderson Mill, 206
Jackson, Ann Eliza, 206
Jackson, Andrew, 40
Jackson, Andrew (US president), 31–32
Jackson, Berkeley, 93
Jackson, Celestia "Less" Hundley
  (author's great-grandmother), 25, 32–
  33, 68, 76–77, 94–95, 101–2, 137, 139, 167,
  177, 180, 183–85; age of, 98; marriage of,
  131, 134–35, 138
Jackson, Charity, 101–2
Jackson, Charles, 40
Jackson, Charles (son of Edward and
  Celestia Jackson), 94, 138, 167
Jackson, C. Mitchell (author's son), 116,
  118–20, 184
Jackson, Edward "Ned" (author's great-
  grandfather), 25, 32, 38, 40, 43–45, 52–
  53, 57–58, 61, 62, 64, 67–68, 73, 76–77,
  85, 89, 92, 94–95, 99, 101, 104, 109, 116,
  132–33, 148, 161, 167–68, 176–77, 179–80,
  182–85, 188, 194, 201–2, 204, 215; age of,
  98; census (1860), disappearance from,
  39; as domestic servant, 42; indentured, possibility of, 41; living quarters
  of, 34, 37; marriage of, 131, 134–35, 138,
  226n10; name of, 206; parents of, 137;
  as slave, 39
Jackson, Elizabeth, 40–41
Jackson, Frankie, 40
Jackson, George, 40
Jackson, George Jr., 40
Jackson, Hugh, 93

Jackson, J., 88
Jackson, John, 69, 102, 145
Jackson, Jordan, 60
Jackson, Madison, 40
Jackson, Martha, 40, 115
Jackson, Martin, 31
Jackson, Mary (author's great-aunt), 102,
  115, 137
Jackson, Millie, 40
Jackson, Nathaniel (author's son), 1, 21,
  32–33, 116, 119–20, 139, 177
Jackson, Nathaniel (author's father), 1–3,
  33, 57, 65, 84, 90, 185–86; birth certifi-
  cate of, 19, 25, 32
Jackson, Nathaniel Henry Sr. (author's
  grandfather), 1–3, 6, 11–13, 15, 19–20, 22–
  24, 33, 57, 65, 84, 93, 102, 116, 131, 139, 161,
  181, 183–84, 207; draft, registered for, 213
Jackson, Polly, 40
Jackson, Raphael, 40
Jackson, Regine, 117, 119
Jackson, Sally. *See* Sally Younger
Jackson, Thomas "Stonewall," 26, 32, 151
Jackson, Virginia Jefferson (author's
  grandmother), 13, 120–21, 125, 139
Jackson, William, 206, 230n9 (chap. 10)
Jacobs, Harriet, 139, 193
Jefferson County, 60
Jefferson, Lucius, 129
Jefferson, Thomas, 33, 47, 54, 57, 67, 192,
  196; prejudice of, 188–89, 191; slavery,
  attitude toward, 191; Phillis Wheatley,
  condemnation of by, 189–91
Jennings, Edmund, 103
Jennings, William, 147
Joe Turner's Come and Gone (Wilson), 193
Johnson, Andrew, 30
Johnson, James Weldon, 55
Johnston, Estelle, 88
Johnston, Helen, 88
Jolson, Al, 183
Jones, Catherine, 147
Jones, Ella, 168
Jones, Lucretia, 167
Jones, Thomas, 42
Joyce, Arthur, 6, 129
Joyce, Richard, 151

Appomattox Regional Library System
Hopewell, Virginia 23860
02/13